The Grand Masters
of French Cuisine

The Grand Masters of French Cuisine
Five Centuries of Great Cooking

Recipes Selected and Adapted by

Céline Vence and Robert Courtine

Edited, with Introductory Notes, by
PHILIP AND MARY HYMAN

G. P. Putnam's Sons • New York

Editors' Preface

Few Frenchmen understand or appreciate the history of their cuisine. Of course, most will admit that cooking is not as good as it was in grandmother's day, but going back more than one or two generations usually bewilders them. The idea of preparing dishes created in the sixteenth, seventeenth, and even eighteenth centuries is a startling one to most Frenchmen, who wrongly believe that cooking "that long ago" must have been heavily spiced and extremely different from food today. Indeed, the old recipes do call for a number of seasonings that have disappeared from French cooking, but by the eighteenth century most of the excesses associated with the Middle Ages had disappeared, and French cooking was very similar to what it is now.

The greatest difference between French cooking now and then is that in the past it was *better*. Cooks were called upon to make a much greater variety of dishes for each meal, using many fewer ingredients than are available today. This meant that cooks had to be more creative. Up until the nineteenth century, for example, menus filled whole pages, and reading them makes one think that they were for dinners designed for gargantuan appetites. The fact is that these menus represent a "smorgasbord" selection that was presented and tasted, but not eaten in its entirety by any guest. This meant that at any meal of consequence, a cook had to prepare a large enough variety of dishes so that *every* taste would be satisfied. Attending such a meal would be like going to any large French restaurant today and ordering *everything* on the menu, then choosing among the foods that are served. This sounds wasteful, and indeed, it was; but these glorious meals were served not in farmhouses but in princely homes where the abundance, variety, and quality of the food were inherent in a certain lifestyle. Of course, formal dinners still exist, and meals that are simply wasteful and showy are not to be praised; but the research and talent that went into meals 200, 300, and 400 years ago should be a source of inspiration for cooks in a completely different context today.

One common objection to the resurrection of old recipes (raised only by people unfamiliar with the history of food) is that ingredients used "then" must be hard to find today. This objection stems from the misconception stated earlier—that French food was once *very* different (almost as foreign as Chinese cooking). In fact, old cookbooks generally call for fewer and more commonly available ingredients than their modern counterparts. The general tendency was for foods to multiply as time went on. Not only were new sources of food discovered (especially in the Americas), but improved means of transportation and storage made a greater variety of foods available to cooks in Europe. Unfortunately, "new" foods and industrialization tended to push out certain varieties of the old staples; for example, where once ten or twelve types of apples were grown, only relatively few are grown commercially today. In the past cooks relied almost entirely on fresh produce grown near where they lived and worked. This, of course, meant that ingredients were limited by the seasons and the general agricultural wealth of the country in which the cook lived. The staples, such as onions, carrots, turnips, celery, thyme, parsley, etc., have not changed, and these old recipes will prove to any skeptics just how much more important creative ideas are than "fancy" ingredients.

One of the reasons France's gastronomic past is so generally misunderstood, even there, is that the books illustrating it are often rare and unavailable to cooks today. A cookbook, like any other practical manual, was written to be used, not admired on a library shelf. Consequently, cookbooks were used until they fell apart and were discarded for newer, more fashionable books. Since each new cookbook pretends to outdo its predecessors, it is not surprising that many of the old books have disappeared. Those used in compiling the recipes that follow are only a very few of many titles that are considered basic to any collection of French cookbooks. Any one of the books cited could furnish easily 100 times more recipes equally appetizing as those that were selected, but space does not allow for a larger sampling here. The aim of this collection is to acquaint modern cooks with some of the past masters of French cooking and give a sampling of their recipes.

A number of the recipes that follow call for spit roasting. It should be remembered that none of the cooks cited here ever cooked on anything approaching a modern stove. Almost all of them worked over an open fire, with pots hanging at different distances above the flames or else buried in the embers. All roasting was done on a spit, and ovens were usually nothing more than a brick enclosure heated by a fire built inside it; the embers were scraped out before the food to be cooked was inserted. It is, of course, preferable to spit-roast meat before an open fire whenever possible, but few cooks today have the facilities for this. Nevertheless, the backyard barbecue pit could be used in many instances to grill fish and meats that otherwise would be placed under the broiler. Whenever possible, the original demands of the recipes should be met; the result not only is more "authentic," but usually tastes better as well.

Some recipes included here are strictly culinary curiosities. Those that call for ingredients unavailable in the United States are few in number; nevertheless, they should interest American cooks. It is important to understand not only what people ate but how they ate it, and a technique used in cooking one food can sometimes be happily applied to another. One thing, however, that should not be tampered with are the cooks' emphasis on the freshness and quality of the ingredients employed. Canned or frozen foods should never be substituted for the fresh food in these recipes. On the other hand, each cook should feel free to vary certain seasonings and garnishes in recipes where no precise measure or ingredient is listed. This brings us to the problem of adapting old recipes in general.

Up until the nineteenth century, cookbooks were generally written for cooks with a firm knowledge of cookery. There were seldom precise instructions for the novice, and ingredients were rarely mentioned in specific quantities. Cooking times were generally ignored, and seasoning was (and always will be) a question of taste. The following recipes are as close to the originals as possible, but since the originals allow for much variation, no two adaptations would be exactly the same. Once a recipe has been tried and mastered, using the information given here, any cook should feel free to adapt it to his or her taste so long as the basic sense and balance of the original are respected.

Despite the many links with French cooking today, the following recipes are full of surprises. The frequent use of anchovies, capers, and vinegar in sauces with both meat and fish has almost disappeared in France today. The surprising, but logical, use of bitter Seville orange juice instead of lemon juice has unfortunately all but vanished, but none of these tastes is ''foreign'' to French cuisine.

This brings us back to the original statement that French cooking in the past (despite certain obvious differences) was not as ''exotic'' as it is often imagined to be. French cooking has always owed its greatness to the moderation which governed its greatest chefs. Excesses are avoided, and tastes are carefully balanced to harmonize rather than struggle with each other. All the following recipes succeed because they respect these principles of balance and moderation, and modern cooks who wish to adapt them in any way should always respect these same principles.

In closing, we would like to return to our earlier remark that French cooking in the past was better than French cooking today. This might be too sweeping a statement since cooking is still an art in France and is constantly evolving. Many of the monotonous ''classics'' developed around the turn of the century are now being challenged by cooks who, consciously or not, are experimenting with ideas like those found in this book. Nothing is better for good cooking than intelligent experimentation, and there is no greater source for inspiration in experimentation than the masterworks cited here. We hope that this collection of recipes will give cooks not only a taste of what great cooking in the past was like, but a sampling of what is to come as well. In the absence of facsimile editions of all the classic cookbooks quoted here, it is hoped that the recipes which follow will sufficiently illustrate the continuity, as well as the variety, that has made French cooking distinct, from its origins until the present day.

PHILIP AND MARY HYMAN

THE GRAND MASTERS
OF FRENCH CUISINE

From 1373 to 1873

1373 TAILLEVENT

entrées *Lait lardé* 73
(Fried Larded Milk)

eggs *Oeufs rôtis à la broche* 85
(Spit-Roasted Eggs)

fish *Pâté d'anguilles* 106
(Eel Pâté)

meat *Galimafrée* 159
(Lamb Gallimaufry)

vegetables *Cretonnée de pois nouveaux* 246
(Green Pea Purée with Chicken)

1392 MENAGIER DE PARIS

entrées *Faux frenon* 73
(False Frenon, or Mixed Meat Casserole)
Tourtes d'herbes 74
(Herb Pie)

fish *Brouet d'anguilles* 106
(Eel Stew)

meat *Porcelet farci* 179
(Roast Suckling Pig with Chestnut Stuffing)

1552 NOSTRADAMUS

desserts and sweets *Coings en quartiers* 265
(Preserved Quinces)

1651 LA VARENNE

soups *Potage d'oignons au lait* 65
(Onion Soup with Milk)

entrées *Flan fin qu'on appelle tarte d'ami* 74
(Cheese Tart, Known as Friend's Tart)
Tourte d'huîtres fraîches 75
(Fresh Oyster Pie)

eggs *Oeufs farcis à l'oseille* 87
(Eggs Stuffed with Sorrel)

fish *Perches au court-bouillon* 107
(Perch in White Wine)
Poissons rôtis sur le gril 107
(Grilled Fish)
Soupresse de poisson 108
(Pressed Fish)

meat *Longe de veau à la marinade* 145
(Marinated Loin Roast of Veal)

	Jarret de veau à l'épigramme 145
	("Epigram" Veal Knuckle)
	Poitrine de veau farcie 147
	(Stuffed Breast of Veal)
variety meats and charcuterie	*Foie de veau fricassé* 195
	(Fricasseed Calf's Liver)
poultry and game	*Foie gras cuit dans les cendres* 206
	(Baked Foie Gras)
vegetables	*Epinards à la crème* 246
	(Creamed Spinach)
desserts and sweets	*Tourte admirable* 267
	(Marzipan Pie)
	Dame Susanne 268
	(Egg Bread Susanne)
	Tourte de frangipane 271
	(Frangipane Pie)
drinks	*Limonade* 284
	(Lemonade)

1654   **BONNEFONS**

entrées	*Beignets de melon* 76
	(Melon Fritters)
	Andouillettes contrefaites 76
	(Mock Sausages)
poultry and game	*Fricassée de poulet* 206
	(Chicken Fricassee)
	Canard en ragoût 207
	(Duck Stew)
vegetables	*Concombres farcis* 247
	(Stuffed Cucumbers)
salads	*"Minor Herbs of All Kinds for Salads"* 260
desserts and sweets	*Petits métiers* 268
	(Little Wafers)

1656   **PIERRE DE LUNE**

entrées	*Tourte de godiveau feuilletée* 77
	(Mixed Meat Pie)
eggs	*Omelette farcie et coupée* 89
	(Stuffed Sliced Omelette)
	Omelette d'asperges 98
	(Asparagus Omelette)
meat	*Boeuf mode* 138
	(Pot Roast)
poultry and game	*Chevreuil* 207
	(Venison in Wine Sauce)
drinks	*Vin des dieux* 284
	(Wine of the Gods)

1662   ESCOLE PARFAITE DES OFFICIERS DE BOUCHE

    eggs   Oeufs pochés à la sauce d'anchois   91
                                           (Poached Eggs with Anchovy Sauce)
                                    Civet d'oeufs à l'huile   98
                                         (Deep-Fried Eggs with Wine Sauce)

1674   L.S.R.

    vegetables   Cardes d'artichauts à la moelle   247
                                      (Cardoons with Bone Marrow)
                                    Asperges en pois verts   248
                                        (Green Pea Style Asparagus)

1691   MASSIALOT

    fish   Saumon en ragoût   108
                                      (Salmon and Oyster Stew)
    poultry and game   Pâté chaud de faisan   208
                                      (Hot Pheasant Pie)
                                    Poulard aux olives   211
                                      (Chicken Stewed with Olives)
    vegetables   Chou farci   248
                                      (Stuffed Cabbage)
                                    Casserole au riz   249
                                    (Rice Casserole)
    desserts and sweets   Benoiles   269
                                    (Egg Fritters)
    drinks   Hypocras blanc   285
                                    (White Hypocras)

1692   AUDIGER

    drinks   Populo   285
                                    (Aniseed and Cinnamon Liqueur)
                                  Ratafia rouge   286
                                    (Red Ratafia)

1733   LA CHAPELLE

    eggs   Oeufs à l'antidame   93
                                    (Eggs with Herbs and Anchovies)
    fish and shellfish   Soles à la sauce aux rois   109
                                    (Sole Stuffed with Anchovies and Herbs)
                                    Turbot à la béchamel   109
                                    (Turbot with Béchamel Sauce)

Maquereaux au fenouil et aux groseilles   110
  (Grilled Mackerel with Fennel and Gooseberries)
Huîtres en coquilles   110
  (Oysters Cooked in Their Shells)
Terrine de lottes   111
  (Burbot and Crayfish Stew)

meat
Filet d'aloyau braisé à la royale   138
  (Braised Fillet of Beef à la Royale)
Côtelettes de veau en surprise   149
  (Surprise Veal Cutlets)
Veau à la bourgeoise   151
  (Loin Roast of Veal with Carrots and Onions)
Ratons de mouton   161
  (Stuffed Lamb Steaks)

poultry and game
Grives au genièvre   213
  (Thrush with Juniper Berries)

1739   *MARIN*

soups
Potage aux moules à la Reyne   65
  (Mussel Soup with Almonds)

entrées
Petits pâtés à la Mazarine   78
  (Veal and Bacon Pastries à la Mazarine)

eggs
Oeufs à l'infante   95
  (Poached Eggs à l'Infante)
Omelette aux huîtres   99
  (Oyster Omelette)

fish and shellfish
Ecrevisses à la poêle   111
  (Sautéed Crayfish with Lamb)
Blanquette de filets de sole   112
  (Fillets of Sole in White Sauce)
Carpe à l'aventure   112
  (Carp Poached in Beer)

meat
Filet de boeuf à la mariée   139
  (Stuffed Fillet of Beef à la Mariée)
Carbonnades de boeuf a la lyonnaise   139
  (Braised Rib Steaks à la Lyonnaise)
Boeuf à la mode paysanne   140
  (Braised Beef Peasant-Style)
Blanquette de veau   153
  (Veal Stewed in White Sauce)
Fricandeau à la bourgeoise   154
  (Glaxed Veal Garnished à la Bourgeoise)
Selle de mouton à la Barberine   163
  (Braised Lamb à la Barberini)
Filet d'agneau à la Condé   165
  (Roast Lamb with Lemon Butter à la Condé)
Jambon en daube   181
  (Braised Ham in Wine)

variety meats and charcuterie
Cervelle de veau au parmesan et à la moutarde   196
  (Calf's Brain with Parmesan and Mustard)
Langue de boeuf aux concombres   196
  (Beef Tongue with Cucumbers)

13

poultry and game	*Poularde en mousseline* 215	
	(Stuffed Chicken Casserole)	
	Lapereaux en brodequins 217	
	(Stuffed Young Rabbit)	
	Civet de lièvre 219	
	(Hare Stew)	
	Poulet au persil 220	
	(Roast Chicken with Herb Butter)	
vegetables	*Haricots en allumettes* 249	
	(Deep-Fried String Beans)	
	Laitues à la dame Simonne 250	
	(Stuffed Lettuce in Cream Sauce)	
desserts and sweets	*Riz meringué* 269	
	(Rice Meringue)	

1740 CUISINIER GASCON

fish	*Truites à la hussarde* 113	
	(Broiled Trout with Rémoulade Sauce)	
meat	*Noix de veau en dés au jambon* 154	
	(Veal and Ham in Wine Sauce)	
	Veau en crottes d'âne roulées à la Neuteau 156	
	(Stuffed Veal Scallops)	
poultry and game	*Poulet à l'oreille* 220	
	(Roast Chicken Stuffed with Oysters)	
vegetables	*Artichauts à la galérienne* 250	
	(Artichokes with Wine and Mushrooms)	

1746 MENON

soups	*Potage à la citrouille* 66	
	(Pumpkin Soup)	
	Potage maigre printanier 66	
	(Spring Soup)	
	Potage à la vierge 67	
	(Virgin Mary's Soup)	
entrées	*Fromage à l'écarlate* 78	
	(Cheese and Crayfish Scarlet)	
	Rôties de Bretagne 79	
	(Breton Toast with Herb Butter)	
eggs	*Omelette au joli coeur* 97	
	(Crayfish Omelette)	
	Oeufs à l'ail 99	
	(Garlic Eggs)	
	Oeufs en matelote 100	
	(Egg and Anchovy Stew)	
	Oeufs au gratin 100	
	(Eggs au Gratin)	
	Oeufs au prévôt 101	
	(Eggs with Ham and Mushrooms)	
	Oeufs à la tripe 101	
	(Eggs and Onions)	

14

fish and shellfish

Filets de morue à la provençale 113
    (Salt Cod in Lemon Butter)
Raie au fromage 114
    (Skate with Cheese Sauce)
Cuisses de grenouilles frites 117
    (Deep-Fried Frogs' Legs)
Brochet en étuvée 118
    (Pike Stew with Anchovies and Capers)
Etuvée de carpes à la chartreuse 120
    (Carp in Red Wine à la Chartreuse)
Escargots de vigne en fricassée de poulet 122
    (Snail and Mushroom Stew)
Truites au four 130
    (Baked Trout with Herb Stuffing)
Moules en beignets 130
    (Mussel Fritters)

meat

Charbonnée de boeuf en papillote 140
    (Rib Roast en Papillote)
Culotte à la braise aux oignons 141
    (Braised Rump Roast with Onions)
Tranche de boeuf à la Camargot 141
    (Braised Beef with Anchovies à la Camargot)
Queue de boeuf en hochepot 142
    (Oxtail Stew)
Brezolles 155
    (Veal Stew with Shallots)
Haricot de mouton 167
    (Lamb and Turnip Stew)
Gigot de mouton à la Ninon 169
    (Marinated Leg of Lamb à la Ninon)
Cochon de lait par quartiers au père Douillet 183
    (Glazed Suckling Pig au Père Douillet)

variety meats and charcuterie

Boudin blanc à la bourgeoise 197
    (Homemade White Sausage)
Fromage de cochon 198
    (Headcheese)

poultry and game

Marinade de pigeons au citron 221
    (Marinated Pigeons with Lemon Sauce)
Oie à la moutarde 221
    (Roast Goose with Mustard)
Canard à la purée verte 223
    (Duck with Split Pea Purée)
Poulet au fromage 225
    (Chicken au Gratin)
Cailles à la cendre 227
    (Cinder-Baked Quail)
Lapin en gâteau 228
    (Rabbit Loaf)
Perdreaux à la Coigny 228
    (Partridge in Wine Sauce)

vegetables

Truffes en puits 251
    (Fresh Truffles with Stuffing)
Artichauts à la barigoule 251
    (Artichokes with Vinaigrette)
Petits pois à la demi-bourgeoise 252
    (Green Peas with Lettuce)

desserts and sweets   *Beignets de feuilles de vigne*   273
                                           (Vine-Leaf Fritters)
drinks   *Vespetro*   286

1765   *DICTIONNAIRE PORTATIF*

eggs   *Oeufs à la bonne femme*   102
                                       (Housewife's Eggs and Onion Soufflé)
                               Oeufs à la monime   102
                                       (Stuffed Omelette and Meat Balls)
fish   *Sardines en caisse*   124
                                       (Sardines—or Smelt—with Fish and Herb Garnish)
                               Barbue marinée   126
                                       (Marinated Flatfish)
meat   *Éclanche de cent feuilles*   171
                                       (Stuffed Leg of Lamb)
                               Côtelettes de porc frais à la cendre   185
                                       (Pork Chops with Mushroom Sauce)
poultry and game   *Poularde en ballon*   229
                                       (Chicken Stuffed en Ballon)

1771   *BUC'HOZ*

vegetables   *Champignons au four*   252
                                       (Stuffed Mushrooms)

1795   *CUISINIERE REPUBLICAINE*

variety meats and charcuterie   *Fraise de veau au gratin de gruyère*   198
                                       (Calf's Ruffle with Gruyère)
vegetables   *Pommes de terre à l'econome*   253
                                       (Potato Patties)

1796   *ISABEAU*

eggs   *Oeufs à la bonne suisse*   103
                                       (Swiss Egg Fondue)
poultry and game   *Cuisses de dindon réveillantes*   231
                                       (Braised Turkey Legs)
                               Faisan en filets au jus d'orange   233
                                       (Pheasant Fillets in Orange Sauce)
desserts and sweets   *Omelette charmante*   274
                                       (Jam and Nut Omelette)
                               Pain des houris   274
                                       (Oriental Nut Cake)

1814   BEAUVILLIERS

eggs   *Oeufs à l'aurore*   103
                             (Egg Casserole)
meat   *Côtelettes de mouton à la Soubise*   175
                             (Lamb Chops à la Soubise)
poultry and game   *Dinde en daube*   242
                             (Stewed Turkey)
                             Canard aux navets à la bourgeoise   242
                             (Duck with Turnips)
desserts and sweets   *Flan de nouilles meringuées*   276
                             (Noodle Meringue Cake)

1820   VIARD

soups   *Potage à la Geaufret*   67
                             (Potato Dumpling Soup)
                             Potage au poisson   68
                             (Fish Soup)
entrées   *Ramequins au fromage*   79
                             (Cheese Ramequins)
fish and shellfish   *Filets de merlan en turban*   129
                             (Whiting Fillets en Turban)
                             Croustade de crevettes   131
                             (Shrimp Croustade)
                             Cabillaud aux fines herbes   131
                             (Baked Cod with Shallots and Mushrooms)
meat   *Côte de boeuf à la gelée*   142
                             (Cold Rib Roast in Meat Jelly)
                             Miroton   143
                             (Beef with Onions)
                             Hachis de boeuf   143
                             (Diced Beef with Eggs)
                             Côtelettes de veau à la Singara   155
                             (Braised Veal Cutlets with Tongue)
                             Tendrons de veau en chartreuse   158
                             (Veal Chartreuse)
                             Cous de mouton à la purée de lentilles   173
                             (Mutton Neck with Lentil Purée)
                             Carrés de porc en couronne   187
                             (Stuffed Crown Pork Roast)
                             Emincés de cochon à l'oignon   189
                             (Pork with Onions)
                             Côtelettes de cochon en crépinettes   191
                             (Pork Chops Wrapped in Onions)
                             Echine de cochon sauce poivrade   194
                             (Pork Chops with Poivrade Sauce)
variety meats and charcuterie *Gras-double en crépinettes*   199
                             (Honeycomb Tripe and Mushroom Patties)
                             Pieds de mouton à la poulette   199
                             (Lamb's Trotters with Mushroom Sauce)
                             Sauté de ris de veau   200
                             (Sautéed Calf's Sweetbread)

	Tête de veau à la tortue 200
	(Mock Turtle Stew)
	Andouille à la béchamel 201
	(Pork Sausage Béchamel)
poultry and game	*Kari de lapereaux* 235
	(Rabbit Curry)
	Salmis de perdreaux 237
	(Partridge Salmi)
	Côtelettes de sanglier sautées 239
	(Sautéed Chops of Wild Boar)
vegetables	*Macédoine à la béchamel* 253
	(Mixed Vegetables in Béchamel Sauce)
desserts and sweets	*Petits puits d'amour* 275
	(Currant, or Apricot, Pastries)
	Biscuit au chocolat 276
	(Chocolate Cake)
drinks	*Ratafia d'oranges* 287
	(Orange Ratafia)
	Fruits à l'eau-de-vie 287
	(Fruit in Alcohol)

1826   **BRILLAT-SAVARIN**

poultry and game	*Bécasses brûlées au rhum à la bacquaise* 241
	(Spit-Roasted Woodcocks with Rum)

1830   **CUISINIER DURAND**

soups	*Soupe garbure aux choux* 68
	(Cabbage Garbure Soup)
	Croûte au pot 69
	(Bouillon with Toasted Bread Crusts)
fish	*Merluche à la branlade en pierre à fusil* 132
	(Salt Cod Purée)
meat	*Gigot de mouton de 7 heures* 177
	(Seven-Hour Lamb)
	Jambon à la broche 193
	(Roast Ham with Wine Sauce)
variety meats and charcuterie	*Pâté de jambon* 202
	(Ham Pâté)
	Terrine de foies de canards 203
	(Duck Liver Terrine)
vegetables	*Ragoût de fèves en grains* 254
	(Lima Bean Stew)
	Friture de salsifis 254
	(Deep-Fried Salsify)
	Feuilles de céleri à la ménagère 255
	(Celery Casserole)
	Pommes d'amour au gratin 255
	(Baked Stuffed Tomatoes)
desserts and sweets	*Pêches au gratin* 277
	(Peaches Baked in Custard)

18

1833   *CAREME*

soups   *Potage de santé*   69
                                  (Health Soup)
                                Potage aux pointes d'asperges   70
                                  (Asparagus Tip Soup)
                                Potage aux herbes   70
                                  (Herb Soup)
fish and shellfish   *Ragoût d'escalopes de homard à la navarin*   132
                                  (Lobster, Eel, and Oyster Stew)
                                Aiguillettes de morue frites   133
                                  (Salt Cod Fritters)
poultry and game   *Soufflé de volaille*   243
                                  (Chicken Soufflé)
vegetables   *Croquettes de pommes de terre*   256
                                  (Potato Croquettes)
desserts and sweets   *Pouding de cabinet*   277
                                  (Raisin Pudding)
                                Solilemme   278
                                  (French Sally Lunn Cake)

1845   *ETIENNE*

fish   *Harengs à la Sainte-Menehould au champagne*   133
                                  (Herring in Champagne Sauce)

1867   *GOUFFE*

soups   *Petite marmite*   71
                                  (Kettle Soup)
entrées   *Bouchées à la purée de sole*   80
                                  (Sole Purée in Pastry Shells)
meat   *Croquettes de bouilli*   144
                                  (Beef Croquettes with Egg Sauce)
                                Filets de boeuf sautés aux olives   144
                                  (Steaks with Olive Sauce)
                                Escalopes de veau aux fines herbes   158
                                  (Veal Scallops in Herb Sauce)
                                Côtelettes de mouton panées et grillées   178
                                  (Grilled Mutton Chops)
                                Filet de porc à la sauce Robert   194
                                  (Braised Pork Roast with Onion Sauce)
variety meats and charcuterie   *Rognons de boeuf sautés*   202
                                  (Sautéed Beef Kidneys)
                                Saucisses au vin blanc   203
                                  (Sausages in White Wine Sauce)
vegetables   *Carottes à la flamande*   256
                                  (Glazed Carrots with Cream)
                                Haricots blancs à la maître d'hôtel   257
                                  (White Beans à la Maître d'Hôtel)
                                Chou-fleur au gratin   257
                                  (Cauliflower au Gratin)

	Aubergines farcies 258
	(Stuffed Eggplants)
	Laitues au jus 258
	(Braised Lettuce)
desserts and sweets	Savarin 279
	(Savarin Cake)
	Pots de crème au citron 279
	(Lemon Custard)
	Croquembouche de gimblettes de génoise 280
	(Genoese Ring-Cookie Basket)
	Tôt fait 280
	(Instant Cake)
	Oeufs à la neige 281
	(Egg Fluff)
	Charlotte de pommes de ménage 281
	(Apple Charlotte)
drinks	Kaldschall à la macédoine 288
	(Wine Fruit Punch)

1870   MONSELET

| shellfish | Coquillage au feu   134 |
| | (Burning Shellfish) |

1873   ALEXANDRE DUMAS

soups	Potage aux tomates et aux queues de crevettes 71
	(Tomato and Shrimp Soup)
fish	Harengs pecs vinaigrette 134
	(Salted Herring in Cress Dressing)
	Carrelet à la sauce normande 135
	(Plaice or Flounder in Norman Sauce)
	Accolade d'anguilles à la broche 135
	(Spit-Roasted Eel)
meat	Poitrine de mouton 178
	(Grilled Breast of Lamb with Shallot Sauce)
poultry	Salade de poulet 243
	(Chicken Salad)
desserts and sweets	Bonnet de Turquie à la Triboulet 282
	(Turk's Hat Cake)
drinks	Punch à la française 288
	(Hot Rum Punch à la Française)

RECIPES

SOUPS

Potage d'oignons au lait   *(La Varenne, 1651)*   *65*
  (Onion Soup with Milk)
Potage aux moules à la Reyne   *(Marin, 1739)*   *65*
  (Mussel Soup with Almonds)
Potage à la citrouille   *(Menon, 1746)*   *66*
  (Pumpkin Soup)
Potage maigre printanier   *(Menon, 1746)*   *66*
  (Spring Soup)
Potage à la vierge   *(Menon, 1746)*   *67*
  (Virgin Mary's Soup)
Potage à la Geaufret   *(Viard, 1820)*   *67*
  (Potato Dumpling Soup)
Potage au poisson   *(Viard, 1820)*   *68*
  (Fish Soup)
Soupe garbure aux choux   *(Cuisinier Durand, 1830)*   *68*
  (Cabbage Garbure Soup)
Croûte au pot   *(Cuisinier Durand, 1830)*   *69*
  (Bouillon with Toasted Bread Crusts)
Potage de santé   *(Carême, 1833)*   *69*
  (Health Soup)
Potage aux pointes d'asperges   *(Carême, 1833)*   *70*
  (Asparagus Tip Soup)
Potage aux herbes   *(Carême, 1833)*   *70*
  (Herb Soup)
Petite marmite   *(Gouffé, 1867)*   *71*
  (Kettle Soup)
Potage aux tomates et aux queues de crevettes   *(Alexandre Dumas, 1873)*   *71*
  (Tomato and Shrimp Soup)

ENTREES

Lait lardé   *(Taillevent, 1373)*   *73*
  (Fried Larded Milk)
Faux frenon   *(Ménagier de Paris, 1392)*   *73*
  (False Frenon, or Mixed Meat Casserole)
Tourte d'herbes   *(Ménagier de Paris, 1392)*   *74*
  (Herb Pie)
Flan fin qu'on appelle tarte d'ami   *(La Varenne, 1651)*   *74*
  (Cheese Tart, Known as Friend's Tart)
Tourte d'huîtres fraîches   *(La Varenne, 1651)*   *75*
  (French Oyster Pie)
Beignets de melon   *(Bonnefons, 1654)*   *76*
  (Melon Fritters)

Andouillettes contrefaites   *(Bonnefons, 1654)*   *76*
   (Mock Sausages)
Tourte de godiveau feuilletée   *(Pierre de Lune, 1656)*   *77*
   (Mixed Meat Pie)
Petits pâtés à la Mazarine   *(Marin, 1739)*   *78*
   (Veal and Bacon Pastries à la Mazarine)
Fromage à l'écarlate   *(Menon, 1746)*   *78*
   (Cheese and Crayfish Scarlet)
Rôties de Bretagne   *(Menon, 1746)*   *79*
   (Breton Toast with Herb Butter)
Ramequins au fromage   *(Viard, 1820)*   *79*
   (Cheese Ramequins)
Bouchées à la purée de sole   *(Gouffé, 1867)*   *80*
   (Sole Purée in Pastry Shells)

EGGS

Oeufs rôtis à la broche   *(Taillevent, 1373)*   *85*
   (Spit-Roasted Eggs)
Oeufs farcis à l'oseille   *(La Varenne, 1651)*   *87*
   (Eggs Stuffed with Sorrel)
Omelette farcie et coupée   *(Pierre de Lune, 1656)*   *89*
   (Stuffed Sliced Omelette)
Oeufs pochés à la sauce d'anchois   *(Escole Parfaite des Officiers de Bouche, 1662)*   *91*
   (Poached Eggs with Anchovy Sauce)
Oeufs à l'antidame   *(La Chapelle, 1733)*   *93*
   (Eggs with Herbs and Anchovies)
Oeufs à l'infante   *(Marin, 1739)*   *95*
   (Poached Eggs à l'Infante)
Omelette au joli coeur   *(Menon, 1746)*   *97*
   (Crayfish Omelette)
Omelette d'asperges   *(Pierre de Lune, 1656)*   *98*
   (Asparagus Omelette)
Civet d'oeufs à l'huile   *(Escole Parfaite des Officiers de Bouche, 1662)*   *98*
   (Deep-Fried Eggs with Wine Sauce)
Omelette aux huîtres   *(Marin, 1739)*   *99*
   (Oyster Omelette)
Oeufs à l'ail   *(Menon, 1746)*   *99*
   (Garlic Eggs)
Oeufs en matelote   *(Menon, 1746)*   *100*
   (Egg and Anchovy Stew)
Oeufs au gratin   *(Menon, 1746)*   *100*
   (Eggs au Gratin)

Oeufs au prévôt   *(Menon, 1746)*   *101*
   (Eggs with Ham and Mushrooms)
Oeufs à la tripe   *(Menon, 1746)*   *101*
   (Eggs and Onions)
Oeufs à la bonne femme   *(Dictionnaire Portatif, 1765)*   *102*
   (Housewife's Eggs and Onion Soufflé)
Oeufs à la monime   *(Dictionnaire Portatif, 1765)*   *102*
   (Stuffed Omelette and Meat Balls)
Oeufs à la bonne suisse   *(Isabeau, 1796)*   *103*
   (Swiss Egg Fondue)
Oeufs à l'aurore   *(Beauvilliers, 1814)*   *103*
   (Egg Casserole)

FISH AND SHELLFISH

Pâté d'anguilles   *(Taillevent, 1373)*   *106*
   (Eel Pâté)
Brouet d'anguilles   *(Ménagier de Paris, 1392)*   *106*
   (Eel Stew)
Perches au court-bouillon   *(La Varenne, 1651)*   *107*
   (Perch in White Wine)
Poissons rôtis sur le gril   *(La Varenne, 1651)*   *107*
   (Grilled Fish)
Soupresse de poisson   *(La Varenne, 1651)*   *108*
   (Pressed Fish)
Saumon en ragoût   *(Massialot, 1691)*   *108*
   (Salmon and Oyster Stew)
Soles à la sauce aux rois   *(La Chapelle, 1733)*   *109*
   (Sole Stuffed with Anchovies and Herbs)
Turbot à la béchamel   *(La Chapelle, 1733)*   *109*
   (Turbot with Béchamel Sauce)
Maquereaux au fenouil et aux groseilles   *(La Chapelle, 1733)*   *110*
   (Grilled Mackerel with Fennel and Gooseberries)
Huîtres en coquilles   *(La Chapelle, 1733)*   *110*
   (Oysters Cooked in Their Shells)
Terrine de lottes   *(La Chapelle, 1733)*   *111*
   (Burbot and Crayfish Stew)
Ecrevisses à la poêle   *(Marin, 1739)*   *111*
   (Sautéed Crayfish with Lamb)
Blanquette de filets de sole   *(Marin, 1739)*   *112*
   (Fillets of Sole in White Sauce)
Carpe à l'aventure   *(Marin, 1739)*   *112*
   (Carp Poached in Beer)
Truites à la hussarde   *(Cuisinier Gascon, 1740)*   *113*
   (Broiled Trout with Rémoulade Sauce)

Filets de morue à la provençale   *(Menon, 1746)*   *114*
  (Salt Cod in Lemon Butter)
Raie au fromage   *(Menon, 1746)*   *114*
  (Skate with Cheese Sauce)
Cuisses de grenouilles frites   *(Menon, 1746)*   *117*
  (Deep-Fried Frogs' Legs)
Brochet en étuvée   *(Menon, 1746)*   *118*
  (Pike Stew with Anchovies and Capers)
Etuvée de carpe à la chartreuse   *(Menon, 1746)*   *120*
  (Carp in Red Wine à la Chartreuse)
Escargots de vigne en fricassée de poulet   *(Menon, 1746)*   *122*
  (Snail and Mushroom Stew)
Sardines en caisse   *(Dictionnaire Portatif, 1765)*   *124*
  (Sardines—or Smelt—with Fish and Herb Garnish)
Barbue Marinée   *(Dictionnaire Portatif, 1765)*   *126*
  (Marinated Flatfish)
Filets de merlan en turban   *(Viard, 1820)*   *129*
  (Whiting Fillets en Turban)
Truites au four   *(Menon, 1746)*   *130*
  (Baked Trout with Herb Stuffing)
Moules en beignets   *(Menon, 1746)*   *130*
  (Mussel Fritters)
Croustade de crevettes   *(Viard, 1820)*   *131*
  (Shrimp Croustade)
Cabillaud aux fines herbes   *(Viard, 1820)*   *131*
  (Baked Cod with Shallots and Mushrooms)
Merluche à la branlade en pierre à fusil   *(Cuisinier Durand, 1830)*   *132*
  (Salt Cod Purée)
Ragoût d'escalopes de homard à la Navarin   *(Carême, 1833)*   *132*
  (Lobster, Eel, and Oyster Stew)
Aiguillettes de morue frites   *(Carême, 1833)*   *133*
  (Salt Cod Fritters)
Harengs à la Sainte-Menehould au champagne   *(Etienne, 1845)*   *133*
  (Herring in Champagne Sauce)
Coquillages au feu   *(Monselet, 1870)*   *134*
  (Burning Shellfish)
Harengs pecs vinaigrette   *(Alexandre Dumas, 1873)*   *134*
  (Salted Herring in Cress Dressing)
Carrelet à la sauce normande   *(Alexandre Dumas, 1873)*   *135*
  (Plaice or Flounder in Norman Sauce)
Accolade d'anguilles à la broche   *(Alexandre Dumas, 1873)*   *135*
  (Spit-Roasted Eel)

BEEF

Boeuf mode   *(Pierre de Lune, 1656)*   *138*
  (Pot Roast)
Filet d'aloyau braisé à la royale   *(La Chapelle, 1733)*   *138*
  (Braised Fillet of Beef à la Royale)
Filet de boeuf à la mariée   *(Marin, 1739)*   *139*
  (Stuffed Fillet of Beef à la Mariée)
Carbonnades de boeuf à la lyonnaise   *(Marin, 1739)*   *139*
  (Braised Rib Steaks à la Lyonnaise)
Boeuf à la mode paysanne   *(Marin, 1739)*   *140*
  (Braised Beef Peasant-Style)
Charbonnée de boeuf en papillote   *(Menon, 1746)*   *140*
  (Rib Roast en Papillote)
Culotte à la braise aux oignons   *(Menon, 1746)*   *141*
  (Braised Rump Roast with Onions)
Tranche de boeuf à la Camargot   *(Menon, 1746)*   *141*
  (Braised Beef with Anchovies à la Camargot)
Queue de boeuf en hochepot   *(Menon, 1746)*   *142*
  (Oxtail Stew)
Côte de boeuf à la gelée   *(Viard, 1820)*   *142*
  (Cold Rib Roast in Meat Jelly)
Miroton   *(Viard, 1820)*   *143*
  (Beef with Onions)
Hachis de boeuf   *(Viard, 1820)*   *143*
  (Diced Beef with Eggs)
Croquettes de bouilli   *(Gouffé, 1867)*   *144*
  (Beef Croquettes with Egg Sauce)
Filets de boeuf sautés aux olives   *(Gouffé, 1867)*   *144*
  (Steaks with Olive Sauce)

VEAL

Longe de veau à la marinade   *(La Varenne, 1651)*   *145*
  (Marinated Loin Roast of Veal)
Jarret de veau à l'épigramme   *(La Varenne, 1651)*   *145*
  ("Epigram" Veal Knuckle)
Poitrine de veau farcie   *(La Varenne, 1651)*   *147*
  (Stuffed Breast of Veal)
Côtelettes de veau en surprise   *(La Chapelle, 1733)*   *149*
  (Surprise Veal Cutlets)
Veau à la bourgeoise   *(La Chapelle, 1733)*   *151*
  (Loin Roast of Veal with Carrots and Onions)
Blanquette de veau   *(Marin, 1739)*   *153*
  (Veal Stewed in White Sauce)

Fricandeau à la bourgeoise   *(Marin, 1739)*   *154*
  (Glazed Veal Garnished à la Bourgeoise)
Noix de veau en dés au jambon   *(Cuisinier Gascon, 1740)*   *154*
  (Veal and Ham in Wine Sauce)
Brezolles   *(Menon, 1746)*   *155*
  (Veal Stew with Shallots)
Côtelettes de veau à la Singara   *(Viard, 1820)*   *155*
  (Braised Veal Cutlets with Tongue)
Veau en crottes d'âne roulées à la Neuteau   *(Cuisinier Gascon, 1740)*   *156*
  (Stuffed Veal Scallops)
Tendrons de veau en chartreuse   *(Viard, 1820)*   *158*
  (Veal Chartreuse)
Escalopes de veau aux fines herbes   *(Gouffé, 1867)*   *158*
  (Veal Scallops in Herb Sauce)

LAMB AND MUTTON

Galimafrée   *(Taillevent, 1373)*   *159*
  (Lamb Gallimaufry)
Ratons de mouton   *(La Chapelle, 1733)*   *161*
  (Stuffed Lamb Steaks)
Selle de mouton à la Barberine   *(Marin, 1739)*   *163*
  (Braised Lamb à la Barberini)
Filet d'agneau à la Condé   *(Marin, 1739)*   *165*
  (Roast Lamb with Lemon Butter à la Condé)
Haricot de mouton   *(Menon, 1746)*   *167*
  (Lamb and Turnip Stew)
Gigot de mouton à la Ninon   *(Menon, 1746)*   *169*
  (Marinated Leg of Lamb à la Ninon)
Eclanche de cent feuilles   *(Dictionnaire Portatif, 1765)*   *171*
  (Stuffed Leg of Lamb)
Cous de mouton à la purée de lentilles   *(Viard, 1820)*   *173*
  (Mutton Neck with Lentil Purée)
Côtelettes de mouton à la Soubise   *(Beauvilliers, 1814)*   *175*
  (Lamb Chops à la Soubise)
Gigot de mouton de 7 heures   *(Cuisinier Durand, 1830)*   *177*
  (Seven-Hour Lamb)
Côtelettes de mouton panées et grillées   *(Gouffé, 1867)*   *178*
  (Grilled Mutton Chops)
Poitrine de mouton   *(Alexandre Dumas, 1873)*   *178*
  (Grilled Breast of Lamb with Shallot Sauce)

PORK

Porcelet farci   *(Ménagier de Paris, 1392)*   *179*
  (Roast Suckling Pig with Chestnut Stuffing)
Jambon en daube   *(Marin, 1739)*   *181*
  (Braised Ham in Wine)
Cochon de lait par quartiers au père Douillet   *(Menon, 1746)*   *183*
  (Glazed Suckling Pig au Père Douillet)
Côtelettes de porc frais à la cendre   *(Dictionnaire Portatif, 1765)*   *185*
  (Pork Chops with Mushroom Sauce)
Carrés de porc en couronne   *(Viard, 1820)*   *187*
  (Stuffed Crown Pork Roast)
Emincés de cochon à l'oignon   *(Viard, 1820)*   *189*
  (Pork with Onions)
Côtelettes de cochon en crépinettes   *(Viard, 1820)*   *191*
  (Pork Chops Wrapped in Onions)
Jambon à la broche   *(Cuisinier Durand, 1830)*   *193*
  (Roast Ham with Wine Sauce)
Echine de cochon sauce poivrade   *(Viard, 1820)*   *194*
  (Pork Chops with Poivrade Sauce)
Filet de porc à la sauce Robert   *(Gouffé, 1867)*   *194*
  (Braised Pork Roast with Onion Sauce)

VARIETY MEATS AND CHARCUTERIE

Foie de veau fricassé   *(La Varenne, 1651)*   *195*
  (Fricasseed Calf's Liver)
Cervelle de veau au parmesan et à la moutarde   *(Marin, 1739)*   *196*
  (Calf's Brain with Parmesan and Mustard)
Langue de boeuf aux concombres   *(Marin, 1739)*   *196*
  (Beef Tongue with Cucumbers)
Boudin blanc à la bourgeoise   *(Menon, 1746)*   *197*
  (Homemade White Sausage)
Fromage de cochon   *(Menon, 1746)*   *198*
  (Headcheese)
Fraise de veau au gratin de gruyère   *(Cuisinière Républicaine, 1795)*   *198*
  (Calf's Ruffle with Gruyère)
Gras-double en crépinettes   *(Viard, 1820)*   *199*
  (Honeycomb Tripe and Mushroom Patties)
Pieds de mouton à la poulette   *(Viard, 1820)*   *199*
  (Lamb's Trotters with Mushroom Sauce)
Sauté de ris de veau   *(Viard, 1820)*   *200*
  (Sautéed Calf's Sweetbread)
Tête de veau à la tortue   *(Viard, 1820)*   *200*
  (Mock Turtle Stew)

Andouille à la béchamel   *(Viard, 1820)*   *201*
    (Pork Sausage Béchamel)
Pâté de jambon   *(Cuisinier Durand, 1830)*   *202*
    (Ham Pâté)
Rognons de boeuf sautés   *(Gouffé, 1867)*   *202*
    (Sautéed Beef Kidneys)
Terrine de foies de canards   *(Cuisinier Durand, 1830)*   *203*
    (Duck Liver Terrine)
Saucisses au vin blanc   *(Gouffé, 1867)*   *203*
    (Sausages in White Wine Sauce)

POULTRY AND GAME

Foie gras cuit dans les cendres   *(La Varenne, 1651)*   *206*
    (Baked Foie Gras)
Fricassée de poulet   *(Bonnefons, 1654)*   *206*
    (Chicken Fricassee)
Canard en ragoût   *(Bonnefons, 1654)*   *207*
    (Duck Stew)
Chevreuil   *(Pierre de Lune, 1656)*   *207*
    (Venison in Wine Sauce)
Pâté chaud de faisan   *(Massialot, 1691)*   *208*
    (Hot Pheasant Pâté)
Poularde aux olives   *(Massialot, 1691)*   *211*
    (Chicken Stewed with Olives)
Grives au genièvre   *(La Chapelle, 1733)*   *213*
    (Thrush with Juniper Berries)
Poularde en mousseline   *(Marin, 1739)*   *215*
    (Stuffed Chicken Casserole)
Lapereaux en brodequins   *(Marin, 1739)*   *217*
    (Stuffed Young Rabbit)
Civet de lièvre   *(Marin, 1739)*   *219*
    (Hare Stew)
Poulet au persil   *(Marin, 1739)*   *220*
    (Roast Chicken with Herb Butter)
Poulet à l'oreille   *(Cuisinier Gascon, 1740)*   *220*
    (Roast Chicken Stuffed with Oysters)
Marinade de pigeons au citron   *(Menon, 1746)*   *221*
    (Marinated Pigeons with Lemon Sauce)
Oie à la moutarde   *(Menon, 1746)*   *221*
    (Roast Goose with Mustard)
Canard à la purée verte   *(Menon, 1746)*   *223*
    (Duck with Split Pea Purée)

Poulet au fromage   *(Menon, 1746)*   *225*
    (Chicken au Gratin)

Cailles à la cendre   *(Menon, 1746)*   *227*
    (Cinder-Baked Quail)

Lapin en gâteau   *(Menon, 1746)*   *228*
    (Rabbit Loaf)

Perdreaux à la Coigny   *(Menon, 1746)*   *228*
    (Partridge in Wine Sauce)

Poularde en ballon   *(Dictionnaire Portatif, 1765)*   *229*
    (Chicken Stuffed en Ballon)

Cuisses de dindon réveillantes   *(Isabeau, 1796)*   *231*
    (Braised Turkey Legs)

Faisan en filets au jus d'orange   *(Isabeau, 1796)*   *233*
    (Pheasant Fillets in Orange Sauce)

Kari de lapereaux   *(Viard, 1820)*   *235*
    (Rabbit Curry)

Salmis de perdreaux   *(Viard, 1820)*   *237*
    (Partridge Salmi)

Côtelettes de sanglier sautées   *(Viard, 1820)*   *239*
    (Sautéed Chops of Wild Boar)

Bécasses brûlées au rhum à la bacquaise   *(Brillat-Savarin, 1826)*   *241*
    (Spit-Roasted Woodcocks with Rum)

Dinde en daube   *(Beauvilliers, 1814)*   *242*
    (Stewed Turkey)

Canard aux navets à la bourgeoise   *(Beauvilliers, 1814)*   *242*
    (Duck with Turnips)

Soufflé de volaille   *(Carême, 1833)*   *243*
    (Chicken Soufflé)

Salade de poulet   *(Alexandre Dumas, 1873)*   *243*
    (Chicken Salad)

VEGETABLES

Cretonnée de pois nouveaux   *(Taillevent, 1373)*   *246*
    (Green Pea Purée with Chicken)

Epinards à la crème   *(La Varenne, 1651)*   *246*
    (Creamed Spinach)

Concombres farcis   *(Bonnefons, 1654)*   *247*
    (Stuffed Cucumbers)

Cardes d'artichauts à la moelle   *(L.S.R., 1674)*   *247*
    (Cardoons with Bone Marrow)

Asperges en pois verts   *(L.S.R., 1674)*   *248*
    (Green Pea Style Asparagus)

Chou farci   *(Massialot, 1691)*   *248*
    (Stuffed Cabbage)

Casserole au riz   *(Massialot, 1691)*   *249*
  (Rice Casserole)
Haricots en allumettes   *(Marin, 1739)*   *249*
  (Deep-Fried String Beans)
Laitues à la dame Simonne   *(Marin, 1739)*   *250*
  (Stuffed Lettuce in Cream Sauce)
Artichauts à la galérienne   *(Cuisinier Gascon, 1740)*   *250*
  (Artichokes with Wine and Mushrooms)
Truffes en puits   *(Menon, 1746)*   *251*
  (Fresh Truffles with Stuffing)
Artichauts à la barigoule   *(Menon, 1746)*   *251*
  (Artichokes with Vinaigrette)
Petits pois à la demi-bourgeoise   *(Menon, 1746)*   *252*
  (Green Peas with Lettuce)
Champignons au four   *(Buc'hoz, 1771)*   *252*
  (Stuffed Mushrooms)
Pommes de terre à l'économe   *(Cuisinière Républicaine, 1795)*   *253*
  (Potato Patties)
Macédoine à la béchamel   *(Viard, 1820)*   *253*
  (Mixed Vegetables in Béchamel Sauce)
Ragoût de fèves en grains   *(Cuisinier Durand, 1830)*   *254*
  (Lima Bean Stew)
Friture de salsifis   *(Cuisinier Durand, 1830)*   *254*
  (Deep-Fried Salsify)
Feuilles de céleri à la ménagère   *(Cuisinier Durand, 1830)*   *255*
  (Celery Casserole)
Pommes d'amour au gratin   *(Cuisinier Durand, 1830)*   *255*
  (Baked Stuffed Tomatoes)
Croquettes de pommes de terre   *(Carême, 1833)*   *256*
  (Potato Croquettes)
Carottes à la flamande   *(Gouffé, 1867)*   *256*
  (Glazed Carrots with Cream)
Haricots blancs à la maître d'hôtel   *(Gouffé, 1867)*   *257*
  (White Beans à la Maître d'Hôtel)
Chou-fleur au gratin   *(Gouffé, 1867)*   *257*
  (Cauliflower au Gratin)
Aubergines farcies   *(Gouffé, 1867)*   *258*
  (Stuffed Eggplants)
Laitues au jus   *(Gouffé, 1867)*   *258*
  (Braised Lettuce)

SALADS

''The Making of Rose Vinegar from the Buds of Red Roses During the Summer''
  (La Pratique de faire toutes confitures, 1550)   *260*
''Minor Herbs of All Kinds for Salads''   *(Bonnefons, 1654)*   *260*

DESSERTS AND SWEETS

Coings en quartiers   *(Nostradamus, 1552)*   *265*
  (Preserved Quinces)
Tourte admirable   *(La Varenne, 1651)*   *267*
  (Marzipan Pie)
Dame Susanne   *(La Varenne, 1651)*   *268*
  (Egg Bread Susanne)
Petits métiers   *(Bonnefons, 1654)*   *268*
  (Little Wafers)
Benoiles   *(Massialot, 1691)*   *269*
  (Egg Fritters)
Riz meringué   *(Marin, 1739)*   *269*
  (Rice Meringue)
Tourte de frangipane   *(La Varenne, 1651)*   *271*
  (Frangipane Pie)
Beignets de feuilles de vigne   *(Menon, 1746)*   *273*
  (Vine-Leaf Fritters)
Omelette charmante   *(Isabeau, 1796)*   *274*
  (Jam and Nut Omelette)
Pain des houris   *(Isabeau, 1796)*   *274*
  (Oriental Nut Cake)
Petits puits d'amour   *(Viard, 1820)*   *275*
  (Currant, or Apricot, Pastries)
Biscuit au chocolat   *(Viard, 1820)*   *276*
  (Chocolate Cake)
Flan de nouilles meringuées   *(Beauvilliers, 1814)*   *276*
  (Noodle Meringue Cake)
Pêches au gratin   *(Cuisinier Durand, 1830)*   *277*
  (Peaches Baked in Custard)
Pouding de cabinet   *(Carême, 1833)*   *277*
  (Raisin Pudding)
Solilemme   *(Carême, 1833)*   *278*
  (French Sally Lunn Cake)
Savarin   *(Gouffé, 1867)*   *279*
  (Savarin Cake)
Pots de crème au citron   *(Gouffé, 1867)*   *279*
  (Lemon Custard)
Croquembouche de gimblettes de génoise   *(Gouffé, 1867)*   *280*
  (Genoese Ring-Cookie Basket)
Tôt fait   *(Gouffé, 1867)*   *280*
  (Instant Cake)
Oeufs à la neige   *(Gouffé, 1867)*   *281*
  (Egg Fluff)
Charlotte de pommes de ménage   *(Gouffé, 1867)*   *281*
  (Apple Charlotte)
Bonnet de Turquie à la Triboulet   *(Alexandre Dumas, 1873)*   *282*
  (Turk's Hat Cake)

DRINKS

Limonade   *(La Varenne, 1651)*   *284*
   (Lemonade)
Vin des dieux   *(Pierre de Lune, 1656)*   *284*
   (Wine of the Gods)
Hypocras blanc   *(Massialot, 1691)*   *285*
   (White Hypocras)
Populo   *(Audiger, 1692)*   *285*
   (Aniseed and Cinnamon Liqueur)
Ratafia rouge   *(Audiger, 1692)*   *286*
   (Red Ratafia)
Vespetro   *(Menon, 1746)*   *286*
Ratafia d'oranges   *(Viard, 1820)*   *287*
   (Orange Ratafia)
Fruits à l'eau-de-vie   *(Viard, 1820)*   *287*
   (Fruit in Alcohol)
Kaldschall à la macédoine   *(Gouffé, 1867)*   *288*
   (Wine Fruit Punch)
Punch à la française   *(Alexandre Dumas, 1873)*   *288*
   (Hot Rum Punch à la Française)

Introduction

Le Viandier

The oldest French cookbook was probably written in 1290 and appeared under the title *Traité où l'on enseigne à faire et appereiller tous boires comme vin, clairet, mouré et autres, ainsi qu'a appareiller et assaisoner toutes viandes selon divers usages de divers pays* ("Treatise Where One Is Taught to Make and Dress All Drinks Such as Wine, Claret, 'Mouré' and Others, as Well as How to Dress and Season All Meats According to the Diverse Uses in Diverse Countries"). Although other books were probably written, the second oldest French book is usually dated 100 years later—1380. This book, *Le Grand Cuisinier de toute cuisine* ("The Great Cookbook of All Kinds of Cooking") was apparently very popular in its day, but all the manuscript copies have been lost. It was printed for the first time in 1540—a fact which has confused some authorities when dating this work. It was in 1490 that the most important of the early cookbooks was printed. The title page contained the following information: *"Ci après sensuyt le viandier pour appareiller toutes manières de viandes que Taillevent, queulx du roi nostre sire fit tant pour abiller et appareiller boully, rosty, poissons de mer et d'eau douce, saulces, espices et aultres choses à ce convenables et nécessaires comme cy après sera dit. . ."* ("Hereafter follows the viandier for dressing all manner of meats that Taillevent, cook to the King our lord made for dressing and preparing boiled meat, roasts, salt water fish and fresh water fish, sauces, spices, and other things agreeable and necessary as it will be shown hereafter. . . .") Today the book is simply referred to as the *Viandier* and its author as Taillevent.

Taillevent's life is surprisingly well documented. We know, for instance, that Taillevent was only his nickname. His real name was Guillaume Tirel, and his career as a chef began when, a boy, he worked as a kitchen helper in the kitchens of the French Queen Jeanne d'Evereux, wife of King Charles IV. No doubt after a long apprenticeship, during which he showed his talent for cooking, and a series of minor posts, Taillevent became cook to King Philippe VI de Valois. In 1349 the king gave Taillevent a house in the village of Saint-Germain-en-Laye, probably as a reward for the excellent food being served to him. When Philippe died, Taillevent entered the service of Charles V, and in 1373 he was appointed the King's cook for the second time in his life. Some authorities believe that it was about this time, late in life, that Taillevent began writing his famous cookbook. He died in 1395

Stone relief on the tomb of Guillaume Tirel, called Taillevent.
(Photo J.L. Charmet © Photeb.)

and was buried in Saint-Germain-en-Laye, where his tombstone is still visible. The stone, now in a local museum, shows Taillevent standing between his two wives (his first wife had died young) and holding a shield decorated with three stewpots and six roses.

A nineteenth-century author (the "Bibliophile Jacob") was no doubt using his own imagination more than any other source when he wrote the following vivid description of this celebrated chef:

Taillevent was short, and so fat, with such a round stomach, back, arms and legs, that you would have thought he was rolling along rather than walking if you saw him at a distance. His enormous head, topped off by a black hat with a turned up brim that rather resembled a mortar board, looked for all the world like a stewpot with its cover. His gray eyes were completely lost in the middle of his fat, red face, and the width of his nose made up for the fact that it was quite short. As for his hair, no one ever saw it, for Taillevent never took his hat off, not even before the King. He had thick legs, like columns, wide dimpled hands, and enormous shoulders. He wore a tight doublet and breeches which nevertheless didn't limit any of his movements, since they were made of the loose, soft, white woolen cloth then used in cooks' uniforms. His linen apron, with a band of decoration, was quite stylish, and a kitchen knife in a leather sheath took the place of a dagger at his belt. A ladle, a larding needle, and the chain from a spit often hung from his belt as well—the eloquent arms of his profession.

36

Le Viandier was reprinted several times during the sixteenth century, and one edition came out as late as 1602—more than 200 years after the author's death. Earlier editions of this work are extremely rare, and in the nineteenth century two erudite scholars published a new version of the book, based on its early manuscripts. One of the manuscripts they consulted had this note scribbled on the last page: *"c'est Viandier fu acheté à Paris par moy, Pierre Buffaut, l'an M CCC IIII^{XX}XII ou pris de vj s. par."* ("This copy of the *Viandier* was bought in Paris by me, Pierre Buffaut, in the year 1392 at the price of six Parisian sous.") This proves that the book was written sometime before 1392, although it was not printed until 1490. It also supports the theory that Taillevent wrote his book during the last years of his service to Charles V.

It is surprising that Taillevent's work was reprinted for so many years after the style of cooking he described had become old-fashioned. Taillevent typically boiled meat before roasting it, thickened sauces with bread instead of flour, and used spices and sugar in quantities that would shock any French chef today.

Woodcut from a 1595 edition of *Le Viandier*.
(Photo J.L. Charmet © Photeb.)

Le Ménagier de Paris

Le Ménagier de Paris ("The Goodman of Paris") is more than just a cookbook. It was written between June 1392 and September 1394 and was unsigned, but references in the text show that the author was a man of a relatively advanced age who had just married a fifteen-year-old orphan. He decided to write a book containing everything his young wife should know about managing a household. He describes his household in great detail. There were several servants, of which the two most important seem to be "Maistre Jehan le despensier," most likely the house steward in charge of domestic expenses, etc., and the young bride's personal maid, Agnès la Béguine. The author warns his wife:

Don't ever hire a chambermaid unless you know first where she comes from, and send servants out to inquire about her, especially as to whether she either gossips or drinks too much. If you have any servants or chambermaids only fifteen to twenty years old, you must be very careful, because at that age they are silly, and know very little of life. They should sleep in a room next to yours which has neither a gable nor a low-set window, and in no case should it look out into the street . . . .

This book, the first of its kind, is of primordial importance to anyone interested in daily life in the Middle Ages. The chapters on cookery reveal that the author of this book was familiar with both *Le Grand Cuisinier de toute cuisine* and the *Viandier*. Unlike Taillevent, however, the author of the *Ménagier* does not particularly care for sugar; he is nevertheless just as fond of spices as the author of the *Viandier*.

Le Ménagier de Paris gives recipes for a variety of dishes, including suckling pig stuffed with egg yolks, chestnuts, sausage meat, cheese, saffron, and ginger; a stew of chicken livers and gizzards cooked in wine and verjuice; an eel stew; etc. The book is also full of detailed advice that shows what a keen interest the author took in food and cooking. For example, he writes: "In winter, coneys [rabbits] hung for eight days are good, and in the summer, four days, but they mustn't have seen the sun." A little farther on he says: "Carp should be very cooked, otherwise it is dangerous to eat it. A carp that has white scales, and not half-yellow, half-red ones, comes from good waters. If it has big eyes that stick out of its head, and the palate and tongue soft and of one piece, then it is good and fat." He goes on: "Pigeons are good in winter. . . . White trout are good in winter, red ones in summer. The best part of the trout is the tail end, while the best part of the carp is the head end. Shad come into season in March."

Illustration of rabbits from the *Traité de chasse,* by Gaston de Foix, called Phoebus.
(Musée Condé, Chantilly, Archives E.B. © Giraudon)

Le Grand Cuisinier de toute cuisine

Although *Le Grand Cuisinier de toute cuisine* ("The Great Cookbook of All Kinds of Cooking") was actually written in 1350, before either the *Viandier* or *Le Ménagier de Paris*, it wasn't published until 1540. The complete title of this book is: *Le Grand Cuisinier de toute cuisine, très utile et prouffitable, contenant la manière d'habiller toutes viandes tant chair que poisson et de servir es banquets et festes, avec un mémoire pour faire un escriteau pour un banquet: composé parplusieurs cuisiniers, revu et corrigé par Pierre Pidoulx, Paris, Jehan Bonfons.* ("The Great Cookbook of All Kinds of Cooking, Very Useful and Profitable Containing the Manner of Dressing All Meats, Both Flesh and Fish, and of Serving Banquets and Feasts, with an Essay on How to Arrange a Menu for a Banquet: Written by Several Cooks, Revised and Corrected by Pierre Pidoulx, Paris, Jehan Bonfons.")

The book is very small, containing only 182 pages. It was reprinted four times under the same title between 1540 and 1575. After that it appeared under such titles as *Livre de cuysine, La Fleur de toute cuysine, Libre et honneste volupté*, etc. Spices are used "in great abundance," as is sugar; bread is still very important in thickening soups and sauces; there are very few vegetables, but a great number of recipes for cakes, especially cheesecakes such as *talmouzes* and jacobine tarts.

Title page of the *Platine*, 1505.
(Photo © B.N., Paris)

Platine

There was a Renaissance in cooking as well as in the other arts. It began in Italy with the publication, in 1474, of a book written in Latin, called *De Honesta voluptate et valetudine*. The author of this book was the historian Barthélémy de Sacchi, better known under the pen name of Baptiste Platine de Crémone.

The book, commonly referred to as the *Platine,* was first published in French in 1505. It was very popular and was still being printed almost 100 years later in 1602. The complete title of the book in French is: *Platine en françois très utile et necessaire pour le corps humain, que traicte de honeste vo-*

lupté et de toutes viandes et choses que l'ome mange, quelles vertus ont, et en quoy nuysent ou prouffitent au corps humain, et comment se doyvent apprester ou appreiller, et de fair à chascune dicelles viandes soit chair ou poysson sa propre saulce et des propriétés et vertus que ont les dites viandes. Et du lieu et place convenable à l'ome pour abiter et de plusieurs gentillesses par quoy l'ome se peut maintenir en prospérité et santé sans avoir grant indigence d'avoir aultre médecin sil est homme de rayson. ("Platine in French, Very Useful and Necessary for the Human Body, Which Treats of Honest Pleasures and of All Meats and Things That Men Eat, What Their Virtues Are, and How They Hurt or Help the Human Body, and How They Should Be Prepared and Dressed, and How to Make for Each One of These Meats, Either Flesh or Fish, Its Own Sauce, and the Properties and Virtues That Each of These Meats Has. And the Best Sites and Places for a Man to Live, and Several Niceties by Which He Can Maintain His Prosperity and Health, with No Need to Have Any Other Doctor, If He Be a Man of Reason.") The book is particularly interesting because Platine enumerates all the various things eaten in the sixteenth century. For example, he mentions fifteen different "salad plants": lettuce, endive, bugloss, purslane, rosemary, mauve, chicory, saxifrage, burnet, sorrel, capers, carrots, parsnips, onions, and leeks. According to the sixteenth-century philosopher Montaigne, "Everything is included under the name of salad."

During the Middle Ages a number of foods were popular which have completely disappeared since. For example, both whale and porpoise were eaten then. Whale blubber was the common fat used by the poorer people, and Platine writes that the porpoise was "a noble fish," mentioning that Pliny considered it the "lightest of all animals, whether under the sea or under the sun." Nevertheless, Platine warns that it is difficult to digest: "It mustn't be eaten as soon as it has been caught, but hung for a few days until its flesh has softened, though it should not be allowed to spoil. It is better if it is a little gamey than if it is fresh, and better roasted than boiled. And it is better boiled in wine than in water."

Platine was full of praise for Catalan cooking. "The Catalans," he writes, "are a people with excellent eating habits." He gives a recipe for Myraux de Catalogne, a sort of stew made with capons, pigeons, and chickens, which "warms the liver, fattens the body, and loosens the belly." He also gives recipes for Partridges à la Catalane and for Mortadelles, a kind of small sausage patty made of veal, chopped with pork fat, thickened with egg yolk, and wrapped in lace fat.

Medieval woodcuts depicting shipment of hay and barrels of wine.
(Photo © Ed. R. Laffont)

Title page of *Le Confiturier français*, by Nostradamus.
(Photo © B.N., Paris)

Le Confiturier français

The Italian influence, which began with Platine, continued to grow throughout the sixteenth-century. The Italians introduced sweets (jams and jellies, pâtés de fruits, and candied fruits) to France at about this time. The first recipe book for sweets was the *Opera nuova intitolata Dificio de recette*, printed in Venice in 1541 and translated into French the same year under the title *Bastiment de recettes* ("Edifice of Recipes"). Ten years later a Parisian bookseller published *Manière de faire toutes confitures* ("Manner of Making All Sorts of Confectionery"). Although the author is unknown, it is assumed to have been written by an Italian then living in France.

Jams, jellies, and sweets of all kinds became more and more fashionable. Making jams and jellies became a snobbish pastime in France. Finally, the first French book on confectionery appeared; it was entitled *Le Confiturier français* ("The French Confectioner") and was written by Nostradamus in 1552. The actual title of the book was *Excellent et moult utile opuscule à tous nécessaires qui désire avoir connaissance de plusieurs exquises recettes* ("Excellent and Most Useful Little Book Necessary to All Those Who Desire to Know a Few Exquisite Recipes"). The first part of the book contains beauty advice; the second is entitled *La façon et manière de faire toutes confitures liquides, tant en sucre, miel qu'en vin cuit* ("The Ways and Methods for Making All Liquid Preserves, with Sugar and Honey, as Well as with Sweet Wines").

Nostradamus (his real name was Michel de Nostre-Dame) was a doctor who had studied medicine in Avignon and Montpellier. He was born in 1503, in Saint-Rémy-de-Provence, and practiced medicine in the town of Salon-de-Provence. But Nostradamus is primarily remembered for his work in astrology. He was both personal physician to Charles IX and court astrologer for a number of years before returning to Salon-de-Provence, where he died in 1566.

Nostradamus' book on confectionery is extremely rare; it contains recipes for preserving "little lemons, and whole oranges," and tells how to make cotignac, pignolat, sugar candy, syrups, candied pears, "touron d'Hespaigne," marzipan tarts, and jellies "both expensive and difficult to make." His recipes are indeed elaborate, but quite practical. Here, for instance, is how he makes cherry jelly:

Take good sugar and pound it to a coarse powder, and put it in a pan, and there should be two pounds, and then take cherries only so much when the stone be removed, as the weight of six to seven pounds, and break them and crush them with clean hands and put them in the pan where the sugar is; and put them on the fire to boil halfway, stirring them with a stick; and when they have boiled thus you pour them through a tight-woven cloth and very clean, and squeeze them a bit; and take what passed through and boil it in another pan over a low fire, and watch it continually to see whether it be cooked; and take care not to set it on a fire too bright nor fierce, for it will boil over or burn.

And when it is cooked: that is known by placing a drop on a piece of marble, and the drop should stay round and firm and not fall hither and thither, and you will see that the drop will be red as the most perfect claret wine. As soon as it is cooked, put it in little glass or wooden vessels.

And when your jelly has cooled off and set, you will have a style and sort of jelly such that no other will be better, nor more excellent in beauty or in goodness.

That is to say, in short: Take two pounds of granulated sugar for every six or seven pounds of cherries, weighed after removing the pits. Crush the cherries with your hand, and put them into a preserving pan with the sugar. Boil until half cooked. Strain the juice through a cloth, pressing it through as you do so. Then put the juice back on a low fire to cook until a drop of it beads on a plate.

One of the reasons this book and others on confectionery were so popular was that anything containing large amounts of sugar was expensive and considered a delicacy. Only cane sugar from the Far East was available then, and it was usually sold in small quantities only by pharmacists. But Nostradamus advises his spendthrift reader: "When making a salad you don't spare the oil, likewise sugar should not be spared in making jams and jellies."

Le Pourtraict de la santé

King Henri IV (reigned 1589–1610) promised that he would make it possible for the poor people of France to put a chicken in their stewpots every Sunday. But "good King Henry's" greatest gift to gastronomy was the encouragement and support he gave to one of the most prominent agronomes of his day, Olivier de Serres, who is credited with popularizing many neglected vegetables in cooking. During the Middle Ages vegetables played only a minor part in any meal, but De Serres encouraged their use in cooking and experimented with new varieties that had never before been grown in France. His book, *Théâtre de l'agriculture et mesnage des champs* ("Theater of Agriculture and Care of the Fields") was printed in 1600 and is said to have revolutionized agriculture in France. De Serres suggested planting rice in the Camargue (in the south of France) and he was the first person in France to talk about the advantages of the potato as food (unsuccessfully it seems, since the potato was not eaten in France until two centuries later).

This brings us to a very important work, *Le Pourtraict de la santé* ("Portrait of Good Health") by Joseph Du Chesne, first published by Claude Morel in Paris in 1606. It is both a dietetic book and a cookbook. Nothing will restore "beaten strength," says Du Chesne, like the juices from a leg of lamb, squeezed out and mixed with a little of the chopped meat itself, fresh bread crumbs, and lemon juice. As far as beef is concerned, the sirloin should be roasted and everything else boiled. He considers poultry the best of all meat and the sole the most delicate of fish (he calls it the partridge of the sea). Next in line come herring and sardines, both of which should be fried in butter and seasoned with lemon juice. Pepper is "the most healthy of spices," but sugar "burns the blood, changes and blackens the teeth, and under its white appearance hides a great blackness. . . ."

Thanks to Du Chesne, we know the eating habits of the French in 1600. They had dinner, or their main meal, around one o'clock, and supper between seven and eight (Du Chesne thought it would be better to have dinner between ten and eleven in the morning and supper around six, then to go to bed around ten). After dinner, he writes, "everyone should stay at the table, without moving, for a good half hour, chatting agreeably with each other."

In 1607 a book entitled *Thrésor de santé ou mesnage de la vie humaine* ("Treasure of Good Health or the Care of Human Life") was published in Lyons. It closely resembles Du Chesne's work, but among the recipes are such regional favorites as Saucisson de Lyon and Andouillettes de Troyes. They are the first examples of regional cooking to be found in print.

LE CVISINIER FRANCOIS,

ENSEIGNANT LA MANIERE de bien apprester & assaifonner les Viandes , qui se seruent aux quatre saisons de l'année, en la table des Grands, & des particuliers.

La maniere de faire le Boüillon pour la nourriture de tous les pots , soit de potage, entrée, ou entre-mets.

Ovs prendrez trumeaux derriere de simier , peu de mouton , & quelques volailles , & suiuant la quantité que vous voulez de boüillon,

Title page of the 1654 edition of *Le Cuisinier François* by Pierre de la Varenne.
(B.N., Paris Photo J.L. Charmet © Photeb.)

Le Cuisinier françois

In 1651 a book appeared which was called *Le Cuisinier françois: Enseignant la manière de bien apprêter et assaisonner toutes sortes de viandes grasses et maigres, légumes, pâtisseries et autres mets qui servent tant sur les tables des Grands que des particuliers* ("The French Cook: Teaching the Manner of Preparing and Seasoning All Sorts of Meats, Both Flesh and Fish, Vegetables, Pastries and Other Dishes Served at the Tables of the Great Lords as Well as Those of Simple Individuals"). The author of the book was a certain La Varenne, head cook to the Marquis d'Uxelles.

François-Pierre de La Varenne had been head cook to this nobleman for ten years before he wrote his book. He is said to have named a mixture of chopped mushrooms, onions, shallots, and parsley, browned rapidly in butter, for his employer, and it is still called a duxelles by cooks today.

In a preface to *Le Cuisinier françois* the publisher writes, "The contents and title of this book are new to Paris." Soups, which were in fact stews, are varied and numerous. Unlike the cooks of the Middle Ages, La Varenne uses only the most common herbs and spices, and in small quantities at that, although he continues to add sugar to meat. Most important, he gives numerous recipes for vegetables, which had been almost entirely neglected until then. La Varenne is generally credited with being the first Frenchman to systematize the art of cooking as it was practiced in his time, and he is responsible for improving and refining the dishes of his day. *Le Cuisinier françois* is often considered the first "modern" French cookbook.

La Varenne's book was extremely popular and was printed more than thirty times between 1651 and 1727. Ironically, La Varenne profited very little from this success. After the death of his master he left Paris and is said to have died in poverty in Dijon in 1678. He was more than sixty years old when he died.

Here is one of La Varenne's recipes, for a Capon Pie:

Take the white meat of a capon and chop it fine. Mix with it two egg yolks, fresh butter, salt, pistachios, and a lot of sugar. If it is too dry, dampen it with a little bouillon. After that, make a very fine, sweet, puff pastry. Line a pie dish with some of it. Put your stuffing into the dish and add some dried currants, then cover the pie with the rest of the puff pastry. Cut a little chimney in the top crust, and cook in a slow oven.

Les Délices de la campagne

Les Délices de la campagne ("The Delights of the Country") was published in Paris by Pierre de Hayes in 1654. The book was written by Nicolas de Bonnefons, valet of King Louis XIV. The work is divided into three parts: The first, dedicated to the "ladies of Paris," deals with breads, rolls, and drinks; the second, with vegetables; the third with meat and fish. *Les Délices de la campagne* bears an overall dedication to the Capuchin friars, and Bonnefons explains that "they show a much greater interest in gardening and farming than any of the other religious orders." He adds: "In recognition of

Seventeeth-century plates illustrating costumes of *Le Rôtisseur, La Cuisinière, Le Boulanger,* and *Le Cuisinier*.
(Bibliothéque des Arts Decoratifs, Paris. Photos J.L. Charmet and Jeanbor © Photeb.)

Habit de Rotisseur

La Cuisiniere   Die Köchin

Le Boulanger du temps de la cherte du Pain

Habit de Cuisinier

the gift I am presenting you here, I hope that you will not forget me in your prayers, so that, having finished my work in this terrestrial paradise, we may be together in that heavenly paradise.''

Bonnefons says, rather sternly: ''A cabbage soup should taste like cabbage, a leek soup like leeks, a turnip soup like turnips; the same applies for all other vegetables. A mixture of tastes should be left to bisques, hashes, panadas, and other disguised dishes which are only to he tasted, not filled up on.'' Bonnefons goes on to give recipes for roast chicken with a light sprinkling of vinegar as the only sauce and chopped calf's kidney seasoned with a little sugar.

Les Délices de la campagne had followed another book by Bonnefons entitled *Le Jardinier françois* (''The French Gardener''). Bonnefons was an amateur gardener interested in experimenting with new varieties of plants. In his books, he advertises seeds from his own garden, and others from Italy, which he says he sells in Paris during the spring, when he visits that city.

Frontispiece of the 1684 edition of *Les Délices de la campagne*, by Nicolas de (B.N., Paris. Photo J.L. Charmet © Photeb.)

''Preparing pastry,'' illustration from *Le Jardinier François*.
(Photo J.L. Charmet © Photeb.)

Le Cuisinier

In 1656, a book appeared simply entitled *Le Cuisinier, Où il est traité de la véritable méthode pour apprester toutes sortes de viandes, gibier, volailles, poissons tant de mer que d'eau douce. Suivant les quatres saisons de l'année. Ensemble la manière de faire toutes sortes de pâtisseries tant froides que chaudes, en perfection* ("The Cook, in Which Is Shown the True Method for Preparing All Sorts of Meat, Game, Poultry, and Both Saltwater and Freshwater Fish. According to the Four Seasons of the Year. As Well as the Best Way to Make all Sorts of Pastries, Both Hot and Cold, to Perfection"). It is attributed to a certain Pierre de Lune, then head cook to the Duke of Rohan.

The following anecdote about Pierre de Lune has come down to us as one of the proofs of his skills in the kitchen. It seems that Hercule de Rohan, the patriarch of the family, was famous for his courage in his younger years, but as he grew older, he became not only senile but stingy. When he was eighty years old, he fell in love with a young lute player, and he asked a friend of his, a certain Mlle. de Clisson, to give a dinner and invite the two of them. Mlle. de Clisson had only one cook, so Hercule said he would send over his cook " with everything that would be necessary." On the appointed day Pierre de Lune arrived, prepared to make a dinner for twelve people with the "necessities" his master had given him . . one little rabbit.

Although Pierre de Lune greatly simplified the art of cooking, he is also credited with the invention of, among other things, the now-famous Beef à la Mode. Pierre de Lune often uses limes in cooking, and he advises garnishing meat with orange slices. He also believes that roast duck should be eaten rare and often adds a bunch of sweet herbs (he calls it a packet) to stews and braised meats. This packet was usually made up of parsley, thyme, chervil, scallions, and a clove, wrapped up and tied inside a strip of fatback. A similar bunch of herbs, called a bouquet garni, is still used in French cooking.

A few years later Pierre de Lune wrote a book entitled *Le Cuisinier a l'espagnole* ("Spanish-Style Cooking"). It contained a number of sweet-sour dishes typical of Spanish cooking then, *e.g.*, a recipe for salt fish cooked with candied fruits. However, his first book, *Le Cuisinier,* proved to be his most popular work and was later plagiarized by numerous authors. In 1662 a book entitled *L'Escole parfaite des officiers de bouche* ("The Perfect School for Officers of the Mouth") appeared, unsigned and with no reference to any author, in which entire chapters of Pierre de Lune's *Cuisinier* are reproduced word for word.

L'Art de bien traiter

L'Art de bien traiter ("The Art of Entertaining") was published in 1674. It is signed with only the initials L. S. R. It is believed these are the initials of a M. Rolland, who was head cook to the Princess of Carignan. Some peole think the author's last name was Robert, rather than Rolland, but in any case *L'Art de bien traiter* is a very interesting document.

The author of *L'Art de bien traiter* observes that "lard is the soul of almost all the best stews." For making salads, he advises using olive oil from Nice and vinegar flavored with tarragon, roses, raspberries, carnations, or elderberries. He criticizes La Varenne, whose book was then extremely popular, and advocates a more refined and simplified approach to cooking.

Le Cuisinier royal et bourgeois

Le Cuisinier royal et bourgeois (translated into English in 1702 as *The Court and Country Cook*) was published in 1691. The author of this book is simply called Massialot; he is said to have been born in Limoges about 1660 and died in Paris in 1733. During his life he was employed by several influential and wealthy people, including the dukes of Chartres and of Orléans.

In the preface to his book, Massialot assures his reader:

It has been established that the cooking in France is far superior to that of other countries. My book gives ample proof that what I say is correct. It is a cookbook which I dare to qualify as royal, since the meals which are described for the different seasons of the year have been served recently at the court, as well as in the homes of princes and other notables. . . .

Le Cuisinier royal et bourgeois is a particularly interesting book because it presents a new stage in the evolution of cooking in France. The herbs and spices he uses are familiar to us today: capers, garlic, rocambole, shallots, scallions, chervil, parsley, cloves, and nutmeg. Dishes are garnished with truffles, morels, and wild mushrooms, as well as with stewed sweetbreads and cocks' combs. Essences of ham and of mushrooms are used as bases for stews and sauces, which are in turn thickened with egg yolk rather than with bread. In short, *Le Cuisinier royal et bourgeois* marks the turning point between seventeenth- and eighteenth-century cooking.

The year following the publication of *Le Cuisinier royal et bourgeois*, Massialot presented another book, *Nouvelles Instructions pour les confitures, les liqueurs, et les fruits* ("New Instructions for Preserves, Liqueurs, and Fruits"). This book was often published as a companion volume to the *Cuisinier royal et bourgeois*. Massialot refined the art of making preserves and candied fruits in a number of ways. For example, he systematically pits cherries before cooking them and parboils orange or lemon peels before candying them in order to remove their bitterness. When he makes pâtés de fruits, Massialot uses equal weights of sugar and fruit, whereas cooks before him used only half as much sugar as fruit.

In 1692 another very interesting book describing the management of a noble household and the service of the table during the second half of the seventeenth century was published under the title of *La Maison réglée, et l'art de diriger la maison d'un grand Seigneur & autres, tant à la ville qu'à la Campagne, et le devoir de tous les Officiers, & autres Domestiques en général. Avec la véritable méthode de faire toutes sortes d'essences, d'Eaux, & de Liqueurs, fortes et rafraichissantes à la mode d'Italie* ("*A Well-Managed House*, and the Art of Managing the Household of a Great Noble and Others, Both in the City and in the Country, with the Duties of All the Domestic Officers and Other Servants in General. With the True Method of Making All Sorts of Essences, Drinks, and Liqueurs, Both

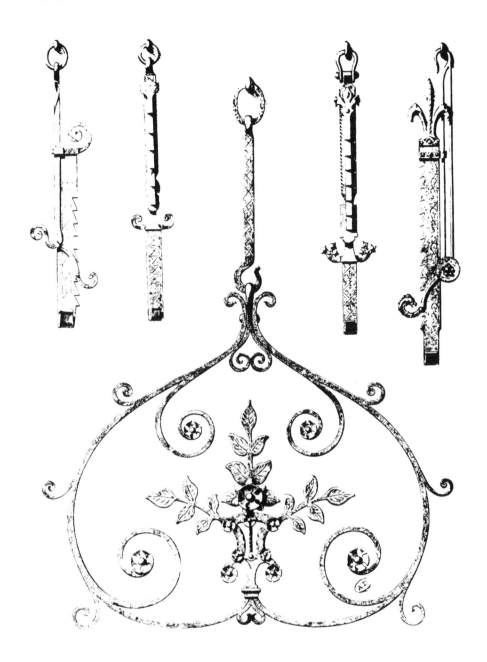

Types of pot-hooks used in the eighteenth century.
(Bibliothèque des Arts decoratifs. Photo J.L. Charmet © Photeb.)

Strong and Refreshing, According to the Latest Italian Fashion''). The recipes for preserves, jams, and jellies differ very little from those of Massialot, but the book's author, Audiger, had traveled widely all over Europe. In Italy he learned the art of distilling flowers, fruits, and berries, as well as the preparation of chocolate, recipes for which are given in his book. In 1680 Audiger is said to have served some of these ''exotic'' preparations to King Louis XIV, who was so pleased that he gave Audiger a little shop in front of the Palais Royal. Audiger made a fortune selling drinks and liqueurs to the king and his court.

After-dinner drinks were even more important then than they are today. The Abbot of Choisy, describing a dinner given in 1666, observed that ''after dinner everyone drank a little glass of rosolio cordial. At the time, coffee and chocolate were completely unknown, and tea was just being introduced.'' In 1671 a little book was published in Lyons with the title *De l'Usage du caphé, du thé et du chocolat* (''The Manner of Making Coffee, Tea, and Chocolate''), but it was not until ten years later, in 1680, that the first café was opened in France. Called the Procope, it was run by an Italian, Francesco Procopio; it is still operated as a restaurant.

The Modern Cook

The eighteenth century was the golden age of French cooking. From this time on, French cooking, like French fashion, was followed and imitated all over Europe.

The Modern Cook was the first cookbook of this new era. Very little is known of its author, Vincent de La Chapelle, except that he was a Frenchman serving as head cook to Lord Chesterfield when his book was first published in London in 1733. Two years later, in 1735, called to serve the Prince of Orange, La Chapelle published a French translation of his book at his own expense. Although the first edition was in fact published in English, the book is in every respect a French cookbook. The full title of the French edition of the book was *Le Cuisinier moderne, qui apprend à donner toutes sortes de repas en gras et maigre, d'une manière plus délicate que ce qui en a été décrit jusqu'a présent (The Modern Cook, Which Teaches How to Prepare All Sorts of Meals, Both Flesh and Fish, in a More Delicate Manner Than Any Other Book Written Until Now)*. Although the recipes in *The Modern Cook* owe a great deal to the work of Massialot, there are a number of original ideas to be found in it, and it was often quoted and copied during the course of the eighteenth century.

Le Festin joyeux

There are always people who want to do things differently. In 1738 a book was published in Paris by a cook named Lebas, who had decided to write all his recipes as poems set to popular tunes of the day. Although the rhymes are rather poor, Lebas explained that his object was "to teach how to make stews and sauces through enjoyment and song." It is somewhat difficult to follow the recipes, because of the rhyme, but they are nevertheless extremely interesting. Here's an example:

Terrine de queues de mouton
(sur l'air de "Je ne veux de Tircis")

Mettez queues de moutons blanchir doucement
Ailes de dindons tout ensemble
Petit lard, choux de Milan,
Et que tout ici se rassemble.
Ayez tranches de boeuf mises dedans un pot,
Ou dans une bonne marmite,
Et que le tout soit aussitôt
Très bien renfermé ensuite,
Que l'assaisonnement: sel, poivre, clous, oignons,
Barde de lard et d'importance,
N'y mettez point de champignons
Pour épargner la dépense.
Enfermez bien cela, etouffez tout sans eau
Que dans son jus cuise la viande:
Ayant bien fermé le vaisseau,
De l'attention cela demande.
Le tout bien cuit, ayez du bon coulis
De veau, de jambon, et ayez essence,
Dégraissez bien ayant tout mis
Et en terrine de fayence.
Arrangez proprement tout ce qui est dessus,
Avec des saucisses fines,
Et les choux dedans et dessus
Servez, elle aura grande mine.

Braised Lambs' Tails and Turkey Wings
(to the tune "I Want No More of Tircis")

Parboil several tails of lamb
Some turkey wings, use just the best,
Pork breast, cabbage from Milan
Should then be mixed in with the rest.
With sliced beef put this in a pan
Or in a stewpot nicely,
Next you should, as best you can
Put on the cover tightly.
Now season it: salt, pepper, cloves,
Some onions and a strip of fat,
But please, no mushrooms, we all know
They're too expensive for all that.
All closed up tight, no water put
For in its juice must cook the meat:
To close a pot seems simple, but
To do it well's no easy feat.
When all is cooked, add essence of ham,
Some cullis of veal, and as you wish
Skim off the fat the best you can,
Then put it in a china dish.
The cabbage should surround the meat,
Now take some sausage pretty
Arrange on top to decorate,
And serve it when it's ready.

Les Dons de Comus

The following year, in 1739, François Marin, cook to Mme. de Gesvres, wrote *Les Dons de Comus ou les delices de la table* ("The Gifts of Comus or the Delights of the Table"). His book contains a preface (supposedly written by two Jesuits) in which the merits of "modern cooking" are proclaimed in a very literary style which was regarded as somewhat ludicrous by many people at the time. In the following editions of the book (there were five, the last being in 1775) the preface was eliminated.

Marin's book is one of the finest books of this period. The recipes are apparently all his own, and he shows prudence and good taste in the use of herbs and spices. He emphasizes the quality of the foods employed in cooking, uses butter generously in making pastries, advises letting chickens hang for a few days before eating them, and (inexplicably) cooks vermicelli for an hour! As for cheeses used in cooking, he prefers parmesan and says: "If parmesan is used, it should be newly made; gruyère should be mild; Brie cheese should be mild and soft; cottage cheese [*fromage blanc*] should be creamy and fresh." *Les Dons de Comus*, originally only one volume, was soon enlarged to three and was an encyclopedic work for the period.

Illustration from *L'Art de découper les alouettes*, 1796.
(B.N., Paris. Photo Jeanbor © Photeb.)

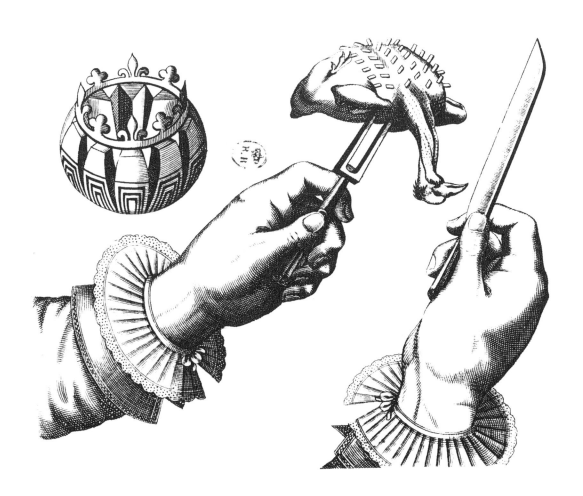

Le Cuisinier gascon

Le Cuisinier gascon (''The Gascon Cook'') is one of the most amusing cookbooks of the eighteenth century. It was published in 1740 at the expense of the Prince de Dombes, to whom it is dedicated. The dedication contains this interesting remark: ''I will shout on all the roofs that you are, milord, one of the best cooks in France.''

It is thought that *Le Cuisinier gascon* was in fact written by the Prince de Dombes himself. Wanting to remain anonymous, the theory goes, he simply attributed his work to a Gascon cook, who then dedicated the book to him. *Le Cuisinier gascon* is remarkable not only for the excellent quality of the recipes, but also for the bizarre names given to some of the dishes, for example, Nasty Chicken, Chicken in Bats' Wings, Chicken in Breeches, Veal in Donkey Droppings Rolled à la Neuteau, etc. There is also a very curious recipe for Stuffed Calf's Eyeballs au Gratin, in which the pupil of each eye is replaced by a whole truffle.

One of the main reasons this book is thought to have been written by the Prince de Dombes himself is that the style and tone of the text are those of a highly educated man. In the foreword, for instance, we find this comment: ''The author of the *Dons de Comus* is knowledgeable; the *Pastissier Anglais* (English Pastry Cook) is witty; I take pride in my taste.''

Menon

Perhaps the greatest, and certainly the most prolific, cook of the eighteenth century was Menon. Fifteen volumes of cookery are attributed to this author alone. His first book, *Nouveau Traité de la cuisine* (''New Treatise on Cooking'') was published in two volumes—the first in 1739 and the second in 1742. The influence of Marin's *Dons de Comus* is quite evident in this work. Then in 1746 Menon wrote an ''Orderly collection of simple and inexpensive recipes which are, nevertheless, very good,'' entitled *La Cuisinière bourgeoise*. Although unsigned, Menon's name appears on the registry papers for this book. It was by far the most popular cookbook written at that time and was reprinted frequently up until the second half of the nineteenth century. Menon wrote several more books, but his most complete and most famous one was the *Soupers de la cour* (''Dining at Court ''), a three- (sometimes four-) volume work first published in 1755. The subtitle of the book is *L'art de travailler toutes sortes d'aliments pour servir les meilleures tables suivant les quatre saisons* (''The Art of Preparing All Sorts of Foodstuffs to Be Served at the Most Refined Tables, According to the Four Seasons''). In all his works, Menon tries to be as clear and precise as possible (a novelty in the eighteenth century). His recipes are varied and refined, and his pastry recipes, especially, are considered remarkable. Some doubt whether one man was capable of writing all that has been attributed to Menon. None of his books were ever signed, and there is no information about Menon at all. Nevertheless, his name is associated with some of the finest works on French cooking.

Le Dictionnaire portatif de cuisine, d'office, et de distillation (''The Portable Dictionary of Cooking, Confectionery, and Distillation'') was an anonymous work published in 1765. It is an extremely interesting book which tries to be a complete guide to cookery. Many of the recipes are taken word for word from earlier books (especially Massialot), but there are many original ideas that seem to be the author's own inventions. The author of this book not only attempts to give recipes for all foods then available, but adds comments on their usefulness and nutritional value.

Take morels, for example. The author of the *Dictionnaire portatif de cuisine* informs us that this mushroom contains ''a lot of oil, very little phlegm, and a great deal of volatile salt, all of which contribute to the pleasant flavor it gives to stews to which it is added.'' He then goes on to give the recipes for preparing them in the following ways:

Morels à l'Italienne (with parsley, a touch of garlic, scallion, and olive oil, served on croutons)
Morels with bacon (arranged alternately on skewers with bits of bacon, and grilled)
Morels stewed with meat, in cream sauce
Morels stewed with vegetables, in cream sauce
Morel soup with croutons
Morels stuffed with chicken
Fried morels (fried in lard, served with the juice of roast lamb poured over them)
Morel pie
Etc.

Cooks today could learn a lot from consulting a list like this one. These delicious mushrooms are too often ignored and, when they are cooked, are usually served in a dull, uninspiring white sauce.

We almost never see recipes for lamprey today. But the *Dictionnaire portatif de cuisine* proposes:

Lamprey with sweet sauce
Lamprey with red sauce (with a roux, scallions, parsley, chopped anchovies, moistened with fish stock, and thickened with a crayfish cullis)
Lamprey with mushrooms (in a wine sauce thickened with the lamprey's blood)
Marinated and fried lamprey
Grilled lamprey (with a sauce of vinegar, mashed anchovies, and parsley)
Stewed lamprey (in a white wine sauce seasoned with nutmeg)

If you ever see the long red berries of the barberry, you probably don't know what to do with them or, for that matter, that anything can be done with them. Yet this book includes recipes for barberry jams, jellies, marmalades, and even ice creams. Here is the recipe for barberry ice cream:

Put a quart of water in a preserving pan and put it on the fire. When it is hot, throw two handfuls of bright red barberries into it, then take the pan off the fire and let the berries infuse until the water has the color and taste of berries. Strain the juice through a very fine sieve or cloth, put it into an ice cream maker, and freeze it.

Desserts of this kind were popular throughout the eighteenth century, and one of the most interesting books on the subject was given the misleading title of *Manuel alimentaire des plantes tant indigenes qu'exotiques* (''Manual on Nutrition, Concerning Both Native and Exotic Plants''). This book, written by Pierre-Joseph Buc'hoz, is actually full of recipes for making desserts, fruit preserves, and liqueurs, as well as a variety of unusual vegetable dishes.

The eighteenth century was a great century for cooking, but the progress made and the refinements added to the art of cooking were briefly interrupted by the French Revolution.

54

In 1789 the French Revolution broke out, and according to one observer at the time, it "served the sovereign people a dish of lentils, seasoned with nothing but the love of their country, which did very little to improve their blandness."

The interest in cooking and gastronomy was temporarily interrupted, but when things had calmed down enough in 1795, a little book entitled *La Cuisinière républicaine* was published. It was written by a Mme. Mérigot, who gives recipes for potatoes (unaccepted until then as food by the French). The growing importance of the potato can be seen in the title of another book published in 1796, *La Petite Cuisinière économe, ou l'art de faire la cuisine au meilleur marché mis à la portée de chacun et contenant l'indication des aliments les plus rapprochés des facultés de tous les citoyens; avec la manière de faire le pain et des instructions claires et faciles sur le traitement et l'appret des pommes de terres dans les temps difficiles* ("The Little Economic Cookbook, or the Art of Cooking Inexpensively in Terms That Everyone Can Understand, and Containing the Most Useful and Available Foodstuffs to Be Had by All Citizens; with the Method of Making Bread, and Clear and Easy Instructions for the Treatment and Preparation of Potatoes in These Difficult Times"). In the same year appeared the *Manuel de la friandise ou les talents de ma Cuisinière Isabeau mis en lumière* ("Manual of Dainty Dishes or the Talent of My Cook Isabeau Brought to Light"). This book closely resembles the traditional cookbooks which had been popular before the Revolution. The reason is obvious; "Isabeau" has simply copied Menon's recipes and given them new titles! There are some new recipes, but Isabeau herself seems to have been more interesting than her cooking. The author of the preface describes her as follows:

> Rosy complexion,
> Lively expression,
> She's the prettiest dish
> In all the kitchen. . . .

And adds, concerning her cooking.

> With veal she prepares
> Fricandeau, roast, and stew,
> And beef sirloin is served
> With a sauce entirely new. . . . [sic!]

Le Cuisinier impérial (Royal, then National)

In 1806 the book which marks the beginning of the nineteenth century and a new era of cooking was published under the title of *Le Cuisinier impérial*. We know little about its author, Viard, except that he was once head cook to the Prince de Condé and that he had traveled a great deal before sitting down to write this work at the age of forty-nine. The book was very successful, rivaling *Le Cuisinière bour-*

Plate from *L'Art de découper les alouettes*, 1796.
(B.N., Paris. Phote Jeanbor © Photeb.)

geoise in the number of editions it eventually went through. The title, however, changed according to the type of government in France at the time. When first published, Napoleon had just been made emperor, hence the title of *Le Cuisinier impérial*. After Napoleon's downfall in 1814, France underwent another brief revolution, and the monarchy was reinstalled under Louis XVIII. Thus, the 1817 edition of this cookbook was retitled *Le Cuisinier Royal*. In 1820, 850 new recipes were added to the book by the ex-cook to the king of Spain, a man named Fouret, whose name appears with Viard's on the title page. In 1831 a M. Delan added 300 more recipes. The book continued to be reprinted regularly, and after the short Revolution of 1848, the Second Republic was installed in France, and the book underwent its third title change, appearing subsequently as *Le Cuisinier National*. In 1875, 300 final recipes were added by Bernardi; the book continued to be published until the very end of the nineteenth century.

One of the things Viard did, certainly one of the things which made the book so popular, was that he often gave two versions of a recipe. After an elaborate preparation, described for accomplished cooks or for those who worked in wealthy households, Viard would give a less complicated and less expensive version "in the bourgeois style," with substitutions for problem ingredients. But many elaborate preparations in Viard's book could not be changed. One of the most often cited is the following recipe for Poached Eggs with Duck Sauce:

> Put twelve ducks on a spit, and roast them until they are almost done, but not quite. Then take them off the spit, and slit the meat to the bone. Press all the juices from the ducks and season with salt and pepper. Heat this sauce, but do not let it boil, and serve it over fifteen poached eggs.

As for the ducks, we will never know what happened to them. . . .

Beauvilliers

In 1814, when Viard's *Cuisinier impérial* was in its fourth edition, Beauvilliers' *L'Art du cuisinier* ("The Cook's Art") appeared for the first time. Beauvilliers had been cook to the Count of Provence before he opened a restaurant in Paris called the Grande Taverne de Londres in 1782 or 1786 (the exact date is not known). The Grande Taverne de Londres is often considered the first true restaurant in Paris; until then the only places which served meals were inns or taverns, frequented almost exclusively by travelers. Beauvilliers quickly became rich and famous, but during the French Revolution and the years following he was forced to close the Grande Taverne de Londres. In 1814 he reopened his restaurant, and the same year he published *L'Art du cuisinier*, considered by many of his contemporaries the best cookbook of its time. Many of the recipes were new; it is Beauvilliers who created Lamb Chops Soubise (lamb chops served on a bed of onion purée), now a classic preparation. His book was translated into English and enjoyed an immense success.

Inspired by his study of architectural engravings, Carême created elaborate candy and spun-sugar centerpieces, such as those on the facing page, These models appeared in *Le Pâtissier royal*, published in Paris in 1815.
(Photothèque Bordas.)

Pavillon Napolitain.

Ruine de Rome antique.

Grande Fontaine chinoise.

Chaumière française.

57

Viard and Beauvilliers set the tone for nineteenth-century cooking, but it was Carême who truly revolutionized the art of French cooking. Marie-Antoine Carême (he signed his books Antonin Carême) was born in Paris on June 8, 1784. The youngest of twenty-five children, he was born into an extremely poor family. When he was ten years old, his father took him to a cabaret on the outskirts of Paris, treated him to a farewell meal, and told him: "Go, my son, and fare well. In this world there are good professions. Leave us to wither away; poverty is our lot, and we will surely die in misery. Great fortunes can be made in this day and age, you just have to be clever to make it, and you are. Go, little one, and maybe this evening or tomorrow a good place will open its doors to you. Go with what God gave you." And he pushed the child outside.

Little Antoine did not go far. The owner of a cheap restaurant took him in and accepted him as a kitchen helper. The child had grown up in poverty and had always been hungry, and here he was surrounded by food. The most humble stews seemed wonderful to him. He worked in this kitchen for five years, then was hired by a slightly better restaurant, where he quickly advanced to a position of authority. His specialty was pastry, but he became a master chef and knowledgeable in all the arts of the kitchen.

Carême writes: "When I was seventeen, I secured a position as chef in charge of making meat pies in the shop of M. Bailly [a famous pastry chef]. This good man was very interested in me; he often allowed me to leave the shop and go copy designs for sculpted sugar pieces in the Print Room of the Bibliothèque Nationale. When he saw that I had talent in this field, he gave me the job of making the centerpieces for the table of the First Consul." The First Consul's name was Napoleon Bonaparte.

When his apprenticeship was completed, Carême took the position of head cook to a M. Lavalette and later to the famous diplomat Talleyrand, for whom he worked for twelve years. The banquets given by Talleyrand became famous. Then Carême went to England, where he was head chef to the crown prince for two years. But the English climate depressed him, and he returned to France. The crown prince ascended to the throne of England as George IV and offered Carême a huge sum of money to come back and be head of his kitchens, but Carême refused—he simply could not be happy in England and felt that he could not work effectively there.

The Carême legend had begun. He was referred to as the Cook of Kings and the King of Cooks. He held positions at the courts of Russia and Austria, cooking for princes and princesses, before taking the position as head cook in the household of the Baron de Rothschild in Paris. In the meantime, he had written several books. In 1815 he wrote *Le Pâtissier royal, ou Traité élémentaire et pratique de la pâtisserie ancienne et moderne* ("The Royal Pastry Cook, or an Elementary and Practical Treatise on Pastry, as Practiced by the Old School and by Modern Cooks"). That same year he published *Le Maître d'Hôtel français* ("The French Majordomo") which compared eighteenth- and nineteenth-century French cooking. Then in 1828, while working for the Baron de Rothschild, he wrote *Le Cuisinier parisien.*

The banquets given by Rothschild were the envy of all Europe. Carême writes: "In this wealthy household, I could spend as much as was necessary in order to prepare things as I wished. This is the only way in which a truly creative cook can fully profit from his talents, for what good is talent if one doesn't have the money with which to buy the best possible provisions?" The Baron de Rothschild bought a château in Ferrières and asked Carême to accompany him there. But Carême refused. His health was failing from the constant work to which he subjected himself. "My last wish," he says," is to finish my days, not in a great château, but in a humble home in Paris. . . . And I still want to write a book on the art of modern cooking." By 1832 he was ill and bedridden, but he managed to dictate his last and most famous book to his daughter. On January 12, 1833, he died, "burned out," it is said, "by the flame of his genius and the heat of the roasting ovens."

L'Art de la cuisine au XIX siècle ("The Art of Cooking in the Nineteenth Century"), his last work, appeared in three volumes between 1833 and 1835. It was meant to be five volumes in all, but Carême died before completing it. Plumery, one of his apprentices and later head cook to the Count of Pahlen, completed the work, using Carême's notes. The last two volumes, by Plumery, appeared in 1843 and 1845.

At about the same time a certain Etienne published a *Traité d'office* ("Management of the Pantry"). Etienne was another student of Carême's, but he specialized in preparing salads, ices, candies, and preserves, which were generally considered separately from both cooking and pastry. His work is a complement to the works of Carême and Plumery and was at one time published with them in a series on cooking in the nineteenth century.

Carême saw himself as the first truly modern cook. He was against garnishing fish dishes with meat or poultry (up through the eighteenth century, this was common practice) and many other practices which had been traditional since the Middle Ages. He perfected the rich *fonds de cuisine* (basic sauces) that were often complex and expensive to prepare. They became the trademark of "classic" French cooking during the century that followed.

But what probably most distinctively characterizes Carême's works is the instructions he gives for the presentation of many of the dishes. He considered cooking a branch of architecture, and many of the centerpieces he created are inspired by Greek and Roman models, with candy columns and spun-sugar fountains. His books are elaborately illustrated with monumental constructions that became all the rage in the first half of the nineteenth century. Unfortunately, food presented in this manner is often cold by the time it is finally served, and later gastronomes were to reproach Carême and his followers for trying to please the eye more than the palate.

Le Cuisinier Durand

In the midst of the publication of Carême's often lofty prose there appeared a very interesting cookbook, simply entitled *Le Cuisinier Durand*. The book was printed at the expense of the author in 1830 and published in Nîmes, where Durand was born in 1768; it is said that when he was only ten years old, he started cooking for the rest of his family. At thirteen he entered the service of the Bishop of Alais and worked as an apprentice to the bishop's chef. After completing his apprenticeship in exemplary style, he worked for a series of notables. Durand rarely left the South of France, and in 1790 he established a restaurant in Nîmes that became famous throughout the country. Toward the very end of his life he decided to codify his recipes in his famous cookbook, of which the full title is *Le Cuisinier Durand: Cuisine du Midi et du Nord (Chef Durand: Cooking in the North and South)*. He explains that few books up until then had recipes for the numerous regional specialties found throughout France. His book is the first to contain many of these regional dishes which had been frowned upon by the more princely chefs of the period. *Le Cuisinier Durand* was a great success (owing to Durand's reputation) and was printed, without any changes in the text, as recently as 1930. Durand's pride and love for his native region are reflected in his recipes, and his work was to inspire many later writers on French regional cuisine.

Food Writers in the Nineteenth Century

People other than professional cooks became more and more interested in the art of cooking and began writing about food. Gastronomic clubs were formed. One of these, of which Balthazar-Laurent Grimod de la Reynière was president, met regularly at the Rocher de Cancale, one of the most famous restaurants of the day. La Reynière, with the help of the other members of his group, wrote the *Almanach des gourmands*, which appeared from 1803 to 1812. This was a series of eight little books in which the best places to eat or buy certain foods were listed and described. Recipes for new dishes were also included and the *Almanach* was written in a very entertaining and intelligent way.

La Reynière is considered the first food writer, but perhaps the most famous food writer of this period, indeed of all time, was Brillat-Savarin. His book *La Physiologie du goût* (translated under two different titles; *The Philosopher in the Kitchen* and *The Physiology of Taste)* was first printed in 1826, but Brillat-Savarin, who died on February 2, 1826, never lived to see its enormous success. *La Physiologie du goût* went through an incredible number of editions and in fact is still being reprinted. It is generally considered the best book on gastronomy ever written; it includes an analysis of taste itself, interesting and entertaining historical anecdotes, and unusual recipes. Brillat-Savarin is often quoted, and many of his comments have become proverbial; for example, "The discovery of a new dish does more for the happiness of mankind than the discovery of a new star."

More than half a century later, in 1859, Charles Monselet, with the help of a number of other writers interested in food, including Alexandre Dumas, wrote *La Cuisine poétique,* including recipes and anecdotes in both prose and verse. Then, from 1863 through 1870, Monselet edited a new *Almanach des gourmands* dedicated to his predecessor, Grimod de la Reynière.

Jules Gouffé

Jules Gouffé, born in 1807, was the son of a pastry cook. After working for his father, he became an apprentice to Carême. He was an excellent student, and in 1840, when he was thirty-three years old, he opened his own pastry shop in Paris. It soon became known as one of the best in the city. In 1855 he decided to retire and sold his shop. But his friends, including Alexandre Dumas, begged him to come out of retirement and made him head cook at the then fashionable Jockey Club. While he was there (and with Dumas' encouragement), he decided to write his *Livre de cuisine* in 1867. In the preface he says:

If, through the reforms and methods I am proposing here, people eat better in years to come, according to
their means and social position; if everyday cooking is more carefully prepared, although economic; and if

on the other hand Haute Cuisine continues in the direction of progress, good taste, and elegance worthy of a century of luxury and enlightenment such as ours, then I will have attained the goal I set for myself. . . .

This declaration is far from being what one might expect from an apprentice of Carême, who reveled in the extravagance of impressive centerpieces. But Jules Gouffé had realized that often the fancy presentation of dishes was detrimental to their taste, and he was one of the first chefs to emphasize the priority of taste over appearance. Gouffé's book was also one of the first cookbooks to contain detailed measurements for every recipe and instructions that even inexperienced cooks could follow. Gouffé's *Livre de cuisine* is considered a masterpiece by chefs today.

Alexandre Dumas

Alexandre Dumas père is better known for his novels—*The Three Musketeers* and *The Count of Monte Cristo,* to name only two—than for his writing on food. Dumas died in 1870, but his *Grand Dictionnaire de cuisine* was not published until 1873. It was his last book, and though it was nearly complete at the time of his death, a large number of recipes had to be corrected. This was the work of A. M. D. J. Vuillemot, a friend and collaborator of Dumas, who is primarily responsible for much of the book's practical content. Dumas was passionately interested in cooking, and he believed that his dictionary was his greatest work. It is full of very amusing anecdotes, and it contains very interesting recipes. But much of the "factual" information it contains is simply wrong, and the recipes tend to be complicated. Nevertheless, the style and fame of its author have made Dumas' *Grand Dictionnaire de cuisine* one of the classics of French gastronomical writing.

Illustration from the 1841 edition of Brillat-Savarin's *La Physiologie du goût.*
(B.N., Paris. Photo J.L. Charmet © Photeb.)

LE CUISINIER.

Soups

From the Middle Ages until the late eighteenth century, soups were often entire meals. The French word for soup, *potage*, originally meant anything cooked in a pot, and early cookbooks often had a long list of *potages* which were, in fact, what we would call meat stews. Today the Pot au feu and the Poule au pot are examples of this kind of soup. Other soups of this kind, for instance, the Petite marmite and Soup garbure aux choux are to be found in the section that follows.

For a long time, the English adopted the term ''pottage'' and used it as the French did. The British, however, had the peculiar habit of soaking a piece of bread in their pottage, which they called a sop. The French mispronounced this word and called the sop a *soupe*. Eventually pottages which were thickened with bread were called *soupes* in France. The English in turn took this ''new'' word from the French and applied it to all ''pottages,'' calling them soups. At this point, neither the French nor the English were sure where the word came from, but it soon gained widespread acceptance in both countries.

The preparation of soups has always been of great importance in France; a French dinner invariably begins with a soup. The quality of the soup is considered essential, since this will allow the diner to form his first impression of the meal that is to come. A good soup does not guarantee that a good dinner is to follow, but a poor soup could ruin the effect of a well-prepared main dish.

Most soups are easy to prepare and call for no more complicated ingredients than vegetables and water. Some soups, however, specify beef bouillon as an important ingredient, and this is often a problem for cooks who don't always have homemade bouillon at hand. The same problem arises in other recipes which call for bouillon, and too often modern cooks resort to bouillon cubes or canned consommé when they don't have the time to prepare bouillon in the traditional manner. Some of the soup recipes given here provide excellent bouillons that can be kept for use either in sauces, main dishes, or other soups (see Petite marmite or Potage de santé). But whenever bouillon is called for, there is a quick and easy way to prepare a substitute that can be used if the real thing is not available:

TO PREPARE QUICK BOUILLON

INGREDIENTS

1 tablespoon butter
1 medium onion, finely chopped
1 medium carrot, finely chopped
1 stalk celery, finely chopped
¼ pound ground beef
4 cups water
1 teaspoon salt
2 peppercorns
¼ bay leaf
1 small sprig thyme

- Melt the butter in a saucepan. Brown the onion, carrot, celery, and ground beef for five minutes over high heat, stirring frequently. Add the water. Bring to a boil, and skim off any foam that appears. Add the salt, peppercorns, bay leaf, and thyme. Cover the pot, and simmer for twenty minutes; then strain out the meat and vegetables.
- Any amount of bouillon can be prepared in this way if these proportions are respected. This bouillon is far superior to any commercial product and will improve the taste of any soup or sauce to which it is added.

POTAGE D'OIGNONS AU LAIT

La Varenne 1651

(Onion Soup with Milk)

Onions have always been a popular ingredient in French cooking. An old French proverb says: *Si tu te trouves san chapon,/Sois content de pain et d'oignons.* ("If you have no capon [chicken], then be glad you have bread and onions.") Today the most familiar French onion dish is probably Parisian onion soup *(gratinée)*. It is very different from the present recipe, however, inasmuch as the onions are cooked with bouillon rather than milk, cheese is sprinkled over the top, and the soup is gratinéed in the oven. La Varenne's recipe for onion soup is simpler and typical of a kind of onion soup still popular throughout France.

Ingredients (for 4 servings): 2 medium onions, peeled. 5 tablespoons butter. 1 cup water. Salt. Pepper. 3 cups milk. 2 cups stale bread crusts or toast, cut into 1-inch squares.

The onions: Slice the onions very thin, making all the slices the same thickness so that they will cook rapidly and evenly. Melt the butter in a saucepan, add the onions, and cook over low heat until they are golden brown. Stir frequently to prevent the onions from burning.

Cooking: When the onions are cooked, pour the water into the saucepan. Add salt and pepper to taste. Simmer for ten minutes. Add the milk. Watch the pan closely, and remove it from the heat as soon as the soup begins to boil.

Croutons: While the onions are cooking, place the bread crusts or toast in a slow oven (325°) for three or four minutes to dry them out completely.

To Serve: As soon as the croutons are removed from the oven, place them in the bottom of a tureen. Pour the soup over the croutons, and serve immediately.

POTAGE AUX MOULES A LA REYNE

Marin 1739

(Mussel Soup with Almonds)

Parsnips are an excellent vegetable which adds flavor to many dishes. From the Middle Ages through the Renaissance, they were especially popular in fish dishes served during Lent. In the eighteenth century they were almost always added to soups, instead of turnips. If you cannot find parsnips, rutabagas can be used instead. Parsnip complements the flavor of the mussels, but what makes this recipe truly original is the addition of almonds to this soup. All the ingredients combine perfectly in an unusual harmony of taste typical of eighteenth-century cooking.

Ingredients (for 4 servings): 2 carrots. 2 medium onions. ¼ pound fresh button mushrooms. 1 medium (½ pound) parsnip or rutabaga. 3 tablespoons butter. 1 teaspoon flour. 4 cups water. 1 quart fresh mussels in their shells. 1 sprig parsley. 4 hard-cooked egg yolks. 12 peeled and blanched almonds. Salt. Black pepper. Several thin slices French or country-style bread.

The soup (first step): Peel and wash the carrots, onions, mushrooms, and parsnip or rutabaga. Cut these vegetables into slices. Melt half the butter in a large saucepan. Add the vegetables, and brown lightly. Sprinkle in the flour, and stir for three minutes. Add the water, and cook for forty minutes.

The mussels: While the soup is cooking, scrape the mussels. Remove all the barnacles, as well as the filaments which mussels use to attach themselves to rocks. Wash the mussels quickly, several times. Do not let them soak in the water. Move them around briskly; otherwise, they may open and lose the salt water inside their shells. Place the remaining butter and the parsley in a second saucepan. Melt the butter on low heat. Place the mussels in this saucepan, and cover the pot. Stir the mussels occasionally, and when all the shells have opened, remove the pan from the heat. Leave a dozen of the mussels in their shells. Remove the others from their shells.

The soup (second step): When the vegetables are cooked, remove them from the pot with a skimmer or slotted spoon. Grind them in a food mill or blender along with the mussels which you have removed from their shells, the egg yolks, and almonds. Pour all these ingredients into the soup. Strain the mussels' cooking liquid, and add this to the soup. Stir. Taste before adding salt, since the salt from the mussels is already in the soup. Add pepper to taste.

To Serve: Place the slices of bread at the bottom of a tureen, along with the twelve mussels in their shells. Pour in a ladleful of soup. Let stand for five minutes. Add the rest of the soup, and serve very hot.

POTAGE A LA CITROUILLE
(Pumpkin Soup)

The pumpkin is a large gourd that can attain a weight of 100 pounds. In the United States it is widely consumed, particularly in pies, but in Europe it is generally used to feed farm animals. Nevertheless, the French, who are totally unfamiliar with pumpkin pie, make an excellent pumpkin soup with a very subtle and delicate flavor. Most French pumpkin soup recipes are similar to this one described by Menon more than 200 years ago.

Ingredients (for 4 servings): 1-pound wedge fresh pumpkin. 4 cups water. 2 tablespoons butter. 2 sugar cubes. Salt. Pepper. 2 cups milk. 2 cups stale French bread or toast, cut into 1-inch squares.

The pumpkin: Remove all the seeds and filaments from the pumpkin wedge. Cut the pumpkin into slices to facilitate peeling; remove the skin to a depth of one-quarter inch so that nothing but the pulp remains. Cut the slices into large cubes. Place the water in a pot. Add the pumpkin, and cook over medium heat for twelve minutes, or until you can easily mash the pumpkin with a fork.

The soup: Grind the cooked pumpkin through a sieve or food mill; then put it back into the pot over very low heat. Add the butter and sugar cubes. Salt and pepper to taste. Add the milk, and simmer for twenty minutes.

To Serve: While the soup is simmering, place the bread or toast in a tureen. (If the bread is not stale enough to be completely dry, place it in the oven for a few minutes to dry out. Otherwise, it will absorb too much liquid and make the soup mushy.) Pour a ladleful of soup into the tureen, and let stand for five minutes. Add the rest of the soup, and serve very hot.

POTAGE MAIGRE PRINTANIER
(Spring Soup)

Numerous herbs once used in cooking are all but forgotten today. Purslane, fresh sorrel, and chervil are fairly uncommon in the United States. If these specific ingredients are not available, substitute fresh green leafy herbs or vegetables of your choice. Always use a variety of herbs when preparing this soup, and do not be afraid to experiment with different combinations.

Ingredients (for 4 servings): 2 pounds unshelled green peas. 2 medium onions. 1 head leafy lettuce. ¼ pound purslane. 1 handful sorrel (2 cups tightly packed). 1 bunch chervil. 1 sprig parsley. 3 tablespoons butter. 4 cups water. Salt. Pepper. 2 cups stale bread or toast cut into 1-inch squares. 4 eggs.

The herbs and vegetables: Shell the green peas. Peel and slice the onions. Wash the lettuce, purslane, sorrel, chervil, and parsley. Discard the purslane stalks, and chop the leaves. Remove the stems of the sorrel leaves. Chop the sorrel leaves together with the chervil, lettuce, and parsley.

Cooking: Place all the herbs and vegetables in a pot with the butter and water. Bring to a boil, and cook over low heat for thirty-five minutes. Leave the pot uncovered; otherwise, the herbs will lose their color. Grind through a sieve or food mill. Salt and pepper to taste.

To Serve: Place the bread or toast in a tureen. Break the eggs into a bowl, and beat them lightly. Gradually add four or five tablespoons of soup to the eggs, stirring constantly with a wooden spoon. This will keep the eggs from forming lumps when they are poured into the hot soup. Remove the pot from the heat. Pour the egg mixture slowly into the soup, stirring constantly. When the mixture is well blended, pour a ladleful of the soup into the tureen with the bread. Let stand for five minutes. Add the rest of the soup, and serve immediately.

POTAGE A LA VIERGE

(Virgin Mary's Soup)

Menon 1746

This is a white soup. The bread, the cream, the white meat of the chicken, the blanched almonds—everything is white. In the eighteenth century, almonds (fresh and ground into a paste) were a major ingredient in a variety of dishes. The whiteness of the soup and the fact that it cooks in a bain-marie (literally, a "Mary bath") might explain the name given to this recipe.

Ingredients (for 4 servings): 4 eggs. 4 cups bouillon. ⅓ cup bread crumbs. 1 chicken breast, cooked, skinned, and boned. 12 peeled and blanched almonds. 6 tablespoons heavy cream. Salt. White pepper. 2½ cups stale bread crusts or toast, cut into 2-inch squares.

The purée: Boil the eggs for nine minutes. Cool the eggs rapidly under running water in order to peel them easily. Keep only the yolks. Pour one cup of the bouillon into a small saucepan along with the bread crumbs. Bring to a boil. Purée the chicken breast in a food mill or blender with the hard-cooked egg yolks, almonds, and the bouillon containing the bread crumbs. Add the cream. Salt and pepper to taste. Keep warm in a double boiler and not over direct heat, because the purée will curdle if it boils.

The soup: Place the bread crusts or toast in a tureen. Pour the remaining bouillon over the bread to dampen, and place in a moderate oven (350°) for fifteen minutes.

To Serve: Remove the tureen from the oven. Add the purée, and stir. Serve immediately.

POTAGE A LA GEAUFRET

(Potato Dumpling Soup)

Viard 1820

The dumplings described below are sometimes called *quenelles* in French, and their delicate flavor hides the fact that they are just a sophisticated way of using leftovers. The cold chicken and cooked potatoes could well have been left from a previous dinner, and the bouillon in recipes like this one should always come from a Pot au feu prepared a day or two in advance.

Ingredients (for 4 servings): 2 medium potatoes. 1 chicken breast, cooked, skinned, and boned. 3 tablespoons butter. 2 egg yolks. Pepper. Nutmeg. A few tablespoons heavy cream (optional). 1 tablespoon flour (optional). 1 egg (optional). Salt. 4 cups bouillon.

The dumplings: Carefully wash the potatoes. Bake them, unpeeled, in a hot oven (425°) for approximately forty-five minutes, or until soft. While the potatoes are baking, thoroughly pound the chicken breast in a mortar, or purée it in a blender. When the potatoes are done, cut them in half. Spoon out the pulp, and add it to the chicken. Pound or beat the mixture vigorously, adding the butter and egg yolks. Add the pepper to taste, and sprinkle with nutmeg, but do not salt. The mixture should now be a smooth paste. Roll this paste into small balls or dumplings. If the paste seems too thick, thin it with the cream. If too thin, add the flour and the egg.

Poaching: Bring some salted water to a boil in a large pot, and add the dumplings; do not let them touch each other. Poach the dumplings gently for thirty minutes, turning them from time to time. Drain.

To Serve: While the dumplings are cooking, heat the bouillon. Taste for proper seasoning. Pour the soup into a tureen. Add the dumplings, and serve.

POTAGE AU POISSON
(Fish Soup)

One of the secrets of making a good fish soup is to use several kinds of fish. In this recipe, for example, Viard uses three types of fish—a flatfish (flounder), a lean fish (whiting), and a fatty fish (conger eel). Any number of fish will do, but the important thing is to use as large a variety as possible.

Fish soup is always cooked quickly over high heat. Nevertheless, many people wrongly believe that making fish soup is a long, involved process. It is, in fact, one of the easiest and quickest soups to prepare. The fennel seeds used in this recipe give a distinctive flavor to the soup, and the taste of the fish is enhanced by the flavor of the spice. Fish soups, such as this one, can be served either at the start of a meal or as a meal in themselves. If there is any fish left over, it should be kept for the next day and used in a salad or reheated with vegetables as a light meal.

Ingredients (for 4 servings): 2 whitings (½ pound each). 1 flounder (1 pound). 4 slices conger eel (totaling 10 ounces). 6 tablespoons olive oil. 2 or 3 sprigs parsley, chopped. 1 medium onion, peeled and chopped. 1 clove garlic, peeled and crushed. ½ bay leaf. 1 pinch fennel seeds. Salt. Pepper. 4 cups water. 2 cups stale bread or toast, cut into 1-inch squares.

Preparing the fish: Carefully bone the whitings and flounder. Wash all the fish. Cut off the tails and fins with scissors. Cut the flounder and whitings into four or five pieces each.

The soup: Slowly heat the olive oil in a saucepan. Add the parsley, onion, and garlic to the olive oil, along with the bay leaf, fennel seeds, and a pinch of salt and pepper. Add the water, and bring to a boil. Place the pieces of fish in the pot, and cook for ten minutes; the liquid should boil rapidly so that the fish will cook through without falling apart.

To Serve: Place the bread or toast in a tureen. Remove the fish from the soup with a skimmer or slotted spoon, and arrange the pieces on a platter. Strain the fish bouillon into the tureen containing the bread. Serve both the fish and the bouillon immediately since they cool quickly.

SOUPE GARBURE AUX CHOUX
(Cabbage Garbure Soup)

Garbure is a local term used in the southwest part of France to designate a soup made with cabbage, ham, bacon, and preserved goose. There are at least ten versions of this soup, depending on the proportions of each ingredient used. This particular recipe comes from one of the earliest French regional cookbooks. The *Cuisinier Durand* helped popularize a number of local specialties that have since spread to the rest of France.

Ingredients (for 6 servings): 1 large cabbage or 2 medium cabbages. 5 tablespoons goose fat or lard. 1 leg of *confit d'oie* (preserved goose) or a ½-pound piece of country ham or salt pork. 8½ cups bouillon (approximately). 1 slice country-style bread, 2 to 3 inches thick. Salt. Pepper.

Cooking the cabbage: Remove any wilted or damaged leaves, and carefully wash the cabbage. Slice the cabbage into large pieces, and place in a pot with the goose fat or lard. Cook over low heat for thirty minutes, stirring occasionally.

The soup: When the cabbage is done, transfer it to another pot. Add the goose leg or, if unavailable, the ham or salt pork. (Country ham and salt pork have to be soaked overnight before being cooked.) Pour enough bouillon over the meat to cover. Cover the pot, and cook over low heat for forty-five minutes.

Simmering the bread: Cut the bread into small, very thin slices. In a small earthenware casserole place alternating layers of bread and cabbage, ending with a layer of cabbage. Taste the bouillon in which the meat and cabbage cooked for proper seasoning. Pour enough bouillon into the casserole barely to cover the top layer of cabbage. Keep the meat warm in the remaining bouillon. Place the casserole in a moderate oven (350°) for fifteen minutes. Check the soup occasionally. If it looks too dry, add a bit more bouillon.

To Serve: Serve the garbure in the earthenware casserole, straight from the oven. The bread should have absorbed all the liquid. In another tureen serve the remaining bouillon, to which no bread has been added. The meat may be either served on a separate platter or buried in the middle of the garbure just before serving.

CROUTE AU POT
(Bouillon with Toasted Bread Crusts)

Cuisinier Durand 1830

Properly speaking, this is not a recipe at all, but a suggestion for using leftover bouillon from a Pot au feu. Croûte au pot is best when the crust from a country-style bread is used—the better the bread crust, the tastier the soup.

Ingredients (for 4 servings): 3 cups bread crusts, cut into 2-inch squares. 4 cups bouillon.

The bread crusts: Before measuring the bread crusts, remove as much of the crumb from the crusts as possible. Put the crusts into a slow oven (325°) until they are a rich golden brown—but not dark brown, for they will then impart an unpleasant taste to the soup.

Simmering the bread: Place the bread crusts in an ovenproof tureen. Pour the bouillon over the bread crusts. Place in a moderate oven (375°) for fifteen minutes.

To Serve: Serve in the tureen as soon as it is removed from the oven.

POTAGE DE SANTE
(Health Soup)

Carême 1833

This soup, which is actually a kind of rich meat bouillon, cooks for a total of nearly seven hours. By the end of this time all the nutrients contained in the meat and vegetables have gone into the bouillon—hence the name "health soup." Up to fifty years ago this type of soup was common in many cookbooks, and before vitamin pills existed, doctors prescribed Health Soup to their patients on a regular basis. Because of the great variety of meat and vegetables used in preparing this soup, the bouillon has much more taste than ordinary beef bouillon, and the time spent making it is certainly justified. The leftover meat and remaining vegetables are excellent for later use in salads.

Ingredients (for 8 servings): 1 chicken (3 pounds), dressed and trussed. 2 large carrots. 2 large turnips. 1 celeriac. 4 leeks. 1 handful sorrel (2 cups tightly packed). 1 bunch chervil leaves. 1 small head leafy lettuce, with leaves separated. ½ pound green asparagus tips. 30 ½-inch squares bread crust. A few beef bones. 1 small veal knuckle. 6 quarts water. Salt. Black pepper. 1 egg white. 1 pinch sugar.

Preparing the ingredients: Roast the chicken, unseasoned, in a hot oven (425°) for thirty minutes. Peel the carrots, turnips, and celeriac. Wash the leeks, sorrel, chervil, lettuce leaves, and asparagus tips. Toast the bread crusts in the oven until they are golden brown.

To begin cooking: Place the beef bones in a large pot, along with the roasted chicken (which gives color to the bouillon) and the veal knuckle. Pour the water into the pot. Bring slowly to a boil, carefully skimming off the foam. When there is no more foam, add one of the carrots, one of the turnips, half the celeriac, two of the leeks, and salt and pepper to taste. Cover and cook gently for five hours.

Final steps: Remove all the vegetables, bones, and meat. In a bowl, beat the egg white with a little cold water. Pour into the pot, stirring vigorously, and simmer for twenty minutes. As it cooks, the egg white will absorb the impurities in the bouillon and clarify it. Meanwhile, dice the remaining carrot, turnip, and celeriac. Slice the lettuce leaves, sorrel, and remaining leeks into thin strips. Strain the soup in order to remove all impurities. Pour the soup back into the pot. Add the diced carrot, turnip, and celeriac, the strips of lettuce, sorrel, and leeks, the chervil leaves, and the asparagus tips. Cook for one hour.

To Serve: Place the croutons in a tureen. Add the sugar to the soup in the pot. Pour the soup over the croutons, and serve very hot.

POTAGE AUX POINTES D'ASPERGES

(Asparagus Tip Soup)

Asparagus has long been treasured as a delicacy. It was a favorite vegetable of the Greeks and Romans (who considered it aphrodisiac), but it was not until the seventeenth century in France that asparagus was cultivated on a large scale. It was the favorite vegetable of Louis XIV, whose gardener built ingenious hothouses so that the king could be served asparagus every day of the year.

Ingredients (for 4 servings): 2 pounds green asparagus. Salt. 3 cups stale bread, cut into ½-inch cubes. 6½ cups bouillon. 1 pinch sugar.

The asparagus: Peel the asparagus, removing any broken or woody parts. Wash the asparagus, and boil them gently in salted water for thirty minutes. Drain carefully. Cut one and a half to two inches off the base of each stalk of asparagus. (Keep these pieces, for they are excellent in stews or omelettes.) Keep the asparagus tips warm.

The croutons: Place the cubes of bread in a moderate oven (375°) until they turn golden brown.

The soup: Bring the bouillon to a boil. Remove from the heat, and stir in the sugar.

To Serve: Arrange the croutons in a tureen. Cover them with the asparagus tips. Pour the bouillon into the tureen. Serve very hot.

POTAGE AUX HERBES

(Herb Soup)

Carême was often called the Cook of Kings and the King of Cooks. This does not imply, however, that everything he made was complicated or elaborate. On the contrary, many of his recipes, such as this one, were quite simple. The use of sugar in this recipe may be surprising, yet it is indispensable, since it counteracts the acidity of the sorrel and enhances the taste of the lettuce and chervil. Although beef or veal bouillon could be used in making this soup, it is best to use chicken bouillon.

Ingredients (for 4 servings): 1½ ounces fresh fatback. 1 pound sorrel. 1 small head leafy lettuce. ½ cup chervil leaves, tightly packed. 4⅓ cups chicken bouillon. 1 sugar cube. 2 cups bread crusts, cut into 1-inch squares. 3 tablespoons soft butter. 4 eggs.

The fatback: Cut the fatback into thin slivers, which will melt more rapidly than large lumps. Place the slivers in a saucepan over very low heat so that the fat will melt without coloring; this takes about fifteen minutes. Strain the melted fat to remove the small particles which remain at the bottom of the saucepan.

The herbs: Carefully wash the sorrel, lettuce, and chervil. Cut them into small pieces with sharp scissors. This way they will retain their natural sugar, which is lost when they are chopped with a knife.

The soup: Pour the melted, strained fat into a pot over low heat. Put the cut herbs in the fat, and stir constantly with a wooden spoon until they begin to turn yellow (about ten minutes). Add the bouillon and the sugar cube. Simmer for thirty minutes.

The bread crusts: Completely remove any crumb from the bread crusts (before they are cut into squares), and scrape both sides so that they will be perfectly smooth. Cut the crusts into one-inch squares, and measure out two cups. Place the squares in a slow oven (325°) until they are dry and golden—but not dark brown.

To Serve: Place the squares of bread crust in a tureen with the butter. Break the eggs into a bowl, and beat them lightly. Gradually add four or five tablespoons of soup to the eggs, stirring constantly so that the eggs do not coagulate. Remove the soup pot from the heat, and pour the egg mixture slowly into the soup, stirring constantly. Pour the soup into the tureen with the bread, and serve immediately.

PETITE MARMITE

(Kettle Soup)

This soup is best in spring, when new carrots, turnips, and young cabbages are in season. It can be made in winter as well, although then it is best to parboil the cabbage before adding it to tl soup, or it will have too strong a taste. At first glance, this recipe seems similar to a Pot au feu, but the addition of the cabbage and oxtail and the absence of a bouquet garni make this soup slightly different from its better-known relative. Nevertheless, the bouillon made here is excellent when used to prepare other soups and sauces.

Ingredients (for 8 servings): 3 pounds beef, sirloin tip or round steak. 1 pound beef short ribs. ¼ pound oxtail. 1 small chicken, dressed and trussed. 2 new carrots. 2 young turnips. 2 leeks. 1 stalk celery. 1 small young cabbage. 2 medium onions. 1 clove. 8 small marrowbones. 5 quarts cold water. Salt. Pepper.

Preparing the ingredients: In a large pot combine the steak, short ribs, oxtail, and chicken. Cover with cold water. Bring to a boil. Carefully skim off the foam; then drain. Peel and wash the carrots, turnips, leeks, celery, cabbage, and onions. Stick the clove into one of the onions.

Cooking: Place all the meat, vegetables, and marrowbones in a large earthenware or cast-iron pot. Pour the five quarts of cold water into the pot. Bring to a boil, and if necessary, skim off the foam once more. Salt and pepper to taste. Cover the pot, and cook over very low heat for two hours and forty-five minutes.

To Serve: Turn off the heat, and allow the pot to stand for a few minutes so that the fat may rise to the surface and be skimmed off. The pot itself may be used in place of a tureen at the table, but it is more practical to serve the soup separately and to serve the meat on a platter, surrounded by the marrowbones and the vegetables. You may also serve a few slices of toast and some additional vegetables. These vegetables must be cooked separately, for the proportions indicated in Gouffé's recipe are precisely those necessary to assure the best taste of the soup.

POTAGE AUX TOMATES ET AUX QUEUES DE CREVETTES

(Tomato and Shrimp Soup)

Alexandre Dumas *père* believed that if his name were to be known to future generations, it would be as a result of his dictionary of cooking, not his literary works. A hundred years have passed since his death, and both his cookbook *and* his novels are still in print. Although his fame as a cookbook author has declined, recipes like this one help justify the reputation he rightly deserves. *Note:* If fish stock is unavailable, use the water in which the shrimp were cooked every time stock is called for.

Ingredients (for 4 servings): Salt. 2 slices lemon. 1 pound live shrimp. 4 medium onions. 1 clove garlic. 3 tablespoons butter. 12 medium tomatoes. 1 bay leaf. 1 sprig thyme. 1 sprig parsley. 1 dash paprika. 5 cups fish stock.

The shrimp: Fill a large pot three-quarters full of lightly salted water. Add the lemon slices, and bring to a boil. Drop the shrimp into the boiling water. After five minutes, lift the shrimp out of the water with a slotted spoon. Keep the water for later use. Peel and clean the shrimp. Remove the heads. (If shrimp water is to be use instead of fish stock, put all the heads and shells of the shrimp back into the water. Continue cooking the water, uncovered, until ready to use.)

The tomatoes: Peel and chop the onions and garlic. Melt the butter in a saucepan. Add the onions and garlic, and sauté over low heat. Wash and quarter the tomatoes. Combine them with the sautéed onions and garlic. Add the bay leaf, thyme, and parsley. Cook, uncovered, for twenty minutes.

The soup: Remove the bay leaf, thyme, and parsley. Grind the tomato mixture through a sieve or food mill. Place this mixture into another pot. Add the paprika, and one cup of the fish stock. Resume cooking. When the mixture has thickened sufficiently, dilute it with the remaining fish stock and two cups of the water in which the shrimp were cooked. Taste for seasoning. Add the peeled shrimp to the soup, bring to a boil, and cook for thirty seconds only.

To Serve: Serve immediately in a tureen.

Entrées

Traditionally, an entrée was a small dish served after the fish course and before the meat course of a meal. Today in France an entrée often means the fish course itself or else any dish served after soup and before meat. In the United States the term is most often applied to the main course of any light meal, thus adding to the confusion that surrounds the use of this word.

However you choose to serve entrées, they should always be dishes that are light and appetizing. The following recipes all fill this requirement and would either be served as a prelude to an elaborate dinner or as a light supper, depending on the occasion and the cook.

LAIT LARDE

(Fried Larded Milk)

Saffron has almost entirely disappeared from French cooking, but in Taillevent's day it was one of the most frequently used ingredients in cooking. Not only did it give a bright yellow color to different foods (medieval cooks were fond of coloring foods), but its taste was more highly esteemed than it is today. Saffron has always been an expensive flavoring, and its popularity in the fourteenth century was due, in part, to its high price. Nobles viewed its presence in different dishes as a sign of wealth, and saffron, as well as many other spices, had a "snob appeal" similar to that of truffles in French cooking today. Taillevent also used ginger in this recipe—another ingredient rarely found in modern French cuisine. It is hard to say whether he meant fresh green ginger or ground dried ginger. Either can be used, but fresh ginger is preferable whenever available.

Ingredients (for 4 servings): ½ pound slab fresh bacon (unsalted and unsmoked). 4 cups milk. 8 eggs. 1 pinch ground ginger or 1 teaspoon fresh grated ginger. 1 pinch saffron. Lard. Salt. Pepper.

The bacon: Remove the rind from the bacon. Cut the bacon into small cubes or rectangles. Lightly grease a skillet with the bacon rind. Place the pieces of bacon in the pan. Brown the bacon well over low heat; then remove from the skillet.

The milk: Bring the milk to a boil. In a large bowl beat the eggs until well blended. Season them with the ginger and saffron. Pour the milk slowly into the bowl with the eggs, stirring constantly with a wooden spoon. Add the bacon. Pour into a soufflé mold. Place the mold in a shallow pan of water, and bake in a slow oven (325°) for thirty-five minutes. Remove from the oven, and allow to cool. Put a small plate directly on top of the Lait lardé; then put a paperweight or similar heavy object on top of the plate in order to compress the milk mixture. Once the weight has been applied, leave overnight before proceeding to the next step.

To Serve: Remove the weight and the plate. Cut the Lait lardé into thin slices. Fry the slices in a little hot lard. Add salt and pepper to taste. Serve very hot.

FAUX FRENON

(False Frenon, or Mixed Meat Casserole)

The French name for this dish continues to baffle etymologists. The word "Frenon" no longer exists in French, and no one knows what it originally meant. To complicate matters, this is a recipe for "false" Frenon! Perhaps Frenon was the name of a now-forgotten dish that had altogether different ingredients and this recipe was a less complicated version of that dish. The author of this recipe does, in fact, say that veal can be used instead of chicken livers and gizzards and that mutton can replace the pork. Is this a clue to what the "real" Frenon contained? We will never know, but this "false" Frenon gives us a good idea of inventive medieval cookery.

Ingredients (for 4 servings): 1 cup dry white wine. 1 cup water. Pepper. 10 ounces lean pork. 5 ounces chicken gizzards, cleaned. 5 ounces chicken livers, cleaned. 3 tablespoons lard. 2½ cups bread crumbs. 1 pinch ground ginger or 1 teaspoon fresh grated ginger. 1 pinch ground cinnamon. 1 pinch ground clove. 1 pinch salt. 4 egg yolks. 2 tablespoons lemon juice. Chopped parsley.

The court-bouillon: Prepare a court-bouillon by combining the wine, water, and pepper. (Do not salt.) Bring to a boil.

The meat: Cut the pork into large chunks. Cut the chicken gizzards into quarters. Poach the gizzards and pork in the boiling court-bouillon for fifteen minutes. Add the chicken livers. Boil for five minutes more; then remove from the heat. Remove all the meat, drain, and chop into very small pieces. Place the chopped meat in a frying pan with the lard, and brown quickly on all sides.

The Faux Frenon: Add the bread crumbs to the chopped meat along with the ginger, cinnamon, clove, salt, egg yolks, and lemon juice. Strain some of the court-bouillon, and mix it very gradually and thoroughly with the chopped meat until the mixture is the consistency of a thick purée. Place over low heat. Bring just to a boil, and remove from the heat.

To Serve: Serve very hot in individual casseroles. Sprinkle each serving lightly with additional cinnamon and chopped parsley.

TOURTE D'HERBES

(Herb Pie)

Ménagier de Paris 1392

In France today a *tourte* is usually a covered pie as opposed to a *tarte,* in which the filling is not covered by a piecrust. When this recipe was written, however, a *tourte* was the name given to anything cooked in a pie pan. This particular *tourte* is a kind of cheesecake that can be seasoned with any leafy green vegetables or herbs.

Ingredients (for 8 servings): 1¾ cups flour. ½ teaspoon salt. 1 tablespoon, plus 1 cup, butter. 4 eggs, separated, keeping 1 egg white apart from the rest. ⅓ cup water (approximately). 8 cups Swiss chard leaves, tightly packed (with midribs removed). 4 cups spinach leaves, tightly packed. 1 cup parsley leaves, tightly packed. ½ cup chervil leaves, tightly packed. 1 small branch fresh fennel. ⅔ cup farmer's cheese or fresh curds. ⅔ cup semisoft goat's-milk cheese or ricotta. 1 pinch pepper. 1 pinch ground ginger or 1 teaspoon fresh grated ginger.

The puff pastry: Place the flour and salt in a bowl. Push the flour against the sides of the bowl until a well is formed in the center. In the well, place one tablespoon of the butter, the white of one egg, and the water (approximately one-third cup—the exact amount depends on the amount of water which can be absorbed by the flour). Mix all the ingredients quickly with the tips of the fingers until a smooth dough is formed. Shape into a ball. Let stand for thirty minutes; then knead gently for ten seconds. Place the dough on a flat, floured surface, and roll out until approximately three-quarters inch thick. Work the remaining butter with the fingers until it is the same consistency as the dough. Flatten the butter into a circle the same size as the dough. Then place the butter on top of the dough. Fold one edge of the dough over the butter, leaving one-third uncovered. Fold the remaining third over the first fold. Carefully roll out the dough into a long rectangle about three-quarters inch thick. Then fold the dough in thirds again, as described above, and turn it a quarter of a turn so that you will be rolling in the direction of the fold when you roll it out. Roll it out again into a long, three-quarter-inch-thick rectangle. Fold in thirds again, and leave in a cool place for fifteen minutes. Roll out the dough twice more, folding it and turning it each time, as above, and then set aside again for fifteen minutes. Roll out twice more, and let stand for a final fifteen minutes. Butter a ten-inch pie pan. Roll out the dough into a circle, and place it in the pan. Place the pan in a moderately hot oven (400°) for ten minutes.

The greens: Carefully wash the Swiss chard, spinach, parsley, chervil, and fennel. Remove all stems, and chop all the greens together.

Filling: Mix the farmer's cheese or curds and the goat's-milk cheese or ricotta together in a large bowl. Add the pepper, ginger, all the chopped greens, and the egg yolks. Beat the three remaining egg whites until they are firm; then fold them carefully into the cheese mixture.

Cooking: Pour the filling into the piecrust. Bake in the same oven (400°) for thirty minutes.

To Serve: The Tourte d'herbes may be served either hot or cold.

FLAN FIN QU'ON APPELLE TARTE D'AMI

(Cheese Tart, Known as Friend's Tart)

La Varenne 1651

Rose water, which is rarely used in cooking today, was a popular flavoring in the seventeenth century. In some old French recipes, *eau de senteur* (scented water) is called for, in which case either orange-flower water or rose water could be used today. Although the following recipe would most likely be thought of as a dessert today, it was common to serve sweet dishes as entrées in La Varenne's day. For those who prefer it, an unsweetened version is included here; in either case this tart would add an original note to any dinner.

Ingredients (for 8 servings): 1¾ cups flour. Salt. ½ pound soft butter. ⅓ cup cold water (approximately). 1 cup grated gruyère or Swiss cheese. ¾ cup farmer's cheese, ricotta, or soft cream cheese. 2 eggs, separated.

For the sweet version: 3 eggs. 5 tablespoons sugar. Rose water or orange-flower water.

The dough: Place three-quarters cup of the flour and a pinch of salt in a large bowl. Use fingers to mix in six and a half tablespoons of the butter until the mixture is crumbly. Add cold water until a soft dough is formed. Roll the dough into a ball, and place in a clean bowl. Cover the bowl with a cloth, and set aside for thirty minutes. Butter a nine-inch pie pan. Roll out the dough, and place it in the pan. Prick the dough all over with a fork.

The cheese filling: Mix the gruyère or Swiss cheese with the farmer's cheese, ricotta, or cream cheese. Add the remaining flour, the remaining butter, and the egg yolks. Beat the egg whites until stiff, and fold them carefully into the cheese mixture.

Cooking the unsweetened version: Put the pie pan containing the dough into a moderately hot oven (400°), and bake for ten minutes. Remove from the oven, and pour in the cheese filling. Replace in the oven, and bake for twenty-five minutes.

Cooking the sweet version: Place the pie pan containing the dough in a moderately hot oven (400°), and bake for ten minutes. Beat the three eggs with three tablespoons of the sugar, and spread this mixture over the piecrust when the latter is removed from the oven. Pour in the cheese filling; then continue baking for twenty-five minutes. Remove from the oven, and sprinkle the surface of the tart, first with the remaining sugar, then with a few drops of rose water or orange-flower water. Replace the tart immediately in the oven for five minutes in order to glaze it.

To Serve: Always serve this tart hot, whether you use it as an entrée or as a dessert.

TOURTE D'HUITRES FRAICHES
(Fresh Oyster Pie)

La Varenne 1651

Although oysters are the main ingredient in this pie, there are almost as many vegetables as oysters in the filling. Today mussels are commonly used in much the same way as oysters were three centuries ago. Any shellfish could be substituted for the oysters in this recipe without compromising the result.

Ingredients (for 10 servings): 1¾ cups flour. Salt. 1 tablespoon, plus 1 cup, butter (for dough). 1 egg white. ⅓ cup water (approximately). 8 artichoke bottoms (see Canard en ragoût, page 207, for preparation). Juice of 1 lemon. 2 pounds asparagus. 1 pound morels or other wild mushrooms. 1 pound fresh button mushrooms. 6 sprigs parsley. 1 scallion. 8 hard-cooked eggs. 6 dozen oysters in shells. ¼ cup butter (for filling). Pepper. Nutmeg. 2 egg yolks. 1 tablespoon vinegar.

The puff pastry: Combine the flour, a pinch of salt, one tablespoon butter, the egg white, and the water. Mix with the tips of the fingers until a smooth dough is formed. Roll it into a ball, and place in a clean bowl. Cover with a cloth, and set aside for thirty minutes. Then place the dough on a table, and flatten it with your hand to a thickness of about three-quarters inch. Work the one cup butter with your hand until soft, and flatten it into a circle the same size as the dough. Place it on the dough. Fold and roll out the dough according to the directions given in the recipe for Tourte d'herbes (page 74). None of the steps should be omitted. Butter two nine-inch pie pans. Roll out the dough into two circles, and line each pie pan with dough. Line each piecrust with waxed paper, and fill the pie pans with dried kidney beans (this will keep the crust from losing its shape). Bake in a moderately hot oven (400°) for ten minutes. Remove from the oven, lift out the paper, and discard the beans or save them for the same use another time.

The garnish: Put the artichoke bottoms in a pot of water seasoned with the lemon juice. Bring to a boil, and cook for thirty minutes. Drain, and cut each artichoke bottom into eight pieces. Peel the asparagus, and cook them for fifteen minutes in boiling salted water. Drain, and cut into pieces. Cut off the sandy end of the morel stems. Rinse; then poach the morels for five minutes. Drain the morels, and set aside. Strain and reserve their cooking liquid. Clean and chop the button mushrooms, parsley, and scallion. Peel the hard-cooked eggs, and cut them into thick slices.

The oysters: Open the oysters, and remove them from their shells. Place them, along with their juice, in a saucepan. Bring barely to a boil over low heat; then remove from the heat.

The tourte: Melt the remaining one-quarter cup butter in a frying pan, and brown the parsley, scallion, and button mushrooms. Add the morels and their cooking liquid, the asparagus, artichoke bottoms, slices of hard-cooked egg, and the oysters and their strained juice. Salt lightly; then add pepper and nutmeg to taste. Remove the pan from the heat. Beat the egg yolks with the vinegar, and mix carefully with the other ingredients, stirring constantly.

Cooking: Pour the contents of the frying pan into the piecrusts, cover with a piece of aluminum foil, and bake in a moderately hot oven (400°) for twenty to twenty-five minutes.

To Serve: Remove the aluminum foil. Remove the pies from the pans, and serve very hot.

BEIGNETS DE MELON

(Melon Fritters)

Either cantaloupe or muskmelon can be used in this recipe. Unfortunately, Bonnefons does not specify what kind of batter was to be used with the melon. The batter recipe that follows is taken from a nineteenth-century cookbook by Viard. It is perfectly suited for this, as well as for any other fritter recipes that call for fresh fruit.

Ingredients (for 4 servings): 1 cup flour. Salt. Pepper. 1 teaspoon vegetable oil. 1 egg, separated. 6 tablespoons beer. 1 ripe cantaloupe or muskmelon. Oil for deep frying. Lemon juice.

The batter (Viard's recipe): Place the flour in a large bowl with a pinch of salt and a pinch of pepper. Make a well in the center. Put the vegetable oil, egg yolk, and beer in the well. Mix the liquid ingredients together, and gradually incorporate the flour. Stir constantly until all the flour has been absorbed and a smooth mixture is formed. The batter should fall from the spoon in a continuous thick stream. (If it is too thick, add a little water.) Beat the egg white until stiff; then fold it into the batter. Let stand in a warm place for two or three hours, so that the beer, which serves as a leaven, has time to ferment the batter slightly.

The melon: Cut the melon into slices, and remove the rind and seeds. Sprinkle with salt.

The fritters: Dip the slices of melon into the batter. Drop the slices in a deep fryer containing very hot oil (the oil should be almost smoking). When the slices rise to the surface of the oil, turn them over. When they are golden brown, remove them with a slotted spoon.

To Serve: Drain the fritters thoroughly. Sprinkle them with lemon juice, and serve very hot.

ANDOUILLETTES CONTREFAITES

(Mock Sausages)

Seventeenth-century cooks were constantly counterfeiting dishes. Chefs went to great lengths to make fish look like meat and meat like fish. This attitude toward the serving and decorating of food has parallel in the architecture of the period, which was essentially trompe-l'oeil. This "sausage"—counterfeit though it may be—is nevertheless delicious. Although potatoes were not used in French cooking until late in the eighteenth century, they have been included in the modernized version of this old recipe since they make the "sausages" easier to form and do not detract from the taste of the other ingredients.

Ingredients (for 4 servings): 1 pound fresh pumpkin. ½ pound (1½ medium) potatoes. 4 eggs. Several sprigs parsley, finely chopped. Several scallions, finely chopped. ¼ pound fresh button mushrooms, finely chopped. 4 tablespoons butter. 1 tablespoon flour. Salt. Pepper. Nutmeg.

The pumpkin: Remove the seeds and the filaments from the pumpkin. Cut the pumpkin into slices, and remove the outer rind from each slice. Cut the slices into large cubes. Place the cubes in a large saucepan. Cover with water, and boil for ten minutes. Drain.

Shaping the sausages: Peel and wash the potatoes. Quarter, then boil them in lightly salted water for twenty minutes. Boil two of the eggs for nine minutes. Cool them under running water; then peel. Grind the pumpkin, potatoes, and hard-cooked eggs through a food mill, or rub them through a sieve. Add the parsley, scallions, and mushrooms. Add the raw eggs, three tablespoons of the butter, and the flour to the ground vegetables. Add salt, pepper, and nutmeg to taste. Stir thoroughly. Shape the mixture into sausagelike patties.

Cooking: Liberally butter an ovenproof dish with the remaining butter. Place the patties in the dish. Cook in a moderately hot oven (400°) for twenty to twenty-five minutes. Turn the patties over halfway through their cooking time. The patties should be golden brown but should not lose their shape or stick to the bottom of the dish.

To Serve: Serve hot as soon as they come out of the oven.

TOURTE DE GODIVEAU FEUILLETEE

Pierre de Lune 1656

(Mixed Meat Pie)

Godiveau is the name given to a variety of mixed meat stuffings that have been used in French cooking for centuries. The origin of this word is unknown, and a godiveau stuffing varies with the availability of ingredients and the personal taste of the chef who prepares it. One thing it always includes is some cut of veal. The following recipe with its use of calf's sweetbreads, artichokes, bone marrow, chicken, and mushrooms might seem elaborate to us today, but it is typical of cooking in the seventeenth and eighteenth centuries. Other vegetables and cuts of meat could be substituted for those called for here as long as the same balance between fatty ingredients (*e.g.*, suet, bacon, etc.) and lean ingredients (*e.g.*, veal, chicken, etc.) are respected.

Ingredients (for 8 servings): 3¾ cups flour. Salt. 1 tablespoon, plus 1 cup, butter. 3 tablespoons water. 3 tablespoons dry white wine. Juice of 2 lemons. 2 medium artichoke bottoms (for preparation see Canard en ragoût, page 207). 10 ounces calf's sweetbreads. 5 ounces fresh slab bacon (unsalted and unsmoked). ½ pound fresh button mushrooms, finely chopped. 2 sprigs parsley, finely chopped. 1 scallion, finely chopped. 1 pound chicken breast, cooked and finely chopped. ¼ pound bone marrow, finely chopped. ¼ pound suet, finely chopped. Pepper. Nutmeg. 1 egg. ½ pound pistachios.

The puff pastry: Mix the flour, a pinch of salt, one tablespoon butter, the water, and white wine. Shape the dough into a ball, place in a covered bowl, and let stand for thirty minutes. Place the dough on a lightly floured table, and use your hands to flatten it to a thickness of about three-quarters inch. Work one cup of butter with your hands until soft. Flatten it into a circle the same size as the dough, and place it on top of the dough. Fold the dough, and roll it out according to the directions given under Tourte d'herbes (page 74). Do not omit any of the steps, but when the dough is set aside for the last time, let it stand for one hour instead of fifteen minutes. Butter a ten-inch pie pan. Divide the dough into two equal halves. Flatten one half, and fit it to the shape of the pan. Cover the bottom and sides of the dough with a sheet of waxed paper, and fill the pan with dried beans. Place the pan in a moderately hot oven (400°) for ten minutes. Remove from the oven, lift out the waxed paper, and discard the beans, or keep them to use in this way another time.

The meat filling: In water seasoned with half the lemon juice, boil the artichoke bottoms for fifteen minutes. Drain, and cut into thin slices. Soak the sweetbreads in cold water for several hours before cooking them. Change the water several times. Then place the sweetbreads in a pot of cold water. Heat the water until it is about to boil; then drain the sweetbreads, and wash them in cold running water. Remove any pieces of skin or fat, and cut the sweetbreads into thin slices. Cut the bacon into small cubes or strips. Melt slowly in a frying pan for twenty minutes. In a bowl mix the bacon and bacon fat, the mushrooms, parsley, scallion, chicken, bone marrow, and suet. Add salt, pepper, and nutmeg to taste. Gently stir in the artichoke bottoms and sweetbreads.

The pie: Fill the piecrust with the meat mixture. Roll out the remaining half of the dough. Dampen the edges, and place the dough over the pie to cover it. Press down along the edges to seal the two crusts together. Make a small hole, for steam to escape, in the center of the upper crust. Make a two-inch-high cylinder with a small piece of aluminum foil, and place this "chimney" in the hole. Beat the egg, and spread with a brush over the upper crust. Bake in a moderate oven (375°) for one hour.

To Serve: Remove the "chimney." Pour the remaining lemon juice into the hole in the upper crust. Shell the pistachios. Place the nuts in boiling water for thirty seconds; then drain them immediately. Remove the thin skins from the nuts, and serve the nuts in a separate dish when serving the pie.

PETITS PATES A LA MAZARINE

(Veal and Bacon Pastries à la Mazarine)

Cardinal Mazarin was a French diplomat who died almost eighty years before this recipe first appeared in print. Nevertheless, it bears his name as a posthumous honor to this famous gourmet. Mazarin was considered one of the greatest gastronomes of his day, and the banquets he hosted rivaled those of the king.

Ingredients (for 4 servings): **For the puff pastry**: 1 cup flour. 1 pinch salt. 1½ teaspoons, plus ½ cup, butter. 1 egg white (optional). 2½ tablespoons water. **For the filling**: ½ pound veal roast. ½ pound fresh lean bacon (unsalted and unsmoked). 3 sprigs parsley. 1 scallion. 1 sprig basil. Salt. Pepper. Nutmeg. 3 eggs. ½ cup heavy cream.

The puff pastry: Since Marin gave no recipe for the puff pastry, follow the instructions given for making it in the recipe for Tourte d'herbes (page 74). Proceed as described in that recipe, but use the amounts of each ingredient listed above.

The filling: Chop the veal and bacon, along with the parsley, scallion, and basil. Add salt, pepper, and nutmeg to taste. Beat in two of the eggs and the cream.

The pastries: Roll out the pastry dough to a thickness a little less than one-quarter inch. With a cookie cutter about two inches in diameter cut sixteen circles out of the dough. Perform this operation with quick, clean strokes, so that the dough does not "smudge" around the edges. Otherwise, the edges will not rise during baking. Divide the filling into eight equal portions. Place these portions on eight of the circles, leaving a small border of dough uncovered around the filling. Moisten this border lightly with a little water. Now place the eight remaining circles over the circles covered with the filling. Pinch the edges with your fingers to seal the top and bottom circles together. Do not pinch too hard, however, for this will prevent the dough from rising during baking.

Baking: Beat the remaining egg with one tablespoon water, and brush the mixture over the top crust of the pastries. Place the pastries on a buttered and floured baking sheet, and bake in a hot oven (425°) for twenty-five minutes.

To Serve: Since timing is important, do not begin baking the pastries more than thirty minutes before they are to be served. They should be served hot as soon as they come from the oven.

FROMAGE A L'ECARLATE

(Cheese and Crayfish Scarlet)

Crayfish (or crawfish as they are called in the South) are a delicacy primarily found in freshwater lakes, rivers, and swamps in Louisiana. Neighboring Southern states can easily obtain live crayfish, but they are difficult to find in the North, except in gourmet restaurants and a few special gourmet fish shops in large metropolitan areas which have them flown in on special order. Even in France (where they are known as *écrevisses*) most live crayfish are imported from other countries in Europe.

Ingredients (for 6 servings): 18 large live crayfish. 10 eggs. 1⅔ cups heavy cream. Juice of 1 lemon. Salt. Pepper. 6½ tablespoons butter. 6 tablespoons bouillon or fish stock. 6 tablespoons dry white wine. Flour.

The crayfish: Place the crayfish in boiling water for two minutes. Drain. Separate the tails from the heads. Peel the tails. Keep the shells in a bowl since they will be used later. Then, using a small, pointed knife, remove the black tubelike bowel in the middle of the crayfish tail. Grind the crayfish heads in a mortar, and strain the resulting juice into a saucepan. Tie the crushed heads in a piece of cheesecloth.

The cheese. Add the eggs to the crayfish juice. Put aside two tablespoons of cream; then pour the remainder into the saucepan. Put the bag containing the crayfish heads into the pan as well. Cook over low heat, stirring constantly with a wooden spoon. Add the lemon juice, continuing to stir. Add salt and pepper to taste. As soon as the cream begins to curdle, remove the bag containing the heads. Line a sieve with a piece of folded cheesecloth. Pour the mixture into the sieve to drain off the whey. Place the strainer containing the curdled cheese over a bowl. Put a small plate on top of the curds, and place a weight (about one-half pound) on the plate. This will press out the remaining whey and form the cheese into a compact mass. Allow to cool.

The crayfish butter: As the cheese is draining and cooling, grind the shells you previously removed from the crayfish tails in a mortar. Put the ground shells in a saucepan with the butter, and place over low heat. Allow the butter to melt without browning. Strain; then set aside to cool.

The crayfish ragout: Pour the bouillon or fish stock and the wine into a saucepan. Add salt and pepper to taste. Simmer for five minutes. Place the shelled crayfish tails into the saucepan, and simmer for five minutes more. Remove from the heat, and stir in the two tablespoons of cream which you set aside earlier. Keep hot, but do not boil.

Cooking the cheese: When the cheese is cold and firm, cut it into slices. Flour the slices on all sides. Fry the slices in a skillet containing the crayfish butter.

To Serve: Arrange the fried slices of cheese on a platter. Pour the crayfish tails over the cheese, and serve immediately.

ROTIES DE BRETAGNE
    (Breton Toast with Herb Butter)

Menon 1746

The coasts of Brittany, in the northwest corner of France, are notoriously rocky. This recipe was originally composed of plants that grew on the Breton cliffs overlooking the sea. Plants such as samphire, white stonecrop, and buckhorn plantain were among the ingredients Menon used in the eighteenth-century version of this dish. These plants still grow along the Brittany coast and in England, but they are rarely commercialized even in the areas that produce them. Today they are thought of simply as decorative plants or weeds. Since none of these plants is available in the United States, this modern version of Menon's recipe calls for a variety of garden herbs that are familiar to American cooks.

Ingredients (for 4 servings): 1 large handful mixed fresh herbs (tarragon, chives, parsley, watercress, etc.). ⅔ cup butter. Juice of 1 lemon. Pepper, coarsely ground. 4 large slices country-style bread (round loaf).

The herb butter: Wash the herbs, and chop them together. Combine the herbs, butter, lemon juice, and pepper to taste by mashing all the ingredients together with a fork. Be careful not to soften the butter too much.

The toast: Toast the bread on both sides over an open fire or under the oven broiler.

To Serve: As soon as the toast is brown and while it is still hot, spread the herb butter on it, and serve immediately.

RAMEQUINS AU FROMAGE
    (Cheese Ramequins)

Viard 1820

Gruyère was not made in France in Viard's time, at least not under that name. (Even today, it would be more accurate to call the French product Comté and to leave the appellation "gruyère" to the Swiss cheese made in the valley of that name.) However, Viard apparently used the authentic gruyère in this recipe, and that is the cheese that should be used instead of any local imitation. He also uses parmesan, which should always be bought fresh in chunks—never grated and packaged. Fresh parmesan has a completely different taste from the powdered cheese that is sold under the same name. If you grate the cheese yourself, you can be sure of its quality.

Ingredients (for 8 servings): 2 cups water. 1 cup butter, cut into pieces. 1 pinch salt. 1¾ cups flour. 8 eggs. 6½ ounces gruyère. 3½ ounces ungrated parmesan. Pepper.

The *chou* pastry dough: Pour the water into a pot. Add the butter and salt. Bring to a boil. As soon as the mixture comes to boil, remove the pot from the heat, and immediately add the flour all at once. Stir the dough vigorously with a wooden spoon until it is smooth and without lumps. Return to the heat, and continue stirring until all excess water has evaporated and the dough comes away from the sides of the pot as you stir it. Remove from the heat, and stir in the eggs one at a time. Each egg should be completely absorbed into the dough before the next one is added.

The ramequins: Dice half the gruyère, and grate the rest. Also grate the parmesan. Add the grated cheeses to the dough. Add pepper to taste.

Baking: Butter and flour a large, shallow baking dish or cookie sheet. Use a teaspoon to place little mounds of the cheese-flavored dough in the baking dish. Arrange them in such a way that they do not touch, for they will swell during baking and, if they are too close together, will stick to each other. Bake in a hot oven (425°) for fifteen minutes.

To Serve: Cover the serving platter with a napkin. Arrange the ramequins in a pyramid on the platter. Serve hot. Serve the diced gruyère on the platter beside the ramequins.

(Sole Purée in Pastry Shells)

Pastry shells served with a meat or fish stuffing in the manner described below are either called *vol-au-vent* or *bouchées* depending on the author of the receipe and the period during which he wrote. Gouffé's recipe is unique in that the filling he uses combines both fish and meat—a common practice in the Middle Ages but unusual in nineteenth-century cookery.

INGREDIENTS

(for 5 servings)

For the puff pastry
1 cup flour
1 pinch salt
1½ teaspoons, plus ½ cup, butter
1 egg white
2½ tablespoons water

For the pastry shells
1 egg
1 tablespoon water

For the purée
1 carrot
1 leek white
½ stalk celery
1 onion
10½ ounces lean veal
1 sprig parsley
¼ bay leaf
1 veal bone
Salt
3 cups cold water
¼ pound butter
2 tablespoons flour
2 ounces fresh button mushrooms
2 tablespoons chopped parsley
2 pounds fillets of sole
Juice of 2 lemons
3 tablespoons milk
6 tablespoons heavy cream

The puff pastry

A detailed description of how to make puff pastry was given earlier in the recipe for Tourte d'herbes (page 74). The reader should consult the instructions given there and follow those directions, using the amount of each ingredient specified here.

The pastry shells

- When the dough has been allowed to stand for the last time, roll it out to a thickness of about one-half inch.
- Butter a cookie sheet.
- Take a cookie cutter (two inches in diameter), dip it into hot water, and press it quickly into the dough. Continue cutting rounds until all the dough is used up. Place the rounds of dough on the cookie sheet.
- Beat the egg with the one tablespoon water. Brush the mixture over the rounds.
- Take a second cookie cutter (one inch in diameter), and dip it in hot water. Place it in the center of one of the rounds, and press down to a depth of a little less than one-sixteenth inch. Do the same with the rest of the rounds.
- Place the rounds in a very hot oven (475°) for fifteen minutes, or until golden brown.
- Remove from the oven, and pry off the lids of the rounds with the point of a knife. Then use a spoon to scoop out the insides of each pastry shell.

The purée of sole

- Peel and slice the carrot, leek white, celery, and onion. Chop the veal into very small pieces, or run it through a meat grinder.
- Put the parsley sprig into a saucepan with the chopped vegetables and veal, also adding the bay leaf, veal bone, and a pinch of salt. Add the cold water. Bring to a boil, and simmer one hour; then strain off the liquid, and reserve.
- Melt one tablespoon of the butter in the same saucepan over low heat; then stir in the flour. Continue stirring until smooth; then pour in the broth that was strained from the veal and vegetables earlier. Continue stirring until the mixture comes to a boil and a thick, smooth sauce is formed.
- Clean and slice the mushrooms. Add them and the chopped parsley to the sauce, and simmer slowly for thirty minutes.
- When the sauce has almost finished cooking, place the fillets of sole in a skillet with three tablespoons of the butter, a pinch of salt, the lemon juice, and milk. Poach the fish for about six minutes.
- Remove the pan containing the sauce from the heat. Add the cream and the remaining butter. Grind the fillets of sole through a sieve or food mill, and stir the purée into the sauce.
- Fill the pastry shells with this mixture, and replace the lids on the shells.

To Serve

- Place the pastry shells in a hot oven (450°) for three or four minutes; then serve immediately.

"Le Récamier"

Eggs

Omelettes and soufflés are practically the only egg dishes most people associate with French cuisine. Nevertheless, boiled, scrambled, poached, and even deep-fried eggs are all typically French. The declining importance of egg cookery in France might be related to the gradual disappearance of dietary laws. For centuries, French cooking was divided into two distinct categories, *la cuisine grasse* (fat cooking) and *la cuisine maigre* (meatless cooking). This division was based on the strict Roman Catholic dietary laws that were enforced throughout the country. Not only were meatless days common, but violators were frequently punished, no matter what their rank in society might be. A debate once raged on whether or not eggs were to be considered *gras* or *maigre*. For many years they were ruled *gras*, thus forbidden in meatless meals—especially during Lent. This gave rise to the custom of giving eggs as presents on Easter Sunday (Easter Sunday being the end of Lent), the egg symbolizing the return to a normal diet. No doubt people's appetite for egg dishes was only whetted the more by these frequent periods of abstention.

Whenever eggs are used in cooking, it is extremely important that they be very fresh. Fresh eggs are readily available today, thanks to modern means of transportation and preservation, but in the past they were harder to find. Ingenious methods were developed in an attempt to ship and store eggs without spoilage. Most methods sought to keep the egg out of contact with the air. This could be done by dipping the egg into hot wax, which would harden and form an airtight seal around the egg, or by burying the egg in sand in order to achieve a similar result. But since these procedures were time-consuming and not always reliable, several tests were commonly employed to check the freshness of eggs sold at the market. Eggs were either held up to a candle, in which case any fecundation of the yolk would be visible, or dropped into a strong saltwater solution, to test their freshness. If the egg was newly laid, it sank to the bottom of the solution; if it was two days old, it rose to the middle; a four-day-old egg touched the surface; and eggs ten days old or more floated on top of the salty water. Needless to say, most consumers had to rely on the honesty of the egg merchants or else have a small hen house of their own. In any case, eggs were seldom stored after their purchase, and even today many French chefs never buy eggs before the day they intend to cook them.

The following recipes are typical of the variety and refinement of egg cookery in France. They illustrate only a few of the uses that can be made of this wholesome food by creative chefs.

This recipe compensates for its complexity by the originality and flavor of the end result. Since spit-roasted eggs tend to be slightly dry, it is best to serve them with melted butter, either plain or with lemon juice added.

INGREDIENTS

(for 4 servings)

8 eggs
1 bouquet fresh herbs (1 sprig each parsley, sweet marjoram, sage, mint)
3 tablespoons butter
1 pinch thyme
1 pinch ground ginger
1 pinch ground saffron
Salt
Pepper

Preparing the shells

- Choose eight fairly large eggs—preferably brown eggs, not because brown eggs are necessarily better, but because their shells are sturdier than those of white eggs.
- Hold an egg over a bowl, and with a pin or small skewer, make a hole a little less than one-quarter inch in diameter at each end. (Make the holes large enough to allow easy insertion of a skewer.) Empty the egg into the bowl by holding it vertically and blowing through the upper hole. Repeat this procedure with each egg.
- Keep the shells.

The filling

- Wash the fresh herbs. Chop finely, and mix thoroughly into the eggs.
- Heat the butter in a skillet, and add the egg mixture. Cook until it is the consistency of a soft omelette. (The eggs will dry as they cook on the skewer.)
- Pour the cooked eggs onto a cutting board, and chop finely, adding the thyme, ginger, saffron, a pinch of salt, and a dash of pepper.

The eggs

- Separate the chopped eggs into eight equal portions.
- Fill the shells carefully with the egg mixture.

Cooking

- Slide each stuffed egg onto a small skewer, or lace two at a time on a larger one.
- Roast the eggs over a low fire for five minutes, or broil them under medium heat, turning occasionally.

To Serve

- Serve the eggs on their skewers—by far the most spectacular way.

"Le Récamier"

OEUFS FARCIS A L'OSEILLE
(Eggs Stuffed with Sorrel)

Since the Middle Ages sorrel has been one of the most commonly used garden vegetables in France. Since sorrel is extremely acid, its taste does not mix well with that of wine. La Varenne suggests mixing other ''herbs'' such as spinach or lettuce with the sorrel if you want to drink wine with this dish.

INGREDIENTS
(for 4 servings)

8 eggs, hard-cooked and peeled
1 large handful ''herbs'' (sorrel,
    lettuce, spinach, or any other
    green leafy vegetable)
5 tablespoons butter
Salt
Pepper
Nutmeg

The eggs
- Cut each egg in half, lengthwise. Remove the yolks, and crush them with a fork.

The filling
- Wash the sorrel and other greens. Drain thoroughly. Remove the stem and thick central rib of the sorrel or spinach leaves. Wilt the greens over low heat in a saucepan with three tablespoons of the butter.
- Add the egg yolks. Salt and pepper to taste, and add a little nutmeg.

To Serve
- Fry the egg whites quickly in the remaining butter.
- Fill each half with a mound of the egg-yolk mixture.
- Arrange on a platter, and serve. To decorate, either wilt some additional sorrel leaves in butter, mix them with a little heavy cream, and place this mixture in the center of the platter; or serve the eggs on small slices of fried French bread trimmed of their crusts.

''Au Châteaubriant''
Lithograph by Picasso

OMELETTE FARCIE ET COUPEE
(Stuffed Sliced Omelette)

This ''omelette'' is really a kind of vegetable quiche without a crust. The lemon juice and sorrel give it a slightly acid flavor. Spinach can be used instead of sorrel for equally good (but less biting) results.

INGREDIENTS

(for 10 servings)

24 eggs
2 large handfuls sorrel (4 cups tightly packed)
1 handful mixed parsley and chervil
½ pound fresh button mushrooms
2 cooked artichoke bottoms
Salt
Black pepper
Nutmeg
6½ tablespoons butter
Juice of 2 lemons
White pepper

The eggs

- Place twelve of the eggs in a pot of boiling water. Cook for nine minutes.
- Cool the eggs under running water, and peel.
- Halve the eggs; remove and reserve the yolks.

The filling

- Wash the sorrel, parsley, and chervil. Remove the stems of the sorrel if the leaves are large.
- Clean the mushrooms.
- Chop all the above ingredients finely, along with the artichoke bottoms and hard-cooked egg yolks.
- Add salt and black pepper to taste and a little nutmeg.
- Melt five and a half tablespoons of the butter in a skillet. Add all the chopped ingredients, and cook for ten minutes. Allow to cool.

The omelette

- Beat the remaining eggs in a large bowl.
- Stir the eggs into the filling.
- Generously butter a very large pie pan with the remaining butter, and pour the omelette into it. If you do not have a pie pan large enough to hold all the filling, use two smaller ones.
- Place in a hot oven (450°) for ten minutes, or until golden brown.

To Serve

- Remove from the oven. Pour the lemon juice over the omelette.
- Sprinkle with the white pepper.
- To serve, slice as though the omelette were a cake.

OEUFS POCHES A LA SAUCE D'ANCHOIS

(Poached Eggs with Anchovy Sauce)

In countries bordering the Mediterranean, anchovies are used in many forms—fresh, marinated, salted, smoked, or, in modern times, as fillets steeped in brine and canned in oil. This recipe originally called for cleaned whole anchovies preserved in salt, but these are very difficult to find in the United States except in some shops catering to ethnic groups from Mediterranean regions. If salted anchovies are used, they have to be soaked in water or milk for four hours before being cooked, but anchovy fillets preserved in oil can be used straight from the can.

INGREDIENTS

(for 4 servings)

16 anchovy fillets in oil
4 tablespoons butter
1 teaspoon flour
Juice of 1 lemon
Salt
Pepper
1 tablespoon white vinegar
8 eggs

Anchovy sauce

- Cut the anchovies into small pieces. Melt the butter in a frying pan. Add the anchovies, and cook gently for twenty minutes.
- Make a paste by rubbing the anchovies through a sieve or pounding them in a mortar.
- Put the anchovy paste back into the pan. Sprinkle with the flour.
- Add the lemon juice and salt and pepper to taste. (Use the salt sparingly since the anchovies tend to be salty.)

Poaching the eggs

- Fill a shallow saucepan three-quarters full of water. Add the vinegar (do not use red vinegar because it will turn the eggs gray).
- Bring to a boil; then reduce the heat, and keep the water at a simmer.
- Break the eggs, one by one, into the water. This must be done with a quick, decisive motion so that the whole egg may be immersed at once and not have time to spread out in the water.
- Poach the eggs for three minutes. Remove them with a slotted spoon, and drain thoroughly.

To Serve

- Carefully place the eggs on a serving platter, and pour the anchovy sauce over them. Or serve the eggs in individual dishes with some of the sauce around them.

OEUFS A L'ANTIDAME
(Eggs with Herbs and Anchovies)

Vincent de La Chapelle was the most famous chef of his day. The publication of his book *The Modern Cook* (1733) marked a turning point in the history of French cooking. This particular dish is an example of the kind of refinement La Chapelle brought to French cooking. The use of simple ingredients and relatively few spices characterizes his approach to cooking.

INGREDIENTS

(for 4 servings)

2 sprigs parsley, finely chopped
1 scallion, finely chopped
8 anchovy fillets in oil, finely
   chopped
1 tablespoon capers, finely chopped
10 eggs
Salt
Pepper
Nutmeg
Juice of 1 lemon
2 tablespoons olive oil

The herbs and anchovies

- Mix the parsley, scallion, anchovies, and capers in a bowl.
- Break four of the eggs, separating the whites from the yolks. Beat the whites until stiff.
- Mix the egg yolks with the herbs. Salt sparingly (the anchovies are already salty). Add pepper to taste and a little nutmeg. Add the lemon juice; then carefully fold in the egg whites.

Cooking

- Put the olive oil in an ovenproof dish. Break the remaining eggs into the dish, and pour the herb preparation over them.
- Place in a hot oven (450°) until the egg whites on top have set, or about ten minutes.

To Serve

- Serve immediately, very hot.

OEUFS A L'INFANTE
(Poached Eggs à l'Infante)

Although this and many other recipes from the eighteenth century call for champagne, it is probable that cooks then used a dry white wine, not the sparkling wine that we are familiar with today. Sparkling wine was not invented until the end of the seventeenth century, and it was a long time before it became as popular as either the dry white wine or the famous red wine that had traditionally come from the Champagne region. In any event, either dry white wine or sparkling champagne can be used in this recipe with different but equally good results.

INGREDIENTS
(for 4 servings)

3 tablespoons butter
1 tablespoon vegetable oil
4 shallots, peeled and chopped
2 cloves garlic, peeled
2 tablespoons parsley, finely
    chopped
1 ⅔ cups bouillon
⅓ cup champagne or dry white wine
Salt
1 tablespoon white vinegar
8 eggs
Juice of 1 orange
Pepper

The sauce

- In a saucepan combine the butter, oil, shallots, garlic, and half the parsley. Place over low heat.
- Add the bouillon and champagne or white wine. Simmer.
- Cook for ten minutes. Salt—but do not pepper.

The eggs

- Add the vinegar to a large saucepan of boiling water.
- Break one of the eggs into a cup. Place the egg in the saucepan of boiling water by lowering the cup to the surface of the water and tipping it until the egg slides in. Repeat the procedure with the remaining eggs, one at a time, as rapidly as possible.
- Cook the eggs for three minutes. Remove with a slotted spoon, and drain the eggs on a cloth.

To Serve

- Trim the eggs with scissors to improve their appearance by making them either perfectly oval or round.
- Place the eggs on a platter.
- Add the orange juice to the sauce. Strain the sauce over the eggs.
- Sprinkle lightly with pepper and the remaining parsley.

Plate by Georges Mathieu

(Crayfish Omelette)

Menon concludes this recipe with the words "Serve with a good sauce." But he does not tell us which good sauce. A sauce made with fresh tomatoes would be very good, or an experienced cook could make a sauce that was flavored and colored by pounding the shells of the crayfish used in preparing this dish. The crayfish themselves might be responsible for the French name of this dish— *au joli coeur* (pretty heart)—since these shellfish were long considered aphrodisiac and were served to "warm the heart" of otherwise timid maidens.

INGREDIENTS

(for 6 servings)

5½ ounces fresh spinach
¾ cup butter
6 tablespoons dry white wine
1 dash cayenne pepper
3 pounds small live crayfish
Several slices stale bread
12 eggs
Salt
Pepper
2 tablespoons heavy cream
   (optional)
10 anchovy fillets in oil

The filling

- Wash the spinach, and remove the central rib and stem of any large leaves. Melt three tablespoons of the butter in a large pot. Gradually add the spinach. Cook for no more than fifteen minutes, stirring occasionally. Drain.
- Place the wine in a saucepan. Add the cayenne pepper. Bring to a boil.
- Wash the crayfish. Drop them into the boiling wine, and cook for eight minutes. Remove them from the liquid. Separate the tails, and shell them. Use a small knife to remove the thin black line from the middle of each tail.
- Cut the bread into small strips. Melt six and a half tablespoons of the butter in a frying pan, and brown the bread over moderate heat, making croutons.

The omelettes

- Make two thin six-egg omelettes as follows:
- Melt one tablespoon of the butter in a large frying pan. In a bowl, quickly beat six of the eggs with salt and pepper to taste (a tablespoon of cream may be added to the eggs, if desired).
- When the butter is very hot, pour the eggs into the pan. Lightly beat the surface of the eggs with a fork, working in circles from the outer edges toward the middle. After a few seconds, move the pan back and forth gently to keep the eggs from sticking.
- When the eggs are set, cook for another four or five seconds; then turn the omelette out onto a plate.
- Prepare a second omelette in the same way.

Filling the omelettes

- Spread spinach over each omelette. Salt and pepper lightly.
- Place five of the anchovy fillets, half the croutons, and half the crayfish tails on the spinach coating one omelette. Arrange the remainder of these ingredients on the spinach on the second omelette.
- Roll the omelettes while they are still hot. Then cut them into slices one and a half to two inches thick.
- Arrange on a platter, and dot with the remaining butter.
- Place in a hot oven (450°) for five minutes.

To Serve

- Serve very hot.

OMELETTE D'ASPERGES

Pierre de Lune 1656

(Asparagus Omelette)

The white or lavender-tipped asparagus is common in France and in classic French cuisine is almost always preferred to the green asparagus. Nonetheless, in some dishes, such as this one, it is preferable to use green asparagus since it has the advantage of being tender along a greater length of the stalk. Asparagus should be cooked as little as possible and remain somewhat crisp when served.

Ingredients (for 4 servings): 1 pound fresh green asparagus. 3 tablespoons butter. 1 tablespoon each finely chopped parsley and chives. Salt. Pepper. Nutmeg. 12 eggs. 4 tablespoons heavy cream. 1 lemon.

The asparagus: Peel the asparagus, starting from the tips and working toward the base. Wash the asparagus, and cook for twenty minutes in boiling salted water. Drain, and cut into one-half-inch pieces. Melt the butter in a frying pan. Add the asparagus and the chopped herbs. Salt and pepper to taste, and add a little nutmeg. Cook until the asparagus pieces begin to brown.

The omelette: Break the eggs into a bowl, and add the cream. Beat the mixture quickly for about one minute. Pour the mixture over the contents of the pan. Raise the edges of the omelette with a fork and tilt the pan from side to side until the eggs are set.

To Serve: This particular omelette should not be folded. When it is cooked, place a round serving platter over the pan, and turn the omelette out with its bottom side up. Garnish with a lemon cut into quarters.

CIVET D'OEUFS A L'HUILE

Escole Parfaite des Officiers de Bouche 1662

(Deep-Fried Eggs with Wine Sauce)

Deep-fried eggs are harder to prepare than scrambled eggs or omelettes, but this method of cooking eggs can be mastered with a little patience and practice. The crispness and unique taste of deep-fried eggs contrast with and improve the flavor of the stewlike sauce that accompanies them in this recipe.

Ingredients (for 4 servings): 4 medium onions, peeled. Oil for deep frying. 3 cups dry wine, red or white. 2 tablespoons red or white wine vinegar. 2 tablespoons lemon juice. Salt. Pepper. 8 eggs.

The sauce: Cut the onions into rings. Dry the rings with a clean cloth to remove all moisture. Deep-fry the onion rings in hot oil. As soon as they brown, remove and drain thoroughly. Discard any of the rings which may have blackened even slightly (these would give a bitter taste to the dish). Place the remaining rings in a saucepan. Cover the onions with the wine. Add red wine vinegar (if you are using red wine) or white (if you are using white wine) and the lemon juice. Salt and pepper to taste. Bring to a boil, and cook until half the liquid has evaporated.

The eggs: Fill a small frying pan halfway with some of the oil in which the onion rings were fried. Heat until the oil is nearly smoking. Break an egg into a saucer. Bring the saucer as close as possible to the surface of the hot oil, and slide the egg into the oil. Dip a wooden spoon into the oil; then quickly fold the white of the egg around the yolk, in such a way that the yolk is completely enveloped. As soon as the white of the egg has solidified and begun to brown, carefully remove the egg with a skimmer or slotted spoon and drain. Repeat this procedure with the remaining eggs. (It will take no more than thirty seconds to cook each egg.)

To Serve: This dish should be served in soup plates. Place two eggs in each plate. Spoon the sauce over the eggs, and serve immediately.

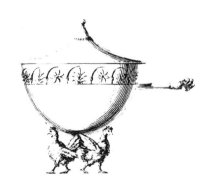

OMELETTE AUX HUITRES

(Oyster Omelette)

Oysters are rarely used in French cooking today, although they are often eaten raw. But in the eighteenth century oysters were frequently cooked and used to garnish stews and egg dishes such as this one. It is essential to drain the oysters thoroughly before they are cooked. Otherwise, the liquid they contain will prevent the oysters from mixing properly with the eggs once the omelette has set, and the general appearance of the dish will be spoiled.

Ingredients (for 6 servings): 36 oysters in their shells. 12 eggs. 4 sprigs fresh parsley, chopped. 2 tablespoons heavy cream. Pepper. 2 cups stale bread, cut into ½-inch cubes. 2 tablespoons butter.

The oysters: Open the oysters over a saucepan in order to catch all their liquid. Remove the oysters from their shells, and put them in the saucepan with their liquid. Place over low heat until the oysters begin to whiten. Drain the oysters. Strain and reserve the liquid.

The eggs: Break the eggs into a large bowl. Add the parsley, cream, and two tablespoons of the liquid in which the oysters cooked. Add pepper to taste. Beat quickly for about one minute.

Cooking: Dry and lightly toast the cubes of bread in a moderate oven (375°). Melt half the butter in a large frying pan. When the butter is quite hot, pour half the beaten eggs into the pan. When the eggs begin to set, add half the oysters and half the croutons. Continue to cook. Fold the omelette and keep hot. Make a second omelette in the same way.

To Serve: Serve very hot.

OEUFS A L'AIL

(Garlic Eggs)

The garlic sauce described in this recipe is very similar to a famous Provençale specialty called *aïoli*. Menon adds anchovies and capers to his sauce, but otherwise, the preparation is identical to the garlic mayonnaise popular in the South of France. This sauce is not to everyone's taste since the garlic dominates the other ingredients, but garlic lovers unite in praising the virtues and flavor of this mixture.

Ingredients (for 4 servings): 10 cloves garlic, peeled. 4 anchovy fillets in oil. 20 capers. Olive oil. 1 tablespoon vinegar. Salt. Pepper. 8 eggs.

The sauce: Place the garlic in a small saucepan. Cover with water, and cook for ten minutes. Strain off the water. Pound the anchovies, capers, and garlic in a mortar until a smooth paste is formed. Add olive oil to the mixture, little by little, stirring constantly until there are approximately four tablespoons of sauce, which should have the consistency of mayonnaise. Add the vinegar. Salt and pepper to taste.

The eggs: Place the eggs in a pot of cold water. Bring to a boil, and cook the eggs for nine minutes. Cool the eggs under running water. Peel the eggs.

To Serve: Pour the sauce into a bowl. Cut the eggs lengthwise, and arrange them in the sauce. Serve cold.

OEUFS EN MATELOTE
(Egg and Anchovy Stew)

This recipe originally called for the addition of carp roe to the onions halfway through their cooking time. But since carp roe is almost impossible to find today (unless you happen to purchase a carp that contains it), it is not included in this version of the recipe. However, if you prefer, you can increase the number of anchovy fillets used in the sauce, and the fish taste will be closer to that of the original recipe. This modified version is nevertheless delicious, and the distinctive taste of the anchovies perfectly complements that of the eggs.

Ingredients (for 4 servings): ¼ pound butter. 1 pound very small onions, peeled. 2 cups bouillon. 2 anchovy fillets in oil, finely chopped. 1 tablespoon capers. 8 thin slices bread. ¾ cup oil for frying. 8 eggs. Salt. Pepper.

The onion stew: Melt two tablespoons of the butter in a heavy saucepan. Add the onions. Cook gently for twenty minutes over low heat, stirring occasionally to prevent burning. Add the bouillon. Cover the saucepan, and simmer for forty-five minutes. Remove the pan from the heat. Add the anchovies and capers.

The croutons: Cut the bread into narrow strips. Melt the remaining butter in a frying pan, and brown the strips of bread, making croutons.

The eggs: Pour the oil into a small frying pan (the oil should be about one-half inch deep). Heat until the oil is almost smoking. As soon as the oil is very hot, lower the heat. Immediately break an egg into a saucer, and slide the egg into the pan near the surface of the oil so that the oil will not splash and the egg will keep its shape. Dip a wooden spoon into the oil; then use it to fold the white of the egg over the yolk. Turn the egg over to brown both sides. As soon as the white is golden brown, remove the egg with a skimmer or slotted spoon, and place it on a serving platter. Salt and pepper lightly. Keep warm. Follow the same procedure for the remaining eggs. The entire operation should not take more than ten minutes.

To Serve: Spoon the onion stew around the eggs, without covering them entirely. Garnish the edge of the platter with the croutons. Serve very hot.

OEUFS AU GRATIN
(Eggs au Gratin)

Eighteenth-century chefs normally had a small army of assistants working under them. Each person had a specific task to perform, and a complicated hierarchy led up to the chef himself, who oversaw everything. This system still exists in French restaurants, but because of the introduction of time-saving appliances to most kitchens, the number of people involved has greatly decreased. Menon, the author of this recipe, probably had at least twenty assistants in the kitchen with him at all times, and the private dinners he prepared were normally for that many guests or more. Under these circumstances little was wasted, since ingredients left over from preparing one dish could easily be used in another. This was probably the case in the following recipe, which calls for eleven eggs and uses only three egg yolks and eight whole eggs. And the three leftover egg whites? They probably went into some dish served later in the meal. Modern cooks can do the same thing or can refrigerate the egg whites (which will prevent them from spoiling) and use them to prepare a dish on a different occasion.

Ingredients (for 4 servings): 2½ cups bread crumbs. 2 sprigs parsley, chopped. 1 scallion, chopped. 1 shallot, peeled and chopped. 2 anchovy fillets in oil, chopped. 11 eggs. 4 tablespoons butter. Salt. Pepper.

The gratin: Mix the bread crumbs, parsley, scallion, shallot, and anchovies. Stir in three egg yolks and three tablespoons of the butter.

Cooking: Butter a shallow ovenproof dish with the remaining butter. Spread the gratin evenly over the bottom of the dish. Place in a hot oven (450°) for ten minutes. Remove from the oven, and break eight eggs into the dish. Add salt and pepper. Return to the oven for five or six minutes, or until the whites have set. The yolks should remain soft.

To Serve: Serve the dish as soon as it comes out of the oven.

OEUFS AU PREVOT

(Eggs with Ham and Mushrooms)

Fried eggs are usually served next to or on top of something else, but in this recipe the garnish is placed on top of the eggs. This is unusual in French cooking, and here the garnish becomes a kind of sauce that improves both the taste and the appearance of the dish.

Ingredients (for 4 servings): 4 medium onions, peeled and finely chopped. 2 ounces fresh fatback or fatty bacon, thinly sliced. ¼ pound fresh button mushrooms, cleaned and sliced. 4 slices ham, finely chopped. 1 tablespoon lard. 8 eggs. Salt. Pepper. Juice of 1 lemon.

The ham and mushrooms: Place the onions and fatback or bacon in a skillet over low heat. When the onions soften, add the mushrooms and ham. Cook for ten minutes.

The eggs: Grease a fireproof dish with the lard. Break the eggs into it so that they completely cover the bottom of the dish. Add salt and pepper to taste. Place over high heat, and baste the egg whites once or twice with the melted lard—be careful not to baste the yolks or they will harden.

To Serve: Pour off the excess fat, and sprinkle the lemon juice over the eggs. Cover the eggs with the ham, mushrooms, and onions. Serve immediately.

OEUFS A LA TRIPE

(Eggs and Onions)

This was one of the most popular recipes of its day, and almost every eighteenth-century French cookbook contained its version of this dish. These recipes differed on whether or not bouillon or milk was used in the sauce served with the eggs. Since fresh milk was not always available, especially in large cities, it is likely that this version, using bouillon, was probably the most common way of preparing this dish in the eighteenth century. If you prefer using milk, follow the same recipe, but omit the vinegar and sprinkle the eggs with parsley before serving. In either case the result is delicious in its simplicity.

Ingredients (for 4 servings): 1 tablespoon butter. 2 tablespoons flour. 2 medium onions, peeled and diced. 1⅔ cups bouillon. 8 eggs. 1 tablespoon vinegar. Salt. Pepper.

The roux: Melt the butter in a saucepan; then stir in the flour. Cook until the mixture turns light brown, stirring constantly with a wooden spoon. Remove from the heat.

The onions: Stir the onions into the roux, and place the pan back on the stove. Add the bouillon. Simmer gently for twenty minutes. The onions should remain white, but should be soft enough to crush with a fork.

The eggs: Place the eggs in a pot of boiling water, and cook for nine minutes. Drain the eggs, and cool them under running water. Peel and slice the eggs.

To Serve: Add the vinegar to the onions. Salt and pepper to taste. Stir well. Add the sliced hard-cooked eggs. Bring just to a boil. Serve very hot.

OEUFS A LA BONNE FEMME
(Housewife's Eggs and Onion Soufflé)

Dictionnaire Portatif 1765

The onion is the French condiment par excellence. Although garlic and shallots rival its appeal in some parts of the country, onions are by far the most widely employed condiment in France. Just as olive oil is said to be the perfect companion to garlic, and butter to shallots, lard is considered best for cooking onions. Even though butter is used in this recipe, lard could be substituted for cooking the onions, and some cooks believe the taste of this dish is, in fact, improved.

Ingredients (for 4 servings): 1 tablespoon butter. 6 medium onions, peeled and diced. 1 pinch flour. 6 tablespoons heavy cream. Salt. Pepper. Nutmeg. 8 eggs, separated.

The onions: Melt the butter in a saucepan. Add the onions, and cook until soft. Do not let the onions brown. Stir in the flour. Remove from the heat, and add the cream, salt and pepper to taste, and a little nutmeg.

Cooking: Stir the egg yolks into the onions. Beat the whites until stiff. Butter a soufflé mold. Gently fold the egg whites into the contents of the saucepan; then pour into the mold. Place the mold in a pan containing about an inch of water, and put it into a moderately hot oven (400°) for ten minutes, or until the eggs are cooked. Test the eggs as you would a custard by sliding a clean knife into the dish. If the blade comes out completely clean, the dish is cooked.

To Serve: Turn out the soufflé onto a serving platter, or serve it in the mold in which it cooked. Serve with a sauce of your choice, such as tomato sauce, white sauce, etc.

OEUFS A LA MONIME
(Stuffed Omelette and Meat Balls)

Dictionnaire Portatif 1765

Leftovers can be transformed into refined dishes by an experienced chef. This recipe is an example of just such a transformation. Any leftover meat can be used in the stuffing described below; even leftover fish can be used if fish bouillon is substituted for the meat stock or bouillon called for here. This 200-year-old recipe is a superb example of creative cooking.

Ingredients (for 6 servings): 3 cups leftover meat (beef, veal, or chicken), chopped. 2 medium onions, peeled and chopped. Salt. Pepper. 16 eggs. 4 sprigs parsley, chopped. 4 scallions, chopped. 1 tablespoon heavy cream. 7 tablespoons butter. Bread crumbs. 1 small lime. 6 French vinegar pickles (cornichons). 1 tablespoon flour. 6 tablespoons bouillon.

The meat stuffing: Mix the meat and onions together until a homogeneous mixture is formed. Sprinkle with salt and pepper. Add two of the eggs, and stir well.

The omelette: Break seven of the eggs into a bowl. Add half the parsley, scallions, and cream. Salt and pepper to taste. Beat well until all the ingredients are combined. Melt two tablespoons of the butter in a large frying pan. When the butter is quite hot, put in the egg mixture, and cook until the eggs have set. Turn the omelette out onto a platter. Cover with one-quarter of the stuffing. Roll the omelette into a sausage shape, and cut it into three pieces. Make a second omelette in exactly the same way, using the remaining eggs and a second quarter of the stuffing. Cut into thirds as well. Melt one tablespoon of the butter in a small saucepan. Dip each piece of omelette into the butter; then roll it in the bread crumbs.

The meat balls: Make six elongated meat balls with the remaining stuffing (half of the original amount). Roll them in the bread crumbs.

Final cooking: Grease a large, shallow baking dish with one tablespoon of the butter. Arrange the breaded pieces of omelette and the meat balls in the dish and place in a hot oven (450°) for ten minutes.

The sauce: Wash the lime, and grate a little of the peel. Coarsely chop the pickles. Melt the remaining butter in a saucepan. Sprinkle in the flour over low heat. Stir constantly until smooth; then pour in the bouillon. Continue stirring until well mixed. Add salt and pepper to taste. Remove from the heat, and add the lime peel and the pickles.

To Serve: Remove the omelette and the meat balls from the oven. Cover with the sauce, and serve.

OEUFS A LA BONNE SUISSE

Isabeau 1796

(Swiss Egg Fondue)

This dish is, in fact, an egg fondue. Although the author calls for champagne, a dry white wine could be used instead. But do not try to economize by using anything but real Swiss gruyère. No other cheese has the taste essential to this dish, and (as the name implies) this recipe loses all its authenticity if anything else is used.

Ingredients (for 4 servings): 4 large slices country-style bread. ¾ cup butter. 6 eggs. ½ pound gruyère, grated. 1 bouquet parsley and scallion, chopped. ⅔ cup champagne or dry white wine. Pepper. Nutmeg.

Preparing the ingredients: Cut the bread into small squares. Fry them in a frying pan with half the butter to make croutons. Break the eggs, separating the whites from the yolks. Beat the whites until stiff.

Cooking the eggs: Melt the remaining butter in a fondue pot. Add the gruyère, chopped herbs, champagne or white wine, pepper to taste, and a pinch of nutmeg. Bring to a boil stirring constantly with a wooden spoon. Continue stirring, lower the heat, and add the egg yolks, then the egg whites. Be very careful, from the time you add the eggs, that the mixture does not come back to a boil.

To Serve: Serve the cheese in the pot in which it cooked. The croutons are served separately, to be dipped into the cheese and eaten immediately.

OEUFS A L'AURORE

Beauvilliers 1814

(Egg Casserole)

Beauvilliers was one of the first great chefs to open his own restaurant. Until the French Revolution in 1789 great cooks were employed in private homes, and public taverns were notorious for the poor quality of their food. Beauvilliers, who was previously chef to the Count of Provence, opened his first restaurant just before the Revolution. This establishment, as well as several others he directed in later years, helped popularize good cooking and made Beauvilliers' name synonymous with fine food.

Ingredients (for 4 servings): 6 tablespoons butter. 2 tablespoons flour. 2 cups milk. Salt. Pepper. Nutmeg. 11 eggs. 1 large slice country-style bread.

The Béchamel sauce: Melt one tablespoon of the butter in a saucepan. Stir in the flour until a smooth paste is formed. Add the milk. Cook for ten minutes, stirring constantly until the sauce comes to a boil. Add salt and pepper to taste, and a little nutmeg. Cover the saucepan. Place the saucepan on very low heat to keep the sauce hot without cooking.

The eggs: Boil eight of the eggs for nine minutes. Cool under running water. Peel. Separate the yolks from the whites. Chop the whites, and place them in the hot Béchamel. Grind the yolks in a mortar with the remaining butter, salt and pepper to taste, and the yolks of two raw eggs.

Cooking: Pour the Béchamel sauce containing the egg whites into a buttered ovenproof dish. Put the ground yolks into a strainer, and hold the strainer over the dish. Then, with a pestle, grind the yolks through the strainer into the dish. Remove the crust from the bread, and cut it into strips. Beat the remaining egg. Dip the bread strips into the egg, and arrange them around the rim of the dish. Place in a hot oven (450°) for ten minutes.

To Serve: Remove from the oven, and serve immediately, very hot. The eggs should be golden brown.

103

Fish and Shellfish

In the Middle Ages most fish sold in Paris were *poissoniers doulx*—literally, "sweet fish"—that is to say, freshwater fish. Because transportation was so slow, few saltwater fish made it to Paris without spoiling. The most popular freshwater fish at that time were eels, barbels, pike, lampreys, loaches, dace, and carp. Among the saltwater fish that were sold in the French capital, herring and mackerel (both fresh and salted) were by far the most important. Salt cod was also sold, but fresh cod was a rarity.

Few shellfish survived the trip to Paris; shrimp were sold in the fourteenth century, but oysters and mussels did not become available until the fifteenth century. At first mussels were not very popular, but oysters (especially raw on the half shell) were all the rage. Lobsters were also highly appreciated by Parisians (when they could get them), but shellfish were reserved almost exclusively for the rich, for even when they were available, they were always very expensive.

One shellfish, however, was extremely popular and not too expensive. This was the only freshwater shellfish—the crayfish—which were caught in the rivers near Paris and were delivered in large quantities to Parisian markets. Many old recipes call for crayfish as a garnish or use them in sauces because of their taste and their bright-red color, which enlivened the presentation of many dishes.

In the past, fish cookery was much more important in France than it is today. Even in regions where fish were scarce, the Catholic Church was very strict about enforcing the meatless days that have now almost disappeared from the calendar. Salt fish (especially cod and herring) were always available when fresh fish could not be had.

One characteristic of fish cooking in the past was the willingness chefs showed to combine different fish in the same dish. Today, the famous bouillabaisse of Marseilles is one of the few reminders of the mixed fish stews that were once popular in France. Combining fish and shellfish was also a common practice, and red wine, instead of white, was often used in cooking fish. All these differences make old recipes for fish extremely interesting.

Although modern cooks often have a greater variety of fish to choose from, cooks in the past had to rely on their own imaginations when a limited number of fish were available. The ideas they came up with are well worth resurrecting by cooks interested in varying menus and discovering new dishes.

PATE D'ANGUILLES
(Eel Pâté)

Almost all pâtés today are made with meat. In the past, pâtés were much more popular (and varied) than they are today. This particular pâté is made in a raised pastry shell (a special pâté mold is needed), and all the ingredients are cooked inside a layer of dough which is both decorative and good to eat.

Ingredients (for 10 servings): 2 freshwater eels (each about 2 pounds). Salt. Pepper. 3 cups dry white wine. 1 pike (4 pounds). 6 eggs. 1⅓ cups heavy cream. 4⅔ cups flour. 1¼ cups soft butter. 1 teaspoon olive oil. 3 tablespoons beer.

Preparing the fish: Clean the eels, and remove the skin. Carefully lift the meat away from the bone, and cut it into slices two to two and a half inches long. Place the slices in a bowl. Sprinkle with salt and pepper, and add the wine. Set aside to marinate for two hours. Wash and clean the pike; then remove the skin. Fillet the pike, and pound the fillets in a mortar until a thick purée is formed. Add four egg yolks, salt and pepper to taste, and the cream to the purée. Mix well. Cover, and set aside for two hours.

The pastry dough: Combine 4 cups of the flour, a pinch of salt, and one cup of the butter. Add approximately three-quarters cup cold water, little by little; the dough should be soft but not sticky. Form the dough into a ball. With the heels of your hand, break the dough into little pieces; then press the pieces together to form a ball again. Repeat this procedure once again; then place the ball of dough in a clean bowl, and cover with a cloth. Set aside for one hour.

The crêpe: Mix the remaining flour with the oil, a pinch of salt, and one egg yolk. Gradually add the beer and three tablespoons water. Set aside for one hour. At the end of that time, fold in one stiffly beaten egg white. Lightly grease a large frying pan with butter, and heat until the butter begins to smoke. Slowly pour in the crêpe batter, tipping the pan from side to side as you do so. When the batter begins to stiffen, turn the crêpe over, and cook for one or two minutes on the other side.

Making the pâté: Butter a rectangular pâté mold. Roll out the dough, and place it in the mold. It should overlap the edge of the mold by one inch along the ends and one side and sufficiently on the other side to cover completely the top of the mold later. Brush the inside surface of the dough with lightly beaten egg white; then spread the crêpe over the pastry dough. Remove the slices of eel from the marinade (keep the marinade for later use). Melt the remaining butter in a hot frying pan. Add the slices of eel, and brown lightly on each side. Beat four egg whites until stiff; then fold them into the pike purée. Put a layer of the purée in the bottom of the pastry shell. Brush the purée with lightly beaten egg white; then cover it with a layer of eel. Continue alternating layers of pike purée and eel slices, brushing each layer with egg white. The top layer should be one of pike purée.

Cooking: Fold the crêpe over the top of the mold; then do the same with the pastry dough. Moisten the one-inch overlap with egg white, fold it over the top, and press down tightly all around the edge of the mold to seal the edges of the dough together. Make a small hole in the middle of the top for the steam to escape through. Then pour the marinade through the hole into the pâté. Roll a small piece of aluminum foil into a two-inch-high cylinder. Fit this ''chimney'' into the hole, and bake the pâté in a slow oven (325°) for two hours.

To Serve: This pâté may be served either hot or cold. If served cold, pour an aspic (made from boiling the heads and fins of the eels and pike with herbs and spices) through the hole in the center of the pastry, as soon as it comes from the oven. Chill for several hours before serving.

BROUET D'ANGUILLES
(Eel Stew)

Any meaty freshwater fish can be used instead of eel in this stew which is similar to the *matelotes* (red wine fish stews) still made in France today.

Ingredients (for 4 servings): 1 freshwater eel (1½ pounds). 3 cups red wine. 1 pinch ground ginger. 1 pinch ground cinnamon. 2 cloves. 1 generous pinch pepper. 1 pinch saffron. ⅔ cup butter. 4 medium onions, peeled and finely chopped. 1 pinch salt. 2 sprigs thyme. 1 bay leaf. Several pieces stale bread, cut into 1-inch squares. 3 sprigs parsley, finely chopped.

The eel: Although the original recipe describes how to kill and skin the eel, it is probably more convenient to have your fish merchant do so. At the same time, he can remove the entrails and cut off the eel's head. Wash the skinned and cleaned eel. Cut the eel into slices one and a half to two inches long.

The wine: Pour the wine into a saucepan. Add the ginger, cinnamon, cloves, pepper, and saffron. Bring to a boil; then remove from the heat.

Cooking: Melt five tablespoons of the butter in a large frying pan, and brown the slices of eel on both sides. Remove from the pan, and set aside. Brown the onions lightly in the pan in which the eel cooked. Add the eel slices to the pan with the onions. Add the salt, thyme, and bay leaf. Pour in the aromatized wine. Cover, and simmer for twenty-five minutes.

To Serve: Melt the remaining butter in another frying pan, and brown the bread on both sides, making croutons. Arrange the croutons in a serving bowl. Drain the eel slices, and place them on the croutons. Keep hot. Pour the cooking liquid through a strainer, and boil for ten minutes longer. Pour this liquid over the eel, and sprinkle with the parsley. Serve immediately.

PERCHES AU COURT-BOUILLON
La Varenne 1651
(Perch in White Wine)

The perch is a freshwater fish, common in the lakes, rivers, and streams of North America and Europe. It is considered by many people the best freshwater fish there is. Unfortunately, perch is very difficult to prepare unless the fish is scaled soon after being caught. Otherwise, the skin hardens and has to be stripped away like the skin of an eel.

Ingredients (for 4 servings): 2 cups dry white wine. 2 cups water. 1 orange. 1 medium onion, peeled and cut into 8 pieces. 10 scallions, washed. 2 cloves. Salt. Pepper. 8 perch (5 to 7 ounces each). 1 egg yolk. 3 tablespoons butter.

The court-bouillon: Combine the wine and water in a saucepan, and bring to a boil. Use a potato peeler to remove the rind from the orange (the juice from the orange will be used later). Put the orange rind and onion into the boiling wine with the scallions, cloves, and some salt and pepper. Boil gently for twenty minutes; then remove from the heat. Set aside to cool.

Preparing the perch: Cut off all the fins, and scale the perch by scraping them from the tail to the head with a knife. Empty the fish through the gills, and wash.

Cooking: Put the fish into the cold court-bouillon, and place over high heat. As soon as the liquid begins to boil, reduce the heat, and poach the fish gently for about fifteen minutes.

To Serve: In a small pan, combine the egg yolk and the juice from the orange. Add a few tablespoons of the warm court-bouillon. Taste for seasoning—add salt and pepper if necessary. Heat the sauce, but do not let it boil. Remove from the heat, and add the butter, divided into small pieces. Remove the skin from the perch, and arrange the fish on a platter. Pour the sauce over them, and serve.

POISSONS ROTIS SUR LE GRIL
La Varenne 1651
(Grilled Fish)

The original recipe for this dish specified the use of weever, a fish with poisonous spines on the dorsal fins but otherwise edible, which is found along all the coasts of France. Since weever is unavailable in the United States, any small fish, such as whiting, makes an admirable substitute.

Ingredients (for 4 servings): 8 whiting (3 to 4 ounces each). ⅛ teaspoon ground cloves. ⅔ cup soft butter. Salt. 3 sprigs parsley, finely chopped. Pepper. 1 tablespoon lemon juice. Several poached gooseberries or fresh currants (optional).

Preparing the fish: Scale and clean the fish. Remove the tails and fins with scissors. Wash the fish in cold water; then wipe them dry. With a very sharp knife, cut four or five slits across the back of each fish, where the meat is thickest. Cut to the bone —but do not cut through the bone.

Cooking: Mix the cloves with half the butter and a little salt. Fill the gashes on the backs of the fish with this mixture. Place the fish on a grill over a hot fire with the gashes facing upward. Grill six or seven minutes on each side. (The fish can also be cooked under the broiler.)

To Serve: Put the parsley in a saucepan with the remaining butter. Add salt and pepper to taste. Heat until the butter barely browns. Add the lemon juice and the gooseberries if desired. Serve the fish on a platter, with the sauce in a separate bowl.

SOUPRESSE DE POISSON
(Pressed Fish)

La Varenne 1651

This is a kind of fish pâté cooked without a mold or terrine. This type of dish was popular during Lent when cooks had to invent meatless substitutes for sausages and pâtés. As the Catholic Church gradually relaxed the rules governing meatless days, this kind of cooking slowly disappeared.

Ingredients (for 8 servings): 4 pounds freshwater fish (carp, eel, etc.). 1 bay leaf. 2 sprigs thyme. 1 medium carrot, scraped and sliced. 1 lemon, scraped and sliced. 4 cups dry white wine, 4 cups water. Salt. Pepper. 2 tablespoons finely chopped parsley. 2 tablespoons finely chopped chives. 2 tablespoons capers. ¾ cup butter. 2 cups bread crumbs. Milk. 1 egg, beaten. Chopped parsley (to garnish). Lemon slices (to garnish).

Preparing the fish: Wash, clean, and skin the fish. (If using eel, cut the skin around the head; then, using a cloth, get a firm grip on the skin, and pull hard toward the tail.) Remove all the bones from the fish. Chop the fish coarsely.

The court-bouillon: In a saucepan combine all the fins, bones, and heads with the bay leaf, thyme, carrot, and lemon. Add the wine and water. Salt and pepper generously.

The pressed fish: Mix the parsley, chives, and capers with the fish; then add the butter. Mix well. Soak the bread crumbs in a mixture of milk and beaten egg. Add these ingredients to the fish. Work the fish and bread-crumb mixture into the shape of a ham. Wrap it tightly in a piece of cheesecloth.

Cooking: Place the fish loaf in the court-bouillon over low heat. Simmer for thirty minutes. Remove from the heat, and allow to cool in the liquid.

To Serve: Lift out the fish loaf, and remove the cheesecloth. Cut the pressed fish into slices. Garnish with chopped parsley and lemon slices.

SAUMON EN RAGOUT
(Salmon and Oyster Stew)

Massialot 1691

Massialot's original recipe calls for the head of a salmon. In the seventeenth century the "head" of a fish included a third of its body along with the head itself. Although once considered a delicacy, the head is rarely eaten today, so this modern version of the recipe uses only a large slice taken from the front half of the fish. Most of the salmon eaten today is canned or smoked, but when it is eaten fresh, it is almost invariably grilled or broiled. This recipe is an example of the imaginative cooking typical of the seventeenth and eighteenth centuries in France. The salmon is braised with lime and served with an oyster stew. Originally the liver of the fish was finely chopped and added to the stew at the same time as the oysters. Since fish are usually cleaned before they are sold, it is almost impossible to find a salmon with the liver still in it, but if you do, or if you yourself fish for salmon, use it by all means; it adds a delicious taste and smoothness to the sauce.

Ingredients (for 8 servings): 2 sprigs parsley. 1 sprig thyme. 1 bay leaf. 1 large slice fresh salmon (about 2 pounds). 1½ cups dry white wine. 1 teaspoon vinegar. 2 cloves. 1 pinch nutmeg. 1 lime, peeled and cut into quarters. Salt. Pepper. 3 tablespoons butter. ¾ pound fresh button mushrooms, finely sliced. 1 tablespoon flour. 1 tablespoon capers. Juice of 1 lemon. 36 oysters in their shells.

The salmon: Tie the parsley, thyme, and bay leaf together, and place this bouquet in the bottom of a casserole with the salmon. Pour in one cup of the wine. Add the vinegar, cloves, nutmeg, and lime. Sprinkle with salt and pepper. Cover the casserole, and place in a moderate oven (350°) for twenty-five minutes.

The oyster stew: Melt the butter in a large frying pan. Add the mushrooms, and sauté for ten minutes, or until all the liquid given off by the mushrooms has evaporated. Sprinkle in the flour. Continue cooking until the mushrooms are golden brown. Add the remaining wine, and simmer for ten minutes more. Add the capers and lemon juice. Remove from the heat. Open the oysters, and carefully pour their juice into a bowl. Strain the juice, and add it to the mushrooms. Add the oysters, stir well, and cover. Poach the oysters for five minutes in the sauce.

To Serve: Remove the salmon from the casserole. Remove the skin, and place the fish on a serving platter. Pour the oyster stew over the fish. Serve very hot.

SOLES A LA SAUCE AUX ROIS

La Chapelle 1733

(Sole Stuffed with Anchovies and Herbs)

The original recipe calls, not for shallots, but for rocambole (or Spanish garlic) whose taste is midway between that of garlic and shallots. Either garlic or shallots can be used in preparing this recipe today.

Ingredients (for 4 servings): 2 sole (¾ pound each). ½ cup butter. 3 sprigs parsley, finely chopped. 1 scallion, finely chopped. 2 shallots or 2 cloves garlic, peeled and finely chopped. 4 anchovy fillets in oil, finely chopped. 2 tablespoons capers, finely chopped. Salt. Pepper. ⅔ cup dry white wine. Juice of 1 orange.

The sole: Cut off the heads of the fish, as close to the gills as possible. Turn the fish so that the dark side is facing upward. With a sharp knife, make a cut across the body just where the tail begins, and pull back the skin about an eighth of an inch. To remove the skin, take hold of the piece of loosened skin with a cloth, and pull quickly toward the head end of the fish. With scissors, cut off the tails and fins. Open the stomachs, and clean the fish; then wash them. On the side from which you have removed the dark skin, make a cut along the backbone of the fish to facilitate cooking. Melt four tablespoons of the butter in a frying pan. Place the fish in the pan, with the white skin facing down. Cook gently for five minutes; then turn the fish over, and cook on the other side for five minutes more. Remove from the heat, but keep hot.

The stuffing: Mix the parsley, scallion, shallots or garlic, anchovies, and capers, Place this mixture in the frying pan in which the fish cooked, and cook for about ten minutes.

Cooking: Through the cut on the side of each fish carefully remove the backbone. Remove the herbs and anchovies from the frying pan, and mix these ingredients with three tablespoons of softened butter. Add salt and pepper to taste. Place half of this mixture inside each fish, and carefully close the flesh over it. Grease an ovenproof serving dish with the remaining butter, and place the fish in the dish (the stuffed side facing upward). Pour the wine over the fish. Cover the dish, and place in a slow oven (325°) for ten minutes.

To Serve: Remove the dish from the oven, and pour the orange juice over the fish. Serve very hot.

TURBOT A LA BECHAMEL

La Chapelle 1733

(Turbot with Béchamel Sauce)

Béchamel sauce was a novelty when this recipe was written. It was supposedly invented by the Marquis de Béchamel in the late seventeenth century. Since turbot is difficult to obtain in the United States because it must be imported, usually frozen and flown in on special order, halibut can be substituted.

Ingredients (for 6 servings): 1 turbot or halibut (3 to 3½ pounds). 3⅓ cup milk. Salt. 3 tablespoons butter. 3 sprigs parsley, chopped. 1 scallion, chopped. 4 shallots, peeled and chopped. 3 tablespoons flour. Pepper. Nutmeg. 1 cup bread crumbs (optional). 3 lemons, quartered (optional).

Preparing the fish: Remove all the fins and the extremity of the tail. Pull out the gills. Turn the fish so that its dark side is facing upward. With a knife, make a slit just behind the gills and remove the intestines. Wash the fish thoroughly. Make an incision on either side of the backbone, on the dark side. If you are using a large fish, break the backbone in two places so that the fish will not lose its shape during cooking. Turn the fish over, and place it in a large frying pan (the white side should face upward). Cover with cold water. Add the milk and a pinch of salt. Slowly bring to a boil; then immediately lower the heat. Poach (do not allow the liquid to boil again) for twenty minutes.

The Béchamel sauce: Melt the butter in a frying pan. Add the parsley, scallion, and shallots, and cook over low heat. When the shallots barely begin to brown—but before they turn color—add the flour. Stir. Pour in three cups of the milk in which the fish cooked. Add salt, pepper, and nutmeg to taste.

The final cooking: Lift the fish from its cooking liquid. Drain, and remove the skin. Make one, two, or three cuts (according to the size of the fish) parallel to the fish's backbone, then the same number of cuts perpendicular to the spine. Slide a broad-bladed knife under each of the squares thus obtained.

To Serve: The fish can be served in either of two ways: (1) Place the fillets in the Béchamel sauce, and allow them to poach, without boiling, for five minutes. Place on a hot platter, and serve immediately. (2) Once the fillets have been removed from the fish, place them in an ovenproof dish. Cover them with the Béchamel sauce, sprinkle with the bread crumbs, and place in a hot oven (450°) for ten minutes. Serve with wedges of lemon.

MAQUEREAUX AU FENOUIL ET AUX GROSEILLES
(Grilled Mackerel with Fennel and Gooseberries)

La Chapelle 1733

Gooseberries were once the traditional accompaniment to mackerel—hence their French name *groseilles à maquereaux* (mackerel currants). The acidity of the gooseberries counteracts the fattiness of the fish, and the two were almost always served together. In La Chapelle's day the fish were wrapped in fennel and grilled over hot coals on an open fire, and it is still preferable to cook them that way. Otherwise, they can be broiled in the oven as described here.

Ingredients (for 4 servings): 4 mackerel (6 to 7 ounces each). Salt. Pepper. ⅔ cup melted butter. ½ pound (approximately 2 cups) gooseberries. 4 tablespoons flour. Nutmeg. 1⅔ cups boiling water. Several fresh fennel leaves, finely chopped. 1 tablespoon vinegar. Several fresh or dried fennel branches.

Preparing the mackerel: Clean the fish, and cut off the heads, tails, and fins. Wash; then wipe dry. With a sharp knife, make a slit about three-quarters inch deep down the length of the mackerel's backs. This will facilitate cooking. Place the fish on a platter. Sprinkle with salt and pepper. Pour two tablespoons of the butter over them. Allow to stand for ten minutes. Turn the mackerel over, and repeat this procedure, using another two tablespoons of the butter.

The sauce: Remove the stems and the tiny points at the other end of the gooseberries. Place them in a pot of boiling water; then poach over low heat. As the gooseberries turn yellowish white and rise to the surface, remove them with a slotted spoon. Cool under running water. Drain, and remove the skins. Pour the remaining butter into a saucepan. Add the flour. Stir constantly to prevent lumps from forming. Remove from the heat. Add salt, pepper, and a little nutmeg. Gradually add the boiling water, stirring constantly. Add the fennel leaves to the sauce, along with the vinegar and gooseberries. Keep hot.

Cooking: Place the mackerel on a bed of fennel branches on the broiler rack. Broil each side for seven or eight minutes (longer if the fish are large).

To Serve: Arrange the mackerel on a serving platter, and pour some of the sauce over them. Serve the rest of the sauce in a sauceboat.

HUITRES EN COQUILLES
(Oysters Cooked in Their Shells)

La Chapelle 1733

In France oysters are almost as varied as wines. They are classified not only by size but by type and the place they come from. In the eighteenth century only the flat *belon* oyster was known, but any large oyster may be used today in this recipe. Fresh oysters in their shells have to be used. Both the salt water inside the shells and the shells themselves are used in cooking the oysters. It is best to open the oysters yourself at home to be sure that none of the liquid they contain is lost.

Ingredients (for 4 servings): 5 tablespoons butter. 3 sprigs parsley, finely chopped. 1 scallion, finely chopped. ½ pound fresh button mushrooms, finely chopped. 36 oysters in their shells. Pepper. Bread crumbs. Lemon slices.

The herbs: Melt two tablespoons of the butter in a saucepan. Add the parsley, scallion, and mushrooms. Cook over low heat until soft. Do not allow the ingredients to brown. Remove from the heat.

The oysters: Open the oysters, and remove them from their shells. Save half of each shell for cooking. Pour the liquid from the shells, through a strainer, into the saucepan containing the herbs. Place the oysters in the saucepan. Add pepper to taste; then stir. Spoon the sauce and oysters into the half shells; the oysters should be covered by the sauce. Sprinkle each shell with bread crumbs, and dot with the remaining butter.

Cooking: Place in a hot oven (475°) for five minutes.

To Serve: Serve with lemon slices.

110

TERRINE DE LOTTES

(Burbot and Crayfish Stew)

The burbot, or eelpout, is a freshwater fish of the rivers and lakes of the northern United States and Europe. In France it was once highly esteemed, and its liver was considered a great delicacy; but one rarely sees modern French recipes for it. If burbot is unavailable, any firm-fleshed freshwater fish may be substituted, but the taste of the stew will be slightly different. La Chapelle's recipe calls for serving the fish simply with a sauce or a stew of your choice. This modern version of his recipe includes instructions for a crayfish stew made to be served with the fish. This combination is typical of La Chapelle's time.

Ingredients (for 4 servings): 1 burbot (1½ to 1¾ pounds). Flour. 3 tablespoons butter. 1 carrot, scraped and diced. 1 stalk celery, trimmed and diced. 1 branch parsley, chopped. 1 medium onion, peeled and diced. 12 crayfish. Salt. Pepper. 1 sprig thyme. ¼ bay leaf. 2 teaspoons cognac. 3 tablespoons dry white wine. 6 tablespoons bouillon. 3 tablespoons heavy cream. Juice of 1 lemon. 3 tablespoons lard.

Preparing the fish: Clean the fish. Put the liver aside for later use. Place the fish in boiling water for three minutes. Drain, and cool under running water. Remove all the skin. Wipe the fish dry, and cut it into large pieces. Roll each piece, as well as the liver, in flour.

The stew: Melt the butter in a saucepan. Add the carrot, celery, parsley, and onion. Cook over medium heat until golden brown. Wash the crayfish quickly; then remove the intestines by pulling out the central fin of the tails. As you clean each crayfish, place it in the saucepan with the vegetables. When all the crayfish have been added to the vegetables, stir thoroughly. Add salt and pepper. Add the thyme and bay leaf. Once the crayfish have turned red, pour the cognac and wine into the saucepan. Boil rapidly until half the cognac and wine has evaporated. Shell the crayfish. Grind the heads and shells in a mortar with the bouillon. Strain, and pour into the saucepan. Simmer for ten minutes. Remove from the heat. Add the cream and lemon juice.

Cooking the fish: Melt the lard in a frying pan. Cook the fish liver for two minutes over very low heat. Turn the liver over, and cook the other side for two minutes; then remove from the pan. Place the pieces of fish in the same pan, and brown on all sides. Add three tablespoons of the crayfish stew, and boil for only a few seconds.

The final cooking: Place the pieces of fish, the liver, and the crayfish in a casserole. Pour the stew from the frying pan into the casserole with the fish. Cover, and bake in a moderately hot oven (400°) for fifteen minutes.

To Serve: Serve very hot in the casserole.

ECREVISSES A LA POELE

(Sautéed Crayfish with Lamb)

Crayfish are almost always boiled in a court-bouillon, whereas here they are simply sautéed in a frying pan. In addition to this, they are garnished, not with other seafood, as might be expected, but with meat. This way of cooking crayfish has virtually disappeared, and the idea of combining meat and fish is practically unheard of today. For centuries, however, preparations such as this one were common and highly appreciated.

Ingredients (for 4 servings): 1 slice ham. 4-ounce slice leg of lamb. 2 ounces fresh slab bacon (unsalted and unsmoked). ¼ pound fresh button mushrooms. 3 sprigs parsley, chopped. 2 tablespoons chopped chives. 4 shallots, peeled and finely chopped. 2 cloves garlic, peeled and finely chopped. 24 large crayfish. Salt. Pepper. 4 tablespoons bouillon.

The preliminary cooking: Cut the ham, lamb, and bacon into small pieces. Melt the pieces of bacon in a frying pan over low heat. Add the mushrooms, parsley, chives, shallots, garlic, ham, and lamb. Cook slowly until barely golden.

The crayfish: Wash the crayfish quickly under running water. Remove the intestines by pulling out the middle fin of the tails. Add the crayfish to the other ingredients in the frying pan. Salt and pepper to taste. Cook for ten minutes.

To Serve: Remove the crayfish from the pan, and arrange on a platter. Pour the bouillon into the pan; bring barely to a boil; then remove from the heat. Pour the sauce over the crayfish, and serve immediately.

BLANQUETTE DE FILETS DE SOLE

(Fillets of Sole in White Sauce)

Marin 1739

Any flatfish can be used in this recipe. Although the procedure for filleting the fish is described below, it is preferable that this be done at the fish store by a professional. Leftover fish of any kind can be served *en blanquette*. If leftovers are used, simply prepare the sauce as described here, and add the fish to it five minutes before serving.

Ingredients (for 8 servings): ⅔ cup butter. 2 cloves garlic, peeled. 3 sprigs parsley. ½ pound small fresh button mushrooms. 1 teaspoon flour. ⅔ cup bouillon. ⅔ cup dry white wine. 4 sole (approximately ¾ pound each). 3 or 4 tablespoons milk. 2 egg yolks. 2 tablespoons heavy cream. Juice of 1 lemon.

The white sauce: Melt three tablespoons of the butter in a frying pan over low heat. Add the garlic (whole), one sprig of the parsley, and the mushrooms. Sprinkle in the flour. Stir. Do not brown. Immediately add the bouillon and the wine. Simmer for twenty minutes.

Preparing the sole: Remove the heads by cutting just behind the gills. Clean the fish; rinse them off; then wipe dry. With the dark side facing up, use a sharp knife to make an incision crosswise where the tail begins. Pull back the skin about one-quarter inch. Take hold of the skin with a cloth and, in one jerk, pull off the entire skin. Turn the fish over, and remove the white skin in the same way. Cut off the fins and the tails.

Precooking the sole: Melt the remaining butter in a large frying pan. Place the fish in the pan, side by side. Add the milk. Cook over very low heat for three minutes on each side. Do not allow the milk to boil.

The final cooking: Cut the fillets along the backbone of the fish. Slide a wide, flexible knife along the bone and detach the fillets. Either leave the fillets whole or cut them into slices about one-half inch wide. When the white sauce has simmered for twenty minutes, place the fillets in the sauce, and simmer for three minutes more.

To Serve: Chop the rest of the parsley. Remove the fillets from the white sauce, and arrange them on a serving platter. Remove the garlic from the white sauce, and discard. Remove the pan from the heat, and add the egg yolks beaten with the cream, the lemon juice, and the chopped parsley. Pour this mixture over the fillets, and serve.

CARPE A L'AVENTURE

(Carp Poached in Beer)

Marin 1739

Carp was one of the most popular freshwater fish in the eighteenth century. It is the first fish people ever tried to raise for use as food. Carp ponds were once common on many estates in Europe, not as ornaments but as food reserves. Carp are still eaten in France, but since their freshness is important, they are always sold live in fish stores that keep them in a large aquarium.

Ingredients (for 8 servings): 1 carp (4 to 4½ pounds). 6½ tablespoons butter. 3 sprigs parsley. 1 scallion. 1 sprig basil. 2 medium onions, peeled and chopped. ½ bay leaf. 1 sprig thyme. Salt. Pepper. Nutmeg. 2 teaspoons brandy. Beer. 2 tablespoons flour. Juice of 1 bitter orange or 1 lemon.

The carp: Cut off the fins and the end of the tail. Scale, and clean the carp through the gills. Cut the body of the carp into four pieces (cut the head in two).

Cooking: Melt three tablespoons of the butter in a large saucepan. Add the parsley, scallion, basil, onions, bay leaf, and thyme. Sprinkle with salt, pepper, and a little nutmeg. Place the fish in the saucepan. Pour in the brandy and enough beer to cover the carp entirely. Bring to a boil, and cook for twenty minutes.

To Serve: Remove the fish from the saucepan, and arrange on a serving platter. Keep hot. Strain the sauce. Boil rapidly for two or three minutes; then remove from the heat. Mix the remaining butter with the flour, and add to the sauce along with the orange or lemon juice. Stir the sauce until smooth; then pour over the carp, and serve.

TRUITES A LA HUSSARDE

Cuisinier Gascon 1740

(Broiled Trout with Rémoulade Sauce)

The rémoulade sauce served with the fish in this recipe is nothing more than a mayonnaise highly seasoned with mustard and capers. This is the *only* rémoulade sauce prepared in France and should not be confused with a Creole version (popular in New Orleans) which contains tomatoes and horseradish. In the eighteenth century rémoulade sauce did not always contain eggs, so (if you like) the fish can be served with a simple oil and vinegar dressing that has been seasoned with both mustard and capers.

Ingredients (for 4 servings): 2 sprigs each parsley, chervil, basil, tarragon, finely chopped. 6½ tablespoons soft butter. Salt. Pepper. 1 cup olive oil. 2 bay leaves, crumbled. 4 trout (6½ to 7 ounces each). 2 eggs. 1 heaping teaspoon Dijon mustard. 1 tablespoon wine vinegar. 1 tablespoon capers.

The butter and herb mixture: Mix half the herbs with the butter. Add salt and pepper.

The marinade: Pour one-half cup of the oil into a deep platter. Add the remaining herbs and the bay leaves.

The trout: Clean the trout, wash them, and wipe dry. Stuff the fish with the butter and herb mixture. Place the fish in the marinade; leave them to soak thirty minutes on each side.

The sauce: Boil an egg in salted water for nine minutes. Cool under running water, and peel. Put the yolk in a small bowl. Crush the yolk with a fork. Add a raw egg yolk, the mustard, vinegar, and a dash of pepper. Slowly (a few drops at a time) stir in the remaining oil. Add the capers.

Cooking: Remove the trout from the marinade. Broil them on a greased rack for six minutes on each side.

To Serve: When done, arrange the fish on a platter. Cover them with the sauce, and serve immediately.

FILETS DE MORUE A LA PROVENCALE

Menon 1746

(Salt Cod in Lemon Butter)

In his dictionary of cooking, Alexandre Dumas wrote: ''The voracity of the cod is equaled only by its fecundity. In a large female fish—weighing sixty to seventy pounds—there are between eight and nine million eggs. If all of these eggs were to hatch, and if each of the hatched codfish grew to maturity in three years, the sea would be so full of cod that one could walk across the Atlantic, without wetting one's feet, on a highway of codfish backs.'' There is little danger, however, of these fish ever multiplying in the way Dumas imagined. Fishermen from all over the world are so active in pursuit of the cod that any such population explosion is impossible. Cod has always been an important food in Europe and America. Because they could be caught in large quantities, they were often salted for shipment and storage. In the eighteenth century fresh cod was rarely eaten since it would always spoil on the journey inland, but recipes like this one for salt cod were extremely common.

Ingredients (for 4 servings): 1 pound salt cod. ⅓ cup butter. 1 clove garlic, peeled and finely chopped. 2 shallots, peeled and finely chopped. 2 tablespoons each finely chopped parsley and chives. ⅓ cup olive oil. Juice of 1 lemon. Salt. Pepper.

Desalting and cooking the cod: Place the salt cod in a large bowl of cold water for twelve hours. Change the water twice during this time. Drain the fish, and place it in a pot with more cold water. Bring to a boil; then lower the heat, and simmer for twenty minutes. Drain.

The lemon butter: Melt two tablespoons of the butter in a frying pan over low heat. Add the garlic, shallots, parsley, and chives. Cook for five minutes, or until they begin to brown. Add the remaining butter, the olive oil, and the cod. Add the lemon juice. Salt and pepper to taste. Cook, without boiling, about ten minutes, to allow the fish to absorb the flavor of the sauce.

To Serve: Serve very hot.

RAIE AU FROMAGE
(Skate with Cheese Sauce)

Skate has always been popular in England, Scotland, and France. The French traditionally prepare this fish with a "black butter" sauce which is generally considered both hard to digest and unhealthy, but nevertheless continues to be popular with this fish. The following recipe is a much more appetizing way of preparing a fish that is still rarely eaten in the United States, though it is popular with some ethnic groups.

INGREDIENTS

(for 4 servings)

½ skate
⅔ cup butter
2 tablespoons flour
2 cups milk
1 clove garlic, peeled and coarsely
    chopped
2 shallots, peeled and coarsely
    chopped
1 sprig basil
2 cloves
1 bay leaf
1 sprig thyme
Salt
Pepper
12 small onions, peeled
6 tablespoons bouillon
3 cups stale bread, cut into ½-inch
    squares
2 cups grated gruyère

Preparing the fish

- Remove the skin of the skate, and cut off the end of the "wing." Wash, and cut into four equal pieces.
- Melt three tablespoons of butter in a frying pan. Add the flour. Stir until smooth. Add the milk.
- Add the garlic, shallots, basil, cloves, bay leaf, thyme, and salt and pepper to taste. Bring to a boil, stirring occasionally.
- Place the skate in the sauce. Lower the heat so that the milk simmers without boiling. After ten minutes, turn the fish over, and simmer for another five minutes. Remove the skate, and set aside.

The cheese sauce

- Cook the onions, covered, for thirty minutes in the bouillon. Drain.
- Fry the squares of bread in the remaining butter, making croutons.
- Strain the sauce. It should be creamy; if not thick enough, boil for a few minutes, stirring constantly.
- Pour half the sauce into an ovenproof dish. Arrange a layer of gruyère over the sauce. Arrange the pieces of skate over the cheese. Place the onions and croutons among the pieces of fish. Cover with the remaining sauce. Sprinkle the rest of the cheese over the top. Brown in a very hot oven (475°) for ten minutes.

To Serve

- Serve the dish as soon as you remove it from the oven.

CUISSES DE GRENOUILLES FRITES
(Deep-Fried Frogs' Legs)

In France the green frog *(Rana esculenta)* and the mute frog are used in cooking. In the United States the bullfrog *(Rana catesbiana)* and the leopard frog *(Rana pipiens)* are used as food. The American frogs are much larger than the French, and the number of frogs' legs needed to make one serving varies, depending on the kind of frog being used. Frogs' legs are so popular in France that they have to be imported into the country to meet the demand. Americans will probably always have a surplus of this particular food, but unfortunately, frogs' legs are not widely commercialized in the United States. A great French chef at the turn of the century found that frogs' legs were highly esteemed by English and American tourists when they were served under a different name. He christened them *nymphes à l'aurore* (nymphs of dawn) on his menus, and their popularity increased overnight.

INGREDIENTS

(for 4 servings)

12 frogs' legs
6 sprigs parsley, chopped
2 scallions, chopped
1 medium onion, peeled and
    chopped
2 cloves garlic, peeled and chopped
2 shallots, peeled and chopped
1 bay leaf
1 sprig thyme
2 cloves
4 tablespoons olive oil
1 tablespoon wine vinegar
⅔ cup flour
1 pinch salt
1 egg, separated
½ cup dry white wine
Oil for deep frying
Fresh parsley (to garnish)
1 lemon, quartered (to garnish)

Marinating the frogs' legs

- Place the frogs' legs in a deep platter. Sprinkle them with the chopped parsley, scallions, onion, garlic, and shallots. Add the bay leaf, thyme, cloves, three tablespoons of the olive oil, and the vinegar.
- Marinate the frogs' legs in this mixture for one hour. Stir frequently.

The batter

- Place the flour and salt in a bowl. Form a well in the center of the flour.
- Place the remaining olive oil and the egg yolk in the well. Stir, incorporating the flour gradually. When all the flour has been absorbed, beat the mixture vigorously until smooth (if too dry, add a little of the wine). Stir in the wine, little by little. Beat the egg white until stiff, and fold it in.
- Let the batter stand while the frogs' legs are marinating.

Cooking

- Drain the frogs' legs, and wipe dry. Heat a pot half full of oil until the oil is almost smoking. Dip the frogs' legs one by one into the batter, and drop them into the hot oil. Do not crowd the pot. Turn the frogs' legs over to brown them evenly.
- When they have fried to a deep golden color, remove from the oil. Keep the fried frogs' legs hot while the rest are cooking.

To Serve

- Serve very hot on a bed of fresh parsley, with the lemon quarters.

(Pike Stew with Anchovies and Capers)

Although pike can weigh up to thirty pounds, those weighing no more than ten pounds are considered the best. This fish has long been notorious for its voracity. It attacks and devours all smaller fish and sometimes becomes a victim of its own greed by its inability to swallow a fish that becomes stuck in its throat. An old story tells of a pike that tried to swallow the head of a swan that was feeding underwater. Since the pike was, of course, incapable of swallowing the head, both the fish and the swan died. The pike has always been considered good eating, but the fish must be extremely fresh. Otherwise, the flesh can develop an unpleasant taste.

INGREDIENTS

(for 4 servings)

1 pike (approximately 2 ½ pounds)
⅔ cup butter
12 small onions, peeled
2 sprigs parsley
1 scallion
1 sprig basil
1 clove garlic, peeled
1 bay leaf
3 cloves
4 cooked artichoke bottoms,
    quartered
¼ pound fresh button mushrooms,
    quartered
Salt
Pepper
12 pieces bread crust, each 1 inch
    square
2 anchovy fillets in oil, finely
    chopped
1 tablespoon capers

The pike

- Scale the pike, and clean it through the gills. Cut the fish into sections about two inches thick. Keep the head.

The stew

- Melt three tablespoons of the butter in a large frying pan. Add the onions, and cook over low heat for ten minutes.
- Tie the parsley, scallion, basil, and garlic in a small piece of cheesecloth. Add this bouquet garni to the onions in the pan. Cook for fifteen minutes more.
- Add the pike (including the head), bay leaf, cloves, artichoke bottoms, and mushrooms. Salt and pepper to taste. Cover the pan, and cook over very low heat for fifteen minutes more.

To Serve

- Fry the bread crusts in three tablespoons of butter. Arrange on a platter.
- Remove the pike from the pan, and place on the bread crusts.
- Remove the cheesecloth bag containing the herbs, as well as the bay leaf and the cloves, from the frying pan, and discard.
- Remove the frying pan from the heat, and stir in the anchovies, capers, and the remaining butter.
- Pour the sauce over the pike, and serve.

"La Bourgogne"

The Carthusian monks in France were famous for their love of good food. Despite a number of strict dietary laws that govern their order (or perhaps because of these restrictions), cooks in the monastery were particularly inventive. This fish dish is typical of Carthusian cooking because of the rich vegetable garnish it contains. The fish should be covered with vegetables for it to be truly presented in the Carthusian fashion. Menon was no doubt trying to ''refine'' this preparation by straining out all the vegetables before serving the carp—an interesting idea but hardly traditional.

INGREDIENTS

(for 4 servings)

1 carp (approximately 3 pounds)
3 cups dry red wine (preferably
  burgundy)
6 ½ tablespoons butter
2 carrots, scraped and thinly sliced
1 parsnip or rutabaga, peeled and
  thinly sliced
2 medium onions, peeled and thinly
  sliced
1 clove garlic, peeled
2 large shallots, peeled and stuck
  with 1 clove each
2 sprigs parsley
1 scallion
Salt
Pepper
⅓ cup water
4 anchovy fillets in oil, chopped
1 tablespoon capers, chopped
2 tablespoons flour

The carp

- Scale the fish, wash it, and cut off the fins. Over a bowl, remove the gills, and clean the fish, letting the blood run into the bowl. Still over the bowl, wash the interior of the fish with one-half cup of the wine.

Cooking

- Melt three tablespoons of the butter in a large frying pan over low heat. Add the carrots, parsnip or rutabaga, onions, garlic, shallots, parsley, and scallion.
- Place the carp on this bed of vegetables. Add salt and pepper to taste.
- Add the mixture of wine and blood, the remaining wine, and the water.
- Simmer for twenty-five minutes.

To Serve

- Mix the anchovies, capers, and flour with the remaining butter, forming a paste.
- Take the carp from the frying pan, and remove the skin. Place the fish on a serving platter. Keep hot.
- Strain the sauce; then boil rapidly for ten minutes. Remove from the heat, and stir in the anchovy paste.
- Pour the sauce over the carp, and serve very hot.

''Charlot, le Roi des Coquillages''
Fresco by Jean Pierre Rémon

   (Snail and Mushroom Stew)

Snails are stewed in their shells in this unusual recipe. If you collect snails yourself, they have to be fed lettuce leaves for several weeks or else starved for several days to be sure they have not eaten plants that are poisonous to humans. It is, of course, preferable to buy live snails from a reputable fish merchant whenever this is possible (they are usually ready for immediate consumption).

INGREDIENTS

(for 4 servings)

1 cup butter
48 snails, washed
½ pound fresh button mushrooms,
    quartered if large
8 sprigs parsley, finely chopped
5 scallions, finely chopped
1 sprig basil, finely chopped
1 clove garlic, peeled and finely
    chopped
2 cloves
1 sprig thyme
1 bay leaf
2 tablespoons flour
2 cups bouillon
1 cup dry white wine
Salt
Pepper
3 egg yolks
3 tablespoons heavy cream
1 tablespoon vinegar

Cooking the snails

- Melt the butter in a large frying pan. Add the snails, and cook for ten minutes over medium heat. Do not allow the butter to brown.
- Add the mushrooms, parsley, scallions, basil, garlic, cloves, thyme, and bay leaf. Sprinkle in the flour.
- Cook for three or four minutes, stirring constantly.
- Pour the bouillon and wine into a pot. Bring to a boil; then add to the snails.
- Salt and pepper to taste.
- Cover, and simmer over low heat for two hours.

To Serve

- A few minutes before the snails are cooked, beat the egg yolks in a bowl with the cream.
- Add two or three tablespoons of the liquid in which the snails are cooking to the egg yolks and cream, stirring constantly.
- Remove the frying pan from the heat. Stirring vigorously, add the contents of the bowl to the snail and mushroom stew.
- Stir in the vinegar, and serve immediately.

Fresh sardines are common in all Mediterranean countries. They are generally grilled over an open fire and served with mustard butter, but in this recipe they are baked between layers of finely chopped fish and herbs. Since fresh sardines are not available in the United States, smelt can be substituted. Each fish can also be cooked by itself, surrounded by the garnish and wrapped in aluminum foil.

INGREDIENTS

(for 6 servings)

2 cups fresh bread crumbs
6 tablespoons milk
11 eggs
⅔ cup butter
½ pound fresh button mushrooms, finely chopped
3 sprigs parsley, finely chopped
1 scallion, finely chopped
1 pound fish fillets, finely chopped
Salt
Pepper
18 fresh sardines or smelt
1 cup dried bread crumbs
Juice of 2 lemons

The fish garnish

- Place the fresh bread crumbs in a large bowl, and add the milk.
- Beat six of the eggs. Melt one tablespoon of the butter in a large frying pan, and make a firmly cooked omelette. (Do not add salt or pepper.)
- Chop the omelette. Add it to the bread-crumb mixture, along with the mushrooms, parsley, scallion, and chopped fish fillets.
- Add salt and pepper to taste. Stir in three egg yolks, mixing the ingredients well together. (Keep the egg whites for later use.)

The sardines or smelt

- Clean and wash the sardines or smelt. Remove the heads. Separate the fillets to remove the bones. Place the two fillets on each other as if the fish were whole.

Cooking

- Spread half of the garnish in a buttered ovenproof dish. Place the sardines or smelt in the dish, and cover them with the rest of the garnish.
- Beat two eggs with the three reserved egg whites, and pour over the top layer of dressing. Sprinkle with the dried bread crumbs.
- Cover with a sheet of greased waxed paper, and bake in a hot oven (425°) for thirty minutes.

To serve

- Melt the remaining butter. Stir in the lemon juice just before serving.
- Serve the dish very hot, with the lemon butter in a sauceboat.

''Paris-Hilton''

In the eighteenth century it was customary to marinate almost all fish before they were cooked. Some authors believe this practice arose because fish were often beginning to spoil by the time they arrived at inland markets. The strong taste of the marinade was meant to ''correct'' any unpleasant taste the fish might have acquired. All this is mere conjecture, since marinated fish, as in this recipe, are delicious, and the use of the marinade can be defended on strictly gastronomic grounds. The original recipe for this dish specifies the use of brill *(barbue)*, which is related to the turbot. However, any flatfish may be used.

INGREDIENTS

(for 6 servings)

1 flounder, halibut, or other flatfish
   (2 pounds)
15 to 20 scallions, chopped
Juice of 2 lemons
3 tablespoons wine vinegar
1 bay leaf
½ pound butter
1 ½ cups bread crumbs
Salt
Pepper
½ pound fresh button mushrooms
6 tablespoons water
12 slices bread
2 lemons, quartered

Preparing the fish

- Cut off the fins and tail of the fish. Pull out the gills. Clean the fish through a cut made just behind the gill on the dark side of the fish. Wash the fish; then make several incisions along the back.
- Place the scallions and the juice of one lemon in a deep platter, with the vinegar and bay leaf.
- Marinate the fish for two hours in this mixture, turning occasionally.

Cooking

- Melt seven tablespoons of the butter.
- Drain the fish, and spread some of the melted butter over one side of it with a basting brush. Sprinkle generously with bread crumbs. Turn the fish over, and do the same with the other side.
- Pour the remaining melted butter into an ovenproof dish. Place the fish in the dish. Add salt and pepper to taste. Bake in a moderate oven (375°) for twenty-five minutes, or until the meat can be lifted easily away from the bone.

Garnishing

- Place the mushrooms in a saucepan with the water, the remaining lemon juice, and two tablespoons of butter. Cook over high heat for five minutes, stirring occasionally. Drain the mushrooms, and chop coarsely.
- Melt the remaining butter in a large frying pan, and fry the bread.

To Serve

- Place the fish on a large platter.
- Cover the slices of fried bread with chopped mushrooms, and put them in the oven for five minutes. Then arrange them around the fish.
- If any of the cooking liquid remains, spoon it over the mushrooms.
- Serve with lemon quarters.

''Jamin''

Both whiting and haddock are small members of the cod family. Either fish can be used in preparing this dish. The unusual mixture of meat and fish in this recipe is entirely justified, since the fatback keeps the fish from drying out when cooking. Fresh fatback should always be used in recipes like this one; salted fatback should be washed and thoroughly desalted if fresh fatback is unavailable.

INGREDIENTS

(for 8 servings)

2 cups fresh bread crumbs
⅓ cup milk
2 pounds whiting or haddock fillets
4 anchovy fillets in oil, cut into pieces
Salt
Pepper
Nutmeg
½ pound butter
2 eggs
½ loaf of bread, unsliced
1 pound fatback, cut into very thin strips
Juice of 2 lemons
1 medium onion, peeled and chopped
2 shallots, peeled and chopped
¼ pound fresh button mushrooms, chopped
1 tablespoon flour
3 tablespoons dry white wine
3 tablespoons bouillon
4 sprigs parsley, chopped

The fish stuffing

- Place the bread crumbs in a saucepan, and add the milk.
- Place over low heat, and stir until a thick, smooth paste is formed. Remove from the heat, and allow to cool.
- Cut two of the fillets into pieces. Pound these pieces with the anchovies in a mortar, along with salt, pepper, and a little nutmeg. Gradually add the bread paste, six tablespoons of the butter, one egg white, and two egg yolks, mixing the ingredients together until smooth.

Cooking

- Cut the bread into the shape of a large cork, with the base slightly larger than the top.
- Cover the bottom of a round ovenproof serving dish with strips of fatback. Wrap another strip of fatback around the bread. Stand the bread on its base in the center of the dish.
- Spread the fish stuffing around the bread, sloping downward from it.
- Place the remaining fillets on the stuffing. The fillets should overlap, but only slightly. Work your way around as though you were wrapping a turban around the bread. The fillets should cover the stuffing entirely.
- In a small saucepan, melt six tablespoons of the butter. Do not allow it to brown. Stir in the lemon juice.
- Sprinkle the lemon butter over the fillets. Then cover them with a layer of fatback strips.
- Butter a sheet of waxed paper, and place it over the dish, so that the heat will not brown the fillets.
- Bake in a hot oven (425°) for twenty minutes.

The sauce

- Melt the remaining butter in a frying pan and cook the onion, shallots, and mushroom until they begin to brown. Salt and pepper to taste. Add a little nutmeg.
- Sprinkle in the flour. Stir.
- Add the wine and bouillon. Simmer gently for fifteen minutes; then add the parsley.

To Serve

- Remove the buttered paper and the top layer of fatback from the fillets. Gently remove the bread from the center of the dish.
- Pour the sauce into the hole left by the piece of bread.
- Serve very hot.

"Le Bristol"

TRUITES AU FOUR
(Baked Trout with Herb Stuffing)

Rainbow, brook, or brown trout can be used in this recipe. On the Atlantic coast a fish belonging to the salmon family, with a red belly, black spots on its sides, and reddish flesh, is often sold as trout. This fish is, in fact, a char and can be cooked in the same way as trout. Note that small fish are used in this recipe, but larger ones can be substituted, in which case all the other ingredients, as well as cooking times, should be changed proportionally.

Ingredients (for 4 servings): 1 cup olive oil. 4 tablespoons finely chopped fresh button mushrooms. 1 clove garlic, peeled and finely chopped. 2 tablespoons each finely chopped parsley, chives, and basil. Salt. Pepper. 3 tablespoons soft butter. 4 trout (6½ to 7 ounces each), cleaned and washed. 2 cups bread crumbs. Juice of 1 lemon.

The marinade: Place the oil, mushrooms, garlic, and half the parsley, chives, and basil in a large earthenware platter. Add salt and pepper. Stir the ingredients together.

The herb butter: Mix the butter with the remaining parsley, chives, and basil, as well as a little salt and pepper.

Preparing the trout: Stuff the trout with the herb butter. Marinate them for two hours, turning occasionally.

Cooking: Remove the trout from the marinade, and roll them in half the bread crumbs. Place them in an ovenproof dish. Pour the marinade over the trout. Cover them with the remaining bread crumbs. Bake in a moderate oven (375°) for twenty minutes, or until the fish comes easily away from the bone when tested.

To Serve: Remove the trout from the oven, and sprinkle them with the lemon juice. Serve in the baking dish.

MOULES EN BEIGNETS
(Mussel Fritters)

Mussels have been called the oysters of the poor. Indeed, they are often extremely cheap, especially in France, where they are the most popular (and cheapest) shellfish. Unlike oysters, mussels are rarely eaten raw in France. They are almost always cooked and served as a garnish with fish or by themselves as an appetizer. Fresh mussels are not available everywhere in the United States, but they are the only kind suitable for preparing this dish. The batter used to coat the mussels, however, can be used with any kind of shellfish that has been partially cooked before deep frying.

Ingredients (for 4 servings): 1 cup flour. 1 pinch salt. 1 tablespoon olive oil. ½ cup dry white wine. 1 tablespoon soft butter. 1 teaspoon flour. 2 shallots, peeled and chopped. 1 clove garlic, peeled and chopped. 1 small carrot, scraped and chopped. 1 small parsnip or turnip, peeled and chopped. 2 tablespoons chopped parsley, chives, tarragon, and basil, mixed. 4 tablespoons vinegar. ½ bay leaf. 1 sprig thyme. Pepper. 1 quart mussels in their shells. Salt. Oil for deep frying. 1 lemon, quartered.

The batter: Place the cup of flour and the pinch of salt in a bowl. Make a well in the center. Stir in the olive oil, then the wine. Continue stirring until smooth. Let stand.

Precooking the mussels: Mix the butter and one teaspoon flour together, forming a paste. Place the shallots, garlic, carrot, parsnip or turnip, and mixed herbs in a large pot. Add the butter and flour mixture, the vinegar, bay leaf, thyme, and pepper. Quickly wash the mussels under running water, scraping them clean and removing any filaments which protrude from their shells. Throw away any mussels which are not tightly closed. As you clean them, place the mussels into the pot containing the vinegar and herbs. Place the pot over low heat. When all the mussels have opened, remove the pot from the heat. Remove the mussels from their shells; then place them back in the pot to marinate for two hours.

Cooking: Fill a deep fryer or large pot with the oil for deep frying. Heat until the oil begins to smoke. Drain the mussels; dip them, one by one, into the batter; then drop them into the hot oil. Do not crowd the pot. Turn the fritters over to brown them evenly. When golden brown, remove them from the pot with a slotted spoon, and drain well. Keep the fried mussels hot while cooking the others.

To Serve: Serve the fritters very hot, sprinkled with salt, pepper, and lemon juice.

CROUSTADE DE CREVETTES

Viard 1820

(Shrimp Croustade)

Croustade, vol-au-vent, and *bouchée* are different names for the same thing. They all are dishes made with pastry shells (using puff pastry) cooked in advance and stuffed with meat or fish in a white sauce just before serving. In France these pastry shells are often sold ready for use in bakeries and charcuteries. They can also be obtained precooked in many bake shops in the United States, where they are called patty shells.

Ingredients (for 8 servings): 1 pound, 10 ounces cooked shrimp. 5 tablespoons soft butter. 6 tablespoons bouillon. 5 tablespoons flour. 3 cups heavy cream. Salt. Pepper. 1 large precooked patty shell or 8 small ones.

The shrimp butter: Peel the shrimp. Take a quarter of the shells, and pound them in a mortar; then stir in the butter. Place in a saucepan with the bouillon over low heat. When the butter has melted, strain the mixture through a piece of damp cheesecloth. After straining the liquid, squeeze the cloth to obtain whatever juices may have stayed with the shells.

The Béchamel sauce: Place the flour in a saucepan. Pour in the shrimp butter little by little, and cook over low heat, stirring constantly until smooth. Cook for ten minutes, stirring occasionally. Do not allow the butter to brown. Add the cream, and increase the heat. Add salt and pepper to taste. Stir in the shrimp.

To Serve: Pour this preparation into a large precooked patty shell, or divide the mixture among eight small ones. Place the pastry in a hot oven (450°) for five minutes. Serve immediately.

CABILLAUD AUX FINES HERBES

Viard 1820

(Baked Cod with Shallots and Mushrooms)

Viard wrote that the cod could be packed in coarse salt for an hour before being cooked. The fish is then washed off, dried, and cooked as described below. This is an excellent idea, since the salt firms up the flesh of the fish and gives it a distinctive taste. This particular way of preparing cod is still popular in France, where the dish is served with a green salad for lunch.

Ingredients (for 8 servings): ½ cup lard. ½ pound fresh button mushrooms, finely chopped. 4 sprigs parsley, finely chopped. 1 cup finely chopped peeled shallots. ⅔ cup butter. 2 ½ cups dry white wine. Salt. Pepper. 1 pinch nutmeg. 1 bay leaf. 1 cod (4 to 4 ½ pounds), scaled and cleaned. 8 tablespoons bread crumbs. 4 lemons, quartered (to garnish).

The mushroom and shallot sauce: Melt the lard in a saucepan. Stir in the mushrooms, parsley, shallots, and one-half cup of the butter. Add one and a half cups of the wine, salt, pepper, the nutmeg, and the bay leaf. Reduce the liquid by half over very high heat, stirring occasionally.

The cod: Wash the cod; wipe it dry; then cut several slits on each side of the fish. Pour the mushroom and herb sauce into an ovenproof baking dish. Add the remaining wine. Place the cod in the dish. Salt and pepper lightly. Sprinkle with the bread crumbs, and dot with the remaining butter. Bake in a hot oven (425°) for thirty-five minutes.

To Serve: Serve in the baking dish, garnished with lemon quarters.

MERLUCHE A LA BRANLADE EN PIERRE A FUSIL

Cuisinier Durand 1830

(Salt Cod Purée)

Today this dish is called a *brandade* and is a specialty of the South of France. Unlike most *brandades* prepared today, this one does not contain any garlic.

Ingredients (for 4 servings): 1 pound salt cod. Juice of 1 lemon. 1 cup olive oil (approximately). 1 cup milk (approximately). Salt. Pepper. 3 sprigs parsley, finely chopped. Croutons.

Desalting the cod: Place the cod in a large bowl of cold water. Soak for twenty-four hours, changing the water six or seven times; then drain.

Cooking the cod: Remove the fins, tail, and bones if there are any. Rinse thoroughly under running water. Cut the cod into ten pieces, and place in a large pot full of cold water. Place over low heat. Skim off any foam that appears. When the water begins to boil, remove from the heat. Cover the pot, and let stand for fifteen minutes.

Preparing the purée: Carefully drain the cod. Remove the skin and any remaining bits of bone. Put the fish in another pot. Sprinkle the lemon juice over the cod. Place over very low heat (or in a double boiler). Do not let boil. Stirring constantly, add oil, drop by drop, until the fish begins to stick together. Still stirring constantly, add milk, drop by drop. Repeat this procedure several times, alternating oil and milk. When the mixture is very creamy, add salt and pepper to taste.

To Serve: Sprinkle the cod with the parsley, and serve with croutons.

RAGOUT D'ESCALOPES DE HOMARD A LA NAVARIN

Carême 1833

(Lobster, Eel, and Oyster Stew)

This dish, created by the greatest cook of his day, is typical of the kind of creative cooking that made Carême famous. It is a prime example of the kind of elaborate dish favored by gourmets in the early nineteenth century.

Ingredients (for 4 servings): 6 sprigs parsley. 1 tablespoon salt. 1 cup champagne. 1 bay leaf. 1 sprig thyme. 3 quarts water. 1 lobster (1½ pounds). ⅔ cup fresh bread crumbs. 2 tablespoons milk. ½ pound fresh button mushrooms. Juice of 1 lemon. ¼ pound butter. 1 small eel (½ pound), skinned and cleaned. Salt. Pepper. Nutmeg. 1 egg. 1 tablespoon heavy cream. 2 cups bouillon. 1 clove garlic, peeled. 2 tablespoons flour. 12 oysters in their shells.

Cooking the lobster: Place the parsley, one tablespoon salt, champagne, bay leaf, thyme, and water in a large pot. Bring to a rapid boil. Fold the lobster's tail against its stomach, and tie it securely in place. Drop the lobster into the boiling mixture, and cook for twenty-five minutes. Remove from the heat. Allow to cool for one hour. Drain. Cut the string, put the lobster on its back, and cut through the membrane along each side of the tail. Remove the tail, and detach it from the head. Cut the tail into one-half-inch slices. Crack the claws; remove and dice the meat. Save the shell and head of the lobster.

The quenelles: Place the bread crumbs in a small saucepan. Add the milk, and place over low heat. Stir continuously until a smooth paste is formed. Remove from the heat. Place the mushrooms, lemon juice, and one tablespoon of the butter in a frying pan, and cook over low heat for five minutes. Drain, keeping the liquid for later use. Purée one-third of the mushrooms. Reserve the rest. Dice the meat of the eel; then pound it in a mortar, along with salt, pepper, and nutmeg. Add the bread paste, puréed mushrooms, three tablespoons of the butter, the egg, and the cream. Mix well. Let stand for one hour; then roll the mixture into small balls, or quenelles. Flour the quenelles. In a wide pot or deep frying pan, bring the bouillon just to a boil. Add the quenelles. Lower the heat, and simmer for ten minutes; then drain. Reserve the liquid.

The sauce: Pound the shell and the head of the lobster in a mortar, and place in a saucepan. Add the garlic, one tablespoon of the butter, and one cup of the bouillon used to cook the quenelles. Boil for ten minutes; then strain. In the same saucepan, melt one tablespoon of the butter; then stir in the flour. Stirring constantly, add the liquid from the lobster shells and the mushrooms' cooking liquid. Simmer for ten minutes, stirring constantly.

The stew: Open the oysters. Remove the meat; strain and reserve the juice. Place the oysters, their juice, the remaining mushrooms, and the meat from the lobster's claws in the sauce.

To Serve: Melt the remaining butter in a frying pan, and sauté the slices of lobster quickly over medium heat. Do not brown. Arrange the lobster on a serving platter with the hot quenelles. Cover with part of the sauce. Serve the rest of the sauce in a separate dish.

132

AIGUILLETTES DE MORUE FRITES

(Salt Cod Fritters)

A cod that has been split open, salted, and hung up to dry soon after being caught is called for in this recipe. Cod that has been filleted, salted, and packaged simply is not as tasty. In any event, it is always best to ask your fish merchant how long he suggests soaking the fish before cooking. Soaking times vary, depending on the age of the fish—it is usually better to soak it too long rather than not long enough.

Ingredients (for 4 servings): 1 pound salt cod, with skin. Several sprigs parsley. Leaves from 1 sprig tarragon. 1 medium onion, peeled and thinly sliced. Salt. Pepper. Nutmeg. 6 tablespoons olive oil. 2 tablespoons wine vinegar. Flour. 1 egg, beaten. Bread crumbs. Oil for deep frying. Additional parsley sprigs. 2 lemons, quartered.

Desalting the cod: Place the cod in a large bowl of cold water. Let stand for twenty-four hours, changing the water six or seven times.

The marinade: Remove the fins and bones from the cod, but do not remove the skin. Cut the cod into strips about one-half inch wide. Place the cod in an earthenware platter. Cover with the parsley, tarragon leaves, and onion slices. Add salt, pepper, and nutmeg to taste, the olive oil, and the vinegar. Marinate for one hour, turning frequently.

Cooking: Drain the strips of codfish. Roll them first in flour, then in the beaten egg, and finally in bread crumbs. Deep-fry in very hot oil until golden brown on all sides.

To serve: Serve the fritters on a bed of parsley, decorated with lemon quarters.

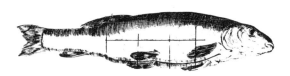

HARENGS A LA SAINTE-MENEHOULD AU CHAMPAGNE

(Herring in Champagne Sauce)

Sainte-Menehould is the gastronomic capital of the Champagne region of France. Many French dishes contain ''Sainte-Menehould'' in their titles; this usually means that they call for the use of bread crumbs at some stage in their preparation. Curiously, this is not the case in this particular recipe. Indeed, it is difficult to determine precisely what the connection is between the present dish and the Sainte-Menehould style of cooking. The dish, naturally enough, calls for cooking the fish in champagne. It is obvious, however, that the author of this recipe was thinking of the dry white wine from Champagne (not the sparkling wine) when he listed the ingredients to be cooked with the fish. Fresh herring are rarely found in the United States, but Etienne himself suggested, at the end of his recipe, that trout could be substituted, although the dish would then differ markedly in texture and taste.

Ingredients (for 4 servings): 3 tablespoons butter. 3 sprigs parsley, finely chopped. 1 carrot, scraped and finely chopped. 1 medium onion, peeled and finely chopped. 1 clove garlic, peeled and finely chopped. Salt. Pepper. Nutmeg. 3 cups dry white wine. 4 herring, with milt. 4 tablespoons flour. 1 tablespoon water.

The sauce: Melt the butter in a saucepan. Add the parsley, carrot, onion, and garlic. Salt and pepper generously. Add a little nutmeg. Cook over medium heat for ten minutes, or until beginning to brown. Add one cup of the wine. Cover; then simmer over very low heat for one hour.

The herring: Clean the herring; reserve the milt. Remove the heads, fins, and tails of the fish. Wash, and wipe dry. Place the milt back inside the fish. Arrange the herring, head to tail, in a generously buttered baking dish with a cover.

Cooking: Strain the sauce, and pour over the fish. Mix the flour and water together to form a soft dough, and seal the dish hermetically in the manner described under Boeuf mode, page 138. Bake in a slow oven (300°) for six hours.

To Serve: Serve very hot, being careful not to break the fish while serving.

COQUILLAGES AU FEU
(Burning Shellfish)

Monselet 1870

Monselet writes that this recipe comes from the west coast of France near Bordeaux, where it is called a finger burner. Today, in the same region, mussels are cooked in pine needles on a wooden plank. To do this, nails are driven through the wood to hold the mussels upright; then the shellfish are covered with the pine needles, which are immediately set on fire. The ashes are blown away with a bellows, and the mussels are served with butter and bread. Some food historians believe this method of cooking shellfish began when fishermen found shell-encrusted planks washed up onto the beach and set them afire in order to remove the shellfish and eat them. It is as likely an explanation as any.

Ingredients (for any number of servings): Some very dry straw. Any shellfish (oysters, mussels, scallops, clams, etc.). Pepper. Bread. Butter.

The shellfish: Place the shellfish flat on the sand, if you are at the seashore, or on the grill of a fireplace or barbecue. Cover the shellfish with a layer of straw.

Cooking: Set fire to the straw. When the straw has burned away, add another layer of straw, and set fire to it.

To Serve: Remove any bits of burned straw sticking to the shells, which will have opened in the flames. Sprinkle with coarsely ground black pepper. Serve immediately with bread and butter.

HARENGS PECS VINAIGRETTE
(Salted Herring in Cress Dressing)

Alexandre Dumas 1873

Freshly salted herring are best in this dish, since they need to soak for only a few hours before being served. Herring that has been salted for a long time may need to soak overnight—ask your fish merchant's advice on soaking times.

Ingredients (for 4 servings): 8 small whole salted herring. 1 cup milk. 1 cup water. 4 apples, peeled, cored, and sliced. Juice of 2 lemons. 2 large onions, peeled and thinly sliced. 1 bunch watercress. 9 tablespoons vegetable oil. 3 tablespoons vinegar. Salt. Pepper.

The herring: Remove the heads, fins, tails, and skins from the herring. Mix the milk and water in a bowl. Add the herring. If the herring are not covered by the liquid, add more milk. Leave the fish to soak for two or three hours.

The garnish: Place the apples in a salad bowl, and pour the lemon juice over them. Place the onions in a separate bowl.

The sauce: Wash the watercress, and chop coarsely. Mix the cress with the oil and vinegar in a third bowl. Salt and pepper lightly.

To Serve: Drain the herring. Wipe them dry, and arrange them on a platter. Serve the apples, onions, and cress dressing at the same time. The dressing should be spooned over the herring as they are served, and the fish should be garnished at the table with both the apples and onions.

CARRELET A LA SAUCE NORMANDE

Alexandre Dumas 1873

(Plaice or Flounder in Norman Sauce)

In this recipe Dumas seems to be ignoring tradition by calling for plaice (summer flounder) instead of sole with his Norman sauce. His sauce is rather unorthodox as well, since a Norman sauce usually contains shrimp and oysters, not mussels, as Dumas suggests.

Ingredients (for 4 servings): 4 small plaice or flounder (6½ to 7 ounces each). 5 tablespoons butter (approximately). Salt. Pepper. 6 tablespoons dry white wine. 12 small fresh button mushrooms. 30 mussels in their shells. 1½ tablespoons flour. 4 egg yolks. 6 tablespoons heavy cream.

Cooking the fish: With a sharp knife, make a small cut crosswise on the dark side of each fish, just above the tail. Take hold of the skin with a cloth, and give a hard pull in the direction of the head to strip off the skin. Clean the fish. Cut off the tails and fins. Wash and wipe dry. Place the fish in a buttered ovenproof dish. Dot with butter. Sprinkle with salt and pepper. Pour the wine over the fish. Bake in a hot oven (400°) for twenty minutes.

The sauce: Melt one tablespoon of the butter in a frying pan over low heat. Add the mushrooms. Cook for about ten minutes, or until they soften; then drain. Place the mushrooms in a bowl for later use. Wash the mussels, and scrape the shells clean. Cook the mussels in a pot over low heat until they open. Strain the liquid they have given off, and keep for later use. Remove the mussels from their shells. Melt one tablespoon of the butter in a saucepan; then stir in the flour. Stir constantly over low heat until smooth. Add the liquid from the mussels. When the fish have finished baking, add their cooking liquid to the sauce as well. Leave the fish in the dish in which they cooked. Remove the saucepan from the heat. Mix the egg yolks and cream in a bowl. Add several spoonfuls of the sauce. Stir well; then pour this mixture into the rest of the sauce, stirring constantly.

To Serve: Add the mushrooms and mussels to the dish containing the fish. Cover with the sauce. Dot with butter. Put the fish back in the oven for two minutes. Serve immediately.

ACCOLADE D'ANGUILLES A LA BROCHE

Alexandre Dumas 1873

(Spit-Roasted Eel)

Accolade is a term still used to describe meat or fish served back to back (for example, two chickens served with their backs touching are called *en accolade*). Dumas' recipe calls for skewering two whole eels back to back on the same skewer, then roasting them over an open fire, but the eels can be cooked in the oven with satisfactory results.

Ingredients (for 5 servings): 2 carrots, scraped and finely chopped. 3 turnips, peeled and finely chopped. 1 Jerusalem artichoke, peeled and finely chopped. 2 quarts boiling water. 1 bay leaf. 1 sprig parsley. Salt. Pepper. 2 cups dry white wine. 2 eels (1½ pounds each). 1 cup sherry. Pinch of nutmeg. Pinch of ground coriander. 3 cups bread crumbs. 1 egg. 1 tablespoon olive oil.

The vegetables: Cook the carrots, turnips, and Jerusalem artichoke for one hour in the boiling water with the bay leaf, parsley, and some salt and pepper. Leave the vegetables to cool in their cooking liquid. Strain out the vegetables, and add the wine to the cooking liquid.

The eels: When you purchase the eels, have your fish merchant skin and clean them and cut off their tails and heads. Wash the eels, and wipe dry. Place the eels back to back and head to tail. Tie them together around a spit or skewer.

Cooking: Pour the liquid prepared earlier into a long ovenproof dish. Place the eels in the dish as well. Bake in a moderate oven (375°) for thirty minutes. Then remove the dish, and allow the eels to cool in their cooking liquid. When they are cool, gently remove them, being careful not to break them.

The sauce: Pour the cooking liquid into a saucepan, and add the sherry, nutmeg, and coriander. Pepper to taste. Boil rapidly until half the liquid has evaporated.

Spit-roasting: Place the bread crumbs in a long platter. In a bowl, beat the egg, one tablespoon of the sauce, and the olive oil. Roll the two skewered eels in the bread crumbs. Baste them with the egg mixture; then roll them in the bread crumbs once more. Wrap the eels in heavily buttered waxed paper. Place them on the turnspit, and turn over an open fire or hot coals for twenty minutes. (The eels can be cooked under a hot broiler, turning frequently, for the same amount of time.)

To Serve: Remove the paper. Remove the skewer, without separating the eels, and place the eels on a long serving platter. Serve accompanied by the sauce.

135

Meat

Although most cooking techniques today can be traced back for centuries, one that was once widely employed has practically disappeared. This was the practice of cooking meat in rapidly boiling water before it was roasted. It seems odd to think that, especially in the Middle Ages, boiling was once the prelude to roasting. There is, however, a certain logic in this practice that does not immediately meet the eye. Meat placed in cold water and slowly brought to a boil loses much of its taste to the cooking liquid, and that is why rich beef bouillon is always prepared with the meat cooked in this way. On the other hand, when beef is dropped into boiling water, the meat juices are sealed inside by the heat of the water, in a way similar to what happens when foods are deep-fried in oil. This second procedure is still used when meat is being boiled as a main dish. The old practice of boiling before roasting could indeed have helped keep juices in the meat that would have otherwise escaped, but an even better explanation for the practice stems from the fact that meat in the past was generally tougher than it is today. The parboiling process would help tenderize the meat, and it only gradually disappeared as selective breeding produced better-quality, tender meat.

Many of the old recipes insist on using expensive cuts of beef in dishes that could be prepared today with almost any stewing cut. This is simply because the stewing cuts in the past were so *very* tough, even after being parboiled, that they could never be served at a formal dinner. This is no longer true, and many old recipes that were prohibitively expensive because of the cut of meat employed can be made by cooks today when cheaper cuts are substituted.

Large quantities of meat were served in France even when the quality was generally low and the prices were high. In the fourteenth century, for example, 30,000 head of cattle, 20,000 calves, 100,000 sheep, and 30,000 hogs were consumed in Paris alone in the course of a year. Until the late eighteenth century pigs were allowed to wander freely through the streets of Paris, and almost every household owned several animals that could be fed on vegetables that were too old and wilted to be sold.

The French have no inhibitions about their food. Tongues, livers, brains, and sweetbreads have always been highly thought of in France, while Americans often shy away from what are called variety meats. In the past, French cooks were even fonder of *triperie* than they are today, and not only were heads, feet, stomachs, and hearts served more often, but there were recipes, such as one for calf's eyeballs, that would surprise and shock even an adventurous French gourmet of today. Many of these eatables that are now looked on with suspicion by some are great delicacies, and when prepared in the appropriate manner, they still delight sophisticated palates that are more concerned with the quality and taste of food than with the social conventions and prejudices that surround it.

Another striking feature of some of these recipes is that they are based on leftovers. Most of the old cookbooks quoted here were written for chefs in well-to-do households, where leftovers were common after stately meals. Excellent dishes were made with ingredients that remained from previous meals, and it was the chef's responsibility to see that the leftover meats were always as appetizing as the dishes from which they were taken.

Cooks today can learn important lessons about domestic economy, nutrition, and cooking techniques by closely studying recipes from the past. Most of these recipes have a direct link to modern French cooking, but they are different enough to make them revealing and exciting for both the novice and the experienced cook alike.

BEEF

BOEUF MODE
(Pot Roast)

Pierre de Lune 1656

Today this recipe is called Boeuf à la mode, but the shorter title used by Pierre de Lune may be its original name since he is credited with inventing the dish. It is now one of the most popular meat dishes in France, but modern recipes differ in several respects from the old version given here. Pierre de Lune adds a whole lime to the meat when it starts cooking, then sprinkles lemon juice over the dish before serving it. This is, indeed, an idea worth trying. On the other hand, since modern recipes always include carrots when preparing this dish, they are mentioned below as a variant. The same is true of the calf's foot which is another modern addition that is essential if the meat is to be served cold, since the calf's foot helps make the beef jelly that is characteristic of cold Boeuf à la mode.

Ingredients (for 7 servings): 6 ounces lightly salted or fresh fatback. 3 pounds rump roast. 4 tablespoons lard. Several scallions. Several sprigs chervil. Several sprigs parsley. 1 sprig thyme. 2 cloves. 6 large fresh button mushrooms. ½ bay leaf. 1 small lime. ⅔ cup dry white wine. 1⅓ cups water. Salt. Pepper. 5 tablespoons flour. Juice of 1 lemon. **Modern additions:** 2 carrots, scraped and quartered. 1 calf's foot, scalded and boned.

Preparing the meat: If salted fatback is used, the layer covered with salt should be sliced off before proceeding to the next step. Cut off the rind from the fatback, and save for later use. Cut the fatback into lardoons about one-eighth inch on each side and one and a half to two inches long. With a larding needle or small knife, insert the fatback into the meat. Heat three tablespoons of the lard in a cast-iron stewpot. Brown the roast on all sides. This should take about fifteen or twenty minutes. (The browning is one of the most important steps in this recipe.)

Cooking: In a large earthenware or cast-iron pot, place the fatback rind, meat, and a bouquet garni made by tying the scallions, chervil, parsley, thyme, and cloves together in a cheesecloth bag. Add the mushrooms, bay leaf, and lime. Pour the wine and water into the pot. Add salt and pepper to taste. (Modern additions: Add the carrots and calf's foot.) Cover the pot, and seal it hermetically in the following manner: Make a dough by mixing four tablespoons of the flour with two teaspoons of water. Roll the dough on a table or between the palms of the hands until a long rope is formed. Place the rope around the top of the pot, moisten with a little water, and press the lid into place. Cook in a slow oven (300°) for four hours—do not open the pot while the meat is cooking.

To Serve: When the roast is cooked, melt the remaining lard in a small saucepan. Add the remaining flour, and stir for three or four minutes. Break the seal around the lid of the pot containing the meat, and remove the lid. Lift out the roast, and put it on a platter. Stir the contents of the saucepan into the pot. Add the lemon juice. Cut the roast into slices, and serve covered with the sauce. (Note: If the calf's foot was included, it should be cut into small pieces and placed around the meat.)

FILET D'ALOYAU BRAISE A LA ROYALE
(Braised Fillet of Beef à la Royale)

La Chapelle 1733

Ingredients (for 12 servings): 6 ounces fatback (for larding). 2 sprigs thyme. ½ bay leaf. 10 peppercorns, coarsely ground. 1 fillet of beef (5 to 5½ pounds). 6 medium onions, peeled. 2 cloves. 6 ounces lean veal. ½ pound fatback, thinly sliced (for barding). 3 sprigs parsley. 1 scallion. Salt. Pepper. 2 cups bouillon.

Larding the beef: Cut the rind from the larding fatback (save it for later use). In a small dish, crumble half the thyme and one-quarter bay leaf. Add the ground peppercorns. Cut the fatback into strips about one-eighth inch on each side and one and a half to two inches long. Roll these strips in the mixture of thyme, bay leaf, and pepper. With a larding needle, insert the strips of fatback into the beef.

Preparations for braising: Cut five of the onions into quarters. Stick the cloves into the remaining onion. Cut the veal into small pieces. Place the reserved fatback rind, half of the barding fat, and the veal in a cast-iron or earthenware pot. Add the onions, parsley, scallion, and the remaining thyme and bay leaf.

Cooking: Place the beef in the pot. Cover it with the remaining slices of barding fat. Add salt and pepper sparingly, because the fatback and bouillon are salty. Pour in the bouillon. Cover the pot with a tight-fitting lid. Cook over very low heat or in a slow oven (275°) for six hours.

To Serve: Remove the meat from the pot, and place it on a serving platter. Keep hot. Remove any grease that may be on the surface of the sauce; then strain the sauce into a small saucepan. Place the saucepan over low heat. Add one or two tablespoons of bouillon, and allow to cook for five minutes. Pour the sauce over the beef, and serve.

FILET DE BOEUF A LA MARIEE

(Stuffed Fillet of Beef à la Mariée)

In the past, many ingredients that are considered unusual today were commonly used. Who, today, would serve a calf's udder? Yet it is used to make an excellent stuffing in the following recipe. In France it is still sold precooked in many butcher shops, but if it is unavailable, sausage meat would be an acceptable substitute in this recipe.

Ingredients (for 12 servings): ½ pound fresh button mushrooms. 6 sprigs parsley, finely chopped. 3 scallions, finely chopped. 10 large basil leaves, finely chopped. 1 pound cooked calf's udder, finely chopped, or sausage meat. 7 tablespoons butter. 3 egg yolks. Salt. Pepper. 1 fillet of beef (5 to 5½ pounds). 6 ounces fatback (for larding). ¼ pound fatback, thinly sliced (for barding). 2 medium onions, peeled and sliced. 2 carrots, scraped and sliced. 2 cups bouillon.

The stuffing: Wash the mushrooms (the original recipe calls for truffles as well). Chop them, and mix with the parsley, scallions, basil, and calf's udder or sausage meat. Stir well. Add the butter, egg yolks, salt, and pepper.

Preparing the beef: Cut the meat in half lengthwise. Remove the rind from the fatback used for larding. Save the rind. Cut the fatback into strips measuring about one-eighth inch on each side and one to one and a half inches long. Lard the two pieces of beef with the fatback. Flatten the meat by tapping it with the flat side of a cleaver. Put half the stuffing on each piece of beef; then place the pieces together like a sandwich. Wrap the meat in a piece of cheesecloth so that it will retain its shape while cooking. Tie string around the meat in several places, and tie off the ends of the cheesecloth.

Cooking: Use a pot that is as close to the size of the meat as possible (an oblong cast-iron stewing pot is ideal). The meat can be close to the sides, but it should not be crowded. Place the rind from the fatback, the slices of barding fat, the onions, and the carrots into the pot. Carefully lay in the piece of meat. Add the bouillon (all but two tablespoons, which should be saved for the sauce). Cover the pot, and cook in a slow oven (325°) for about one hour.

To Serve: Carefully remove the meat. Remove the cheesecloth. Place the meat on a serving dish. Keep hot. Strain the sauce into a small saucepan. Add the reserved bouillon, and cook over medium heat for five minutes. Pour the sauce over the beef, and serve.

CARBONNADES DE BOEUF A LA LYONNAISE

(Braised Rib Steaks à la Lyonnaise)

Carbonnade was originally a name given to meat that was grilled over an open fire. The name was later applied to various meat stews such as this one described by Marin. Although the original recipe calls for rib steaks, a cheaper cut can be used, and sausage meat can be substituted for the calf's udder.

Ingredients (for 4 servings): 6 ounces lean veal. 6 ounces cooked calf's udder or sausage meat. ¼ pound fatback. 4 tablespoons mixed herbs (watercress, parsley, tarragon, chervil, chives), all finely chopped together. Salt. Pepper. Nutmeg. Ground basil. 1 egg yolk. Several thin slices fatback (for barding). 4 rib steaks (6 ounces each).

The stuffing: Chop the veal, udder or sausage meat, and fatback together. Mix with the herbs. Add salt and pepper to taste, a little nutmeg, and a pinch of basil. Mix well, and stir in the egg yolk.

Cooking: Select a deep cast-iron pot slightly larger than the diameter of the steaks. Cover the bottom of the pot with the slices of barding fatback. Spread a thin layer of the stuffing—about one-fifth of it—over the fatback. Put one of the rib steaks into the pot; then spread a thin layer of the stuffing over it. Continue laying in the steaks and stuffing in this manner. The last layer should be of stuffing. Cover the pot and cook over low heat for forty-five minutes.

To Serve: Carefully lift out, in a single block, the alternating layers of rib steak and stuffing. Skim the excess fat from the sauce remaining in the pot, then pour the sauce over the meat. Serve with boiled or baked potatoes.

BOEUF A LA MODE PAYSANNE
(Braised Beef Peasant-Style)

Marin 1739

This recipe is typical of a number of slow-cooking meat dishes still popular in many rural parts of France. Here the meat is cooked for nine hours in a slow oven—the meat can either be left to cook overnight or started cooking early in the morning for dinner that evening. In either case, the cook has nothing to do but watch the clock and remove the pot from the oven when the time is up.

Ingredients (for 8 servings): 3 pounds rump roast or any stewing cut. ½ pound fresh lean slab bacon, unsmoked and unsalted. 2 bay leaves. 4 cloves. Salt. Pepper. 6 tablespoons water. 1 tablespoon brandy. Flour.

Preparing and cooking the meat: Cut the meat and bacon into very thin slices. Cover the bottom of a small cast-iron or earthenware pot with the slices of bacon. Place the slices of beef in a symmetrical pattern on top of the bacon. Add the bay leaves (broken into large pieces), the cloves, and salt and pepper to taste. Mix the water and brandy together. Pour into the pot with the meat. Seal the pot hermetically (use a paste made of flour and water as described in the recipe for Boeuf mode, page 138). Place in a slow oven (275°), and cook for nine hours.

To Serve: Serve in the pot in which the beef cooked just as it comes from the oven.

CHARBONNEE DE BOEUF EN PAPILLOTE
(Rib Roast en Papillote)

Menon 1746

Meat and fish were often cooked *en papillote* during the eighteenth century. This form of cooking always entailed wrapping the meat in a paper case, which would ensure that no meat juices were lost and would keep the meat from drying out. As in this recipe, the meat was often precooked before it was wrapped in paper and put in the oven. The final stage of cooking was usually just a means of reheating the meat with the ingredients that were to flavor it. This was a favorite way of reheating leftovers that ought to be tried today.

Ingredients (for 8 servings): 1 standing rib roast (4½ to 5 pounds). Bouillon. 4 sprigs parsley, finely chopped. 1 scallion, finely chopped. 5 to 6 basil leaves, finely chopped. 4 shallots, peeled and finely chopped. ¼ pound fresh button mushrooms, finely chopped. 3 tablespoons vegetable oil. Salt. Pepper. 3 tablespoons lard.

Precooking the beef: Place the roast in a stewpot approximately its size. Pour in bouillon to cover (the narrower the pot, the less bouillon you will need). Cover with a tight-fitting lid. Allow to simmer, without boiling, for forty-five minutes (longer if you like meat well done). Remove the meat. Continue cooking the sauce until it thickens and becomes slightly syrupy.

The marinade: Mix the parsley, scallion, basil, shallots, and mushrooms with the oil. Marinate the meat for one hour in this mixture (thirty minutes on each side).

Cooking: Place the roast on a large sheet of waxed paper. Pour the reduced bouillon and the marinade over the meat. Add salt and pepper. Fold the sheet of paper so that it encloses the roast, and tie it closed. (Aluminum foil can be used instead of waxed paper, in which case the outside need not be greased.) Melt the lard over low heat. With a basting brush, grease the outside of the waxed paper. Preheat the broiler for about fifteen minutes, which will bring the oven heat to its highest point. Place the meat in the center of the oven, and cook it for thirty minutes, turning the meat over once.

To Serve: Place the wrapped roast on a platter. Open it at the table, and serve.

CULOTTE A LA BRAISE AUX OIGNONS

Menon 1746

(Braised Rump Roast with Onions)

Menon states that red onions are best in this recipe, but yellow onions are just as good. They both have a sweeter taste than white onions. On the other hand, Menon does not specify what kind of white wine to use in the cooking. In the eighteenth century, French wines were generally sweeter than they are today, and this dish is improved if a slightly sweet (rather than dry) white wine is used—for example, a sauterne.

Ingredients (for 6 or 7 servings): 6 ounces lean veal. 3 to 4 scallions. 2 or 3 sprigs parsley. 1 clove garlic, peeled. 1 sprig thyme. 2 cloves. 6 ounces thinly sliced fatback or 4 tablespoons lard. 3 pounds rump roast. 30 small onions, peeled. 2 cups slightly sweet white wine. 4 cups bouillon. 2 tablespoons flour.

Braising: Cut the veal into small pieces. Make a bouquet garni by tying the scallions, parsley, garlic, and thyme together. Stick the cloves into the garlic. Place the bouquet in a pot with the fatback or lard and the veal. Cook, covered, over low heat for thirty minutes.

Cooking: Place the roast in the pot with the cooked ingredients. Brown on all sides, over low heat, for about fifteen minutes. Add the onions. Pour in the wine. Raise the heat slightly until the wine boils. Boil the wine for two or three minutes. Reduce the heat, and add the bouillon (keep two tablespoons of bouillon for use in the sauce). Cover the pot with a tight-fitting lid. Cook in a slow oven (300°) for three hours.

To Serve: Remove the roast and place upright on a serving platter. Surround with the onions. Strain the sauce and skim off whatever fat comes to the surface. Place the flour in a bowl, and stir in the reserved bouillon. Pour this mixture into the sauce. Stir. Bring to a boil; then remove from the heat. Serve the sauce in a separate dish.

TRANCHE DE BOEUF A LA CAMARGOT

Menon 1746

(Braised Beef with Anchovies à la Camargot)

Some food writers believe this dish was named for a once-famous dancer named Camargot who was a contemporary of the author of the recipe. Another theory suggests the name is simply a corruption of Camargue, a small area in the South of France where anchovies are often used in cooking. Indeed, the meat in this recipe is larded with anchovies, but this was a common practice in French cooking until the nineteenth century. The true origin of the name of this dish will no doubt remain a mystery until the etymology of cooking terms and the names of dishes are studied systematically by historians.

Ingredients (for 6 or 7 servings): **For the meat:** ¼ pound fatback (for larding). 3 pounds rump roast. 25 anchovy fillets in oil. 6 ounces thinly sliced fatback (for barding) or ⅔ cup lard. 1 scallion. 1 sprig parsley. 1 sprig basil. 2 cloves garlic, peeled. 2 shallots, peeled. 1 bay leaf. 1 sprig thyme. 6 tablespoons dry white wine. 3 cups bouillon. Pepper. **For the sauce:** 3 tablespoons butter. 2 tablespoons flour. 1 tablespoon capers.

Preparing the meat: Remove the rind from the larding fatback. Save the rind for later use. Cut the fatback into strips about one-eighth inch on each side and one and a half to two inches long. Using a larding needle or small knife, insert the fatback strips into the roast. Lard the roast with the anchovy fillets in the same manner.

Cooking: Place the fatback rind in a cast-iron pot along with the barding fat or lard. Begin cooking over low heat. When the fat is hot, add the meat, and brown it on all sides for approximately fifteen minutes. Add all the remaining ingredients listed for cooking the meat. Cover the pot with a tight-fitting lid. Cook in a slow oven (325°) for four hours.

To Serve: Remove the meat from the pot. Melt the butter in a small saucepan, and stir in the flour. Continue stirring until the mixture is smooth and begins to color. Strain the juice from the pot in which the meat cooked, and add to the butter and flour mixture. Stir and bring to a boil. Taste for seasoning. If the sauce seems too thick, add several tablespoons of bouillon. Add the capers to the sauce at the last minute. Serve the meat covered with the sauce.

QUEUE DE BOEUF EN HOCHEPOT

(Oxtail Stew)

Menon 1746

In the northern regions of France (Picardy and Flanders), oxtail is traditionally cooked with beer instead of bouillon. Although Menon's recipe does not mention it, beer can be used without changing the basic character of the dish.

Ingredients (for 8 servings): 2 oxtails. 6½ cups bouillon (approximately). ½ bay leaf. 1 sprig thyme. 2 cloves. 1 small green cabbage (about 2 pounds). 3 carrots, scraped. 3 turnips, peeled. 1 parsnip, peeled (optional). 2 large onions, peeled. Salt. Pepper. 3 tablespoons butter. 2 tablespoons flour. 1 large handful parsley, chopped.

Preparing the oxtails: Cut the oxtails into pieces four inches long. Put them in a large pot of boiling water, and cook for ten minutes. Drain.

The first step in cooking the oxtails: Place the pieces of oxtail in a large cast-iron stewpot. Pour in enough bouillon to cover. Add the bay leaf, thyme, and cloves. Bring to a boil over medium heat. Skim off the foam which rises to the surface. When there is no more foam, cover, and cook in a slow oven (300°) for two hours and thirty minutes.

The vegetables: While the oxtails are cooking, clean the cabbage, and cut it in half. Put the cabbage into a large pot of boiling water and cook for ten minutes. Drain. Cut the carrots, turnips, parsnip, and onions into quarters.

Finishing the cooking: Remove the pot containing the oxtails from the oven, and take out the bay leaf and thyme. Add all the vegetables (there should still be enough bouillon to cover the oxtails). Salt and pepper to taste. Replace the lid, and return the pot to the oven to cook for two hours and thirty minutes longer.

To Serve: Use a slotted spoon to remove the vegetables from the pot. Drain thoroughly; then arrange them on a serving platter. Place the pieces of oxtail on top of the vegetables. Melt the butter in a small saucepan. Stir in the flour. Strain the bouillon in which the oxtails cooked. Stir it into the butter and flour mixture until a smooth sauce is formed. Bring to a boil. Add the parsley to the sauce before serving. Serve very hot, with the sauce in a separate dish.

COTE DE BOEUF A LA GELEE

(Cold Rib Roast in Meat Jelly)

Viard 1820

When a French recipe calls for brandy, either cognac or armagnac is generally understood. But any good brandy is acceptable.

Ingredients (for 8 servings): ¼ pound fatback (for larding). 1 rib roast (4½ pounds). ¼ pound thinly sliced fatback (for barding). ¼ pound fresh pork rind. 1 calf's foot, cleaned and parboiled. 6 ounces veal knuckle. 1 large bouquet parsley. 4 small carrots, scraped. 2 medium onions, peeled and stuck with 2 cloves each. 1 clove garlic, peeled. 1 bay leaf. 1 sprig thyme. Salt. Pepper. 2 teaspoons brandy. 3 cups dry white wine. ¾ cup bouillon. 2 egg whites.

Preparing the rib roast: Remove the rind from the fatback, and save it for later use. Cut the fatback into strips about one-eighth inch on each side and one and a half to two inches long. Using a larding needle or sharp knife, insert the fatback strips into the roast. Wrap the meat in thin slices of barding fat. Tie the fat to the roast. Wrap the entire roast in a large piece of cheesecloth. Tie strings around the cheesecloth so that the roast will keep its shape, and tie off the ends of the cloth.

Cooking: In a pot large enough to hold the roast, but not too deep, place the fresh pork rind and the rind from the fatback. Add the roast, calf's foot, and veal knuckle. Add the parsley, carrots, the onions stuck with cloves, the garlic, bay leaf, and thyme. Add salt and pepper to taste. Pour in the brandy, wine, and bouillon. Cover the pot, and cook in a slow oven (325°) for five hours.

The jelly: When the roast is finished, carefully remove it. Take off the cheesecloth and the slices of barding fat. Place the meat in a serving dish. Strain the roast's cooking liquid into a saucepan, and leave to cool for fifteen minutes so that the excess fat will rise to the surface. Spoon off the fat. In a bowl, beat the egg whites with a little water until foamy. Stir the egg whites into the saucepan with the cooking liquid. Place over low heat, and bring to a boil, stirring frequently. Remove from the heat. Strain the sauce through a damp cloth. Pour the sauce over the meat, and allow to cool.

To Serve: Serve cold.

MIROTON

(Beef with Onions)

This dish is traditionally prepared the day after a Pot au feu has been cooked or anytime leftover boiled beef is available. It used to be made with leftover lamb or pork, and even fish was once used in Miroton. Today only leftover beef is prepared in this manner, and though rarely seen on restaurant menus, it is perhaps one of the most popular dishes in France.

Ingredients (for 4 servings): 2 tablespoons lard or 3 tablespoons butter. 2 large onions, peeled and thinly sliced. 1 tablespoon flour. ¾ cup bouillon. 1 tablespoon vinegar. Salt. Pepper. 1 pound boiled beef, with all fat removed. Juice of 1 lemon.

The onions: Melt the lard or butter in a frying pan. Add the onions. Stir occasionally until the onions begin to brown. Sprinkle in the flour, and cook slowly for five minutes, stirring frequently. Add the bouillon and vinegar. Stir, and cook for fifteen minutes more. Add salt and pepper to taste.

The beef: Cut the meat into very thin slices. Add the slices to the onions. Lower the heat as much as possible. Cover the pan, and cook very slowly for twenty-five to thirty minutes. The sauce should be quite thick at the end of this time.

To Serve: Stir the lemon juice into the pan, and serve.

HACHIS DE BOEUF

(Diced Beef with Eggs)

This is an excellent example of leftover cookery. The eggs that are served with this dish make it more filling—especially when there is only a little leftover beef in the sauce. It is also possible to prepare this dish with fresh meat, in which case a top-quality lean cut of beef should be used. Croutons can be added to the dish before serving, or the beef and eggs can be served on toast.

Ingredients (for 4 servings): 5 tablespoons butter. 1 medium carrot, scraped and diced. 3 sprigs parsley, chopped. 1 scallion, chopped. 1 small onion, peeled and diced. 2 shallots, peeled and diced. 2 ounces fresh lean bacon (unsmoked and unsalted), diced. ½ bay leaf. 1 small sprig thyme. 4 medium fresh button mushrooms, cleaned and diced. 2 tablespoons flour. 1⅓ cups dry white wine. 2 cups bouillon. 4 eggs. 1¼ pounds (approximately 2½ cups) diced boiled beef. Salt. Pepper.

The sauce: Over low heat, melt two tablespoons of the butter in a saucepan. Add the carrots, parsley, scallion, onion, shallots, and bacon, along with the bay leaf and thyme. Brown all the ingredients, stirring occasionally. Add the mushrooms, stir, and cook for another minute. Sprinkle in the flour. Cook for ten minutes more, stirring occasionally. Pour in the wine and bouillon. Simmer for one hour. At the end of this time, there should be about one cup of sauce remaining in the saucepan.

The eggs: Bring a pot of water to a boil. Add the eggs. Cook for nine minutes from the time the water comes back to a boil; then remove the eggs. Cool the eggs slightly under running water, and peel them.

The beef: Remove the thyme and bay leaf from the sauce. Add the beef. Salt and pepper to taste. Cook for five to six minutes, stirring constantly. Remove from the heat, and stir in the remaining butter.

To Serve: Serve the meat and sauce in a dish surrounded by the eggs.

CROQUETTES DE BOUILLI

(Beef Croquettes with Egg Sauce)

Brillat-Savarin, a famous gastronome in the early nineteenth century, refused to eat boiled beef. "It is meat without its juices," he wrote. Few people would agree with this opinion today, and since most French cooks prepare a Pot au feu at least once a week, one can assume that boiled beef is as popular as ever. Leftovers are always welcome in French cooking, and this is yet another excellent way of using boiled beef.

Ingredients (for 8 servings): 2 tablespoons butter. 3 tablespoons flour. 1⅔ cups bouillon. 3 eggs, separated. 3 sprigs parsley, finely chopped (for the croquettes). 1¾ pounds (approximately 3¼ cups) boiled beef, finely chopped. Salt. Pepper. 2½ cups bread crumbs. 1 tablespoon vegetable oil. 1 tablespoon water. Oil for deep frying. 1 tablespoon finely chopped parsley (to garnish).

The sauce: Melt two-thirds of the butter in a saucepan over low heat. Stir in the flour. Add the bouillon, and cook for fifteen minutes, stirring constantly. Remove from the heat, and add the remaining butter and the egg yolks.

The croquettes: Add the parsley and beef to the sauce. Add salt and pepper to taste. Spread the croquette mixture on a cutting board in a layer about two inches thick. Allow to cool.

The batter: Cut the croquette mixture into sixteen equal parts. Then roll each croquette in the bread crumbs, forming it into a small cylinder. Beat the egg whites until foamy with a pinch of salt, a dash of pepper, the vegetable oil, and the water. Dip each of the croquettes into this mixture; then roll once more in the bread crumbs.

Cooking: Heat the oil for frying in a deep fryer or pot. Place the croquettes in the oil when it begins to smoke. Fry them quickly, turning them with a slotted spoon. When they are golden brown, remove the croquettes, and drain.

To Serve: Arrange the croquettes on a platter. Sprinkle with the parsley for garnish, and serve immediately.

FILETS DE BOEUF SAUTES AUX OLIVES

(Steaks with Olive Sauce)

Jules Gouffé's cookbook was one of the first systematic and truly practical books on cooking. He divided it into two sections—the first on "home cooking" and the second on *grande cuisine*. This recipe is an example of Gouffé's idea of home cooking. It is surprisingly easy to prepare, and most important, it is delicious.

Ingredients (for 4 servings): 24 green olives, pitted. 1 tablespoon butter. Salt. Pepper. 4 tenderloin steaks (filet mignon), 2 inches thick. 1 tablespoon flour. 6 tablespoons bouillon.

The olives: Drop the olives into boiling water, and cook for five minutes. Drain.

Cooking: Melt the butter in a frying pan over high heat. Salt and pepper the steaks, and place them in the pan. Cook for four minutes on each side (longer if you like the meat well done).

The sauce: Place the steaks on a serving platter. Keep hot. Add the flour to the pan. Stir. Stir in the bouillon, over moderate heat. Add the olives, and cook for two minutes.

To Serve: Serve the sauce in a separate dish, or pour it over the steaks.

VEAL

LONGE DE VEAU A LA MARINADE
(Marinated Loin Roast of Veal)

La Varenne 1651

Today restaurants would serve this magnificent dish with French fries or some other kind of potato. It would be much more interesting to follow La Varenne's suggestion and accompany the veal with asparagus. But depending on what is in season, chard, Jerusalem artichokes, okra, or broccoli would also be excellent with this dish.

Ingredients (for 10 servings): 1 sprig rosemary. 1 sprig sage. Juice of 1 lemon. Juice of 1 orange. 2 medium onions, peeled and finely chopped. ⅛ teaspoon ground cloves. 6 tablespoons wine vinegar. Pepper. ¼ pound fatback. 3 pounds loin roast of veal. Salt. 3 tablespoons bread crumbs. ¾ cup bouillon.

The marinade: Remove the leaves from the rosemary and sage. Place them in a large bowl with the lemon juice, orange juice, onions, cloves, vinegar, and a little pepper. Cut the fatback into strips suitable for larding the veal. Using a larding needle or small knife, insert these strips into the veal. Place the veal in the marinade, and leave for four to five hours, turning occasionally.

Cooking: Put the veal in a roasting pan. Place in a moderately hot oven (400°) for one hour and thirty minutes. Baste occasionally with the marinade and the drippings from the roast. Salt the veal about halfway through the cooking time.

To Serve: Mix the bread crumbs with the bouillon, and add to the roasting pan. Boil for five minutes. Place the veal on a serving platter. Serve the sauce from the pan in a separate dish.

JARRET DE VEAU A L'EPIGRAMME
("Epigram" Veal Knuckle)

La Varenne 1651

Legend has it that a French nobleman was once talking with one of his status-seeking peers and said, "I dined yesterday with a poet who regaled us with a choice epigram." The listener was so impressed that he immediately went home and asked his cook, "How is it that you never send any epigrams to my table?" And so, the story goes, this same cook invented the "epigram" of veal for his pretentious master. This anecdote probably has more charm to it than truth, but it is the only explanation we have for the name of this particular dish.

Ingredients (for 8 servings): Flour. 8 large slices veal knuckle. 3 tablespoons lard. 1 large onion, peeled and quartered. 2 sprigs parsley. 1 sprig thyme. 1 bay leaf. 1 clove. 1 tablespoon capers. Salt. Pepper. Bouillon.

Preparing the veal: Flour the slices of veal on both sides. Brown them in a pan with the hot lard.

Cooking: Arrange the veal in a cast-iron pot. Add the onion, parsley, thyme, bay leaf, clove, capers, salt, and pepper. If there is any lard left in the pan, pour that in as well. Pour in enough bouillon to cover the veal. Cover the pot with a tight-fitting lid. Cook in a moderate oven (350°) for three hours.

To Serve: Serve in the pot in which the veal was cooked.

De la teste de Veau

This is still the most common (and practical) way of preparing a breast of veal in France. Today, however, most cooks use sausage meat in the stuffing instead of the mixture of lean veal and suet La Varenne describes. The stuffing is finer and tastier when veal and suet are used, but you can substitute sausage meat if you choose. Once the veal has been stuffed, La Varenne writes, it can either be boiled with a variety of fresh vegetables (as in this recipe) or roasted on a spit or in the oven. If either of these last alternatives is chosen, the meat should be rubbed with lard before being cooked and should be basted often to keep it from drying out.

INGREDIENTS

(for 12 to 15 servings)

3 pounds boned breast of veal
½ pound lean veal (round or rump), diced
½ pound beef suet, diced
1 cup stale bread, broken into small pieces
2 tablespoons bouillon or dry white wine
¼ pound fresh button mushrooms, diced
Several sprigs parsley, finely chopped
1 scallion, finely chopped
1 tablespoon capers
2 egg yolks
Salt
Pepper
4 carrots, scraped and quartered
2 turnips, peeled and quartered
4 leeks, quartered
1 large onion, peeled and quartered
1 sprig thyme
1 bay leaf
2 cloves

The meat

- The veal must be boned and a "pocket" created by careful separation of the first layer of meat from those beneath it. (An experienced butcher should be able to do this if you tell him to prepare the veal for stuffing.)

The stuffing

- Mix the lean veal and the beef suet together.
- Soak the bread until soft in the bouillon or wine. Squeeze out the liquid from the bread before combining it with the other ingredients.
- Add the mushrooms, parsley, scallion, capers, and soaked bread to the diced meat.
- Mix all the ingredients thoroughly. Add the egg yolks, salt, and pepper. Mix well.

Cooking

- Place the stuffing in the "pocket" of the breast of veal. Sew the pocket closed—but not too tightly, since the stuffing will expand during cooking.
- Place the veal in a large pot of rapidly boiling water. Cook over medium heat, removing the foam as it appears.
- Add the carrots, turnips, leeks, onion, thyme, bay leaf, and cloves to the pot with the meat. Salt and pepper lightly.
- Cook slowly for two hours and thirty minutes.

To Serve

- Drain the veal, and cut into slices.
- Serve on a platter, surrounded by the vegetables with which it cooked.

"Ambassade d'Auvergne et du Rouergue"

COTELETTES DE VEAU EN SURPRISE

(Surprise Veal Cutlets)

These cutlets are made by chopping several different ingredients together and then shaping the mixture on a bone so that it resembles a veal chop. This technique is common in Russian cooking where many cutlets are made this way, but it is surprising to find such a recipe in a French cookbook. One theory is that this way of making cutlets was, in fact, a French invention that was adopted by Russian cooks. It is more probable, however, that this way of cooking meat was developed independently in both countries and simply fell out of favor in France while it continued to gain popularity in Russia.

INGREDIENTS

(for 8 servings)

8 veal chops with bones
2 tablespoons chopped beef suet
5 tablespoons lard
2 cups stale bread crusts, broken into small pieces
6 tablespoons milk
Several sprigs parsley, finely chopped
Several scallions, finely chopped
½ pound fresh button mushrooms, finely chopped
Salt
Pepper
8 slices ham, diced
1½ tablespoons butter
2 tablespoons flour
1 cup bouillon
2 eggs
2 cups bread crumbs (approximately)
Parsley sprigs (to garnish)

The veal

- Remove the bones from the veal chops. Cut the meat into small pieces. Place the pieces of meat in a frying pan with the bones, suet, and two tablespoons of the lard. Cook until the meat begins to brown.
- Soak the bread crusts in the milk until soft. Squeeze out most of the liquid; then add the crusts, chopped parsley, scallions, and mushrooms to the pan containing the meat. Salt and pepper lightly. Stir over moderate heat for a few minutes.
- Remove from the heat. Take the bones from the pan. Mix all the ingredients in the pan thoroughly.

The ham

- Place the ham in a saucepan with the butter. Cook until the ham begins to brown.
- Sprinkle in the flour, stirring constantly until well blended. Pour in the bouillon, and bring to a boil, stirring constantly. Cook for ten minutes more; then remove from the heat, and cool.

Cooking

- Combine the veal mixture and the ham.
- Divide into eight equal parts, and mold the chopped ingredients into the shape of cutlets.
- Beat the eggs in a shallow bowl. Place the bread crumbs in another.
- Coat each of the cutlets first with the eggs and then with the bread crumbs. Insert one of the bones into each of the cutlets.
- Melt the remaining lard in a frying pan. Add the cutlets, and cook until both sides are golden brown (about six minutes on a side).

To Serve

- Serve very hot, garnished with sprigs of parsley.

(Loin Roast of Veal with Carrots and Onions)

La Chapelle specifies that the meat used in this recipe should come from a "female calf." It would be interesting to know the difference between the meat of a calf which will develop into a cow and that of a calf which will grow into a bull. Today good veal is so rare that fine points like this seem irrelevant. The best most cooks can hope for is to find good-quality veal of any kind.

INGREDIENTS

(for 6 servings)

6 ounces fatback
2 sprigs thyme
Salt
Pepper
2 pounds loin roast of veal
6½ tablespoons butter
4 carrots, scraped and quartered
3 medium onions, peeled and
    quartered
3 sprigs parsley and 1 scallion, tied
    together
⅔ cup bouillon

Preparing the veal

- Cut the fatback into strips about the length and width of the little finger. Crumble the leaves of the thyme, and sprinkle them over the fatback strips. Salt and pepper lightly.
- Using a larding needle or small knife, insert the fatback into the veal.

Cooking

- Melt half the butter in a cast-iron pot (the size of the roast). Add the carrots, onions, parsley, and scallion. Place the larded veal in the pot.
- Pour in the bouillon. Salt and pepper to taste. Cover, and cook in a moderate oven (375°) for two hours.

To Serve

- Remove the parsley and scallion. Take the meat from the pot and place it on a serving platter. Cut it into slices.
- Add the remaining butter to the pot in which the veal cooked. Arrange the vegetables around the meat. Cover both the meat and vegetables with the sauce.

BLANQUETTE DE VEAU

(Veal Stewed in White Sauce)

Although the original recipe calls for leftover veal, this modern version begins by cooking the veal, then making the sauce. If you have leftover veal (from a roast, for example), it can be prepared *en blanquette* by simply omitting the section of the recipe dealing with the cooking of the meat and by preparing the onions, carrots, and mushrooms in a separate pan with a little butter and water. In this case bouillon (preferably prepared from veal or chicken) will have to be made separately for use in the sauce.

INGREDIENTS

(for 4 servings)

1¾ pounds breast of veal, cut into 2-inch squares
Salt
1 carrot, scraped and quartered
1 medium onion, peeled and stuck with 1 clove
1 sprig thyme
1 bay leaf
¼ pound fresh button mushrooms, cleaned
6 tablespoons water
6 tablespoons butter
16 small white onions, peeled
4 tablespoons flour
Juice of 1 lemon
2 egg yolks
6 tablespoons heavy cream
Pepper
Nutmeg
3 sprigs parsley, finely chopped

Cooking

- Place the veal in a large saucepan. Add enough water to cover. Salt lightly.
- Bring to a boil over gentle heat. Skim off the foam.
- Add the carrot, the onion with the clove, thyme, and bay leaf. Simmer for one hour and thirty minutes.
- Place the mushrooms in a small saucepan with the water, a pinch of salt, and two tablespoons of the butter. Bring to a boil, and cook for five minutes.
- In another saucepan, melt one tablespoon of the butter, and cook the small onions for thirty-five minutes over low heat, stirring occasionally. The onions should cook thoroughly, but without browning.

The sauce

- Remove the veal from the saucepan, and place in a serving bowl. Keep hot.
- Melt the remaining butter in a pot. Add the flour, and cook over low heat, stirring until the mixture is smooth. Do not allow to color.
- Stir in the liquid in which the veal cooked. Add the mushrooms and their cooking liquid. Add the onions as well. Simmer over low heat for fifteen minutes.
- Remove from the heat. Mix the lemon juice, egg yolks, and cream in a bowl. Add a tablespoon of the sauce, and stir; then pour these ingredients into the pot with the rest of the sauce. Add a little pepper and nutmeg.

To Serve

- Pour the sauce over the veal.
- Sprinkle with the parsley, and serve.

FRICANDEAU A LA BOURGEOISE

Marin 1739

(Glazed Veal Garnished à la Bourgeoise)

Veal cooked in the following manner becomes so soft that it is traditionally eaten with a spoon. This recipe calls for a garnish made of mushrooms and sweetbreads (sweetbreads were frequently used as a garnish in the eighteenth century). A *fricandeau* such as this one is always served on a bed of freshly puréed sorrel. If sorrel is unavailable, spinach is a good substitute. Not only does the taste of these vegetables go perfectly with the taste of the veal, but the dark green of the spinach or sorrel forms a perfect background for the glazed meat.

Ingredients (for 6 servings): 10 ounces sweetbreads. ¼ pound fatback. 3 pounds round roast of veal. ½ pound fresh button mushrooms, cleaned. 3 sprigs parsley. 1 scallion, stuck with 2 cloves. Bouillon. 1 teaspoon flour.

The sweetbreads: Leave the sweetbreads in a bowl of cold water for several hours before cooking them. Drain; then place them in a pot of cold water, and bring to a boil. As soon as the water boils, drain the sweetbreads, and cool under running water. Remove whatever fat and skin remain on the sweetbreads; then cut them into thin slices.

The veal: Cut the fatback into small strips (lardoons), and using a larding needle or small knife, insert them into the veal. Lard only one side of the veal, and do not go all the way through the meat; the ends of the fatback should protrude slightly.

Cooking: Place the veal in a saucepan, with the larded side up. Add the sweetbreads and mushrooms. Tie the parsley and the scallion stuck with cloves together, and add to the pot with the meat. Pour in just enough bouillon to cover the meat, but leave the ends of the fatback uncovered. Cover, and simmer over low heat. After fifteen minutes, remove the sweetbreads and mushrooms. Save for later use. Replace the lid on the saucepan, and simmer for two hours more. At the end of this time the sauce should be on the point of caramelizing. Turn the veal, and allow it to cook for five minutes on the larded side. Glaze the veal in the concentrated meat sauce remaining in the pan; then remove and keep it warm while you prepare the sauce.

The sauce: Sprinkle the flour into the saucepan. Stir. Add the remaining bouillon. Salt and pepper to taste. Place the sweetbreads and mushrooms back in the sauce, and simmer for ten minutes.

To Serve: Cover the meat with several spoonfuls of the sauce. Arrange the mushrooms and sweetbreads around the meat. Serve the rest of the sauce in a separate bowl.

NOIX DE VEAU EN DES AU JAMBON

Cuisinier Gascon 1740

(Veal and Ham in Wine Sauce)

Ham is rarely served hot in French restaurants today. In the past ham was often cooked and served whole or mixed with other meat as in the following recipe. In a short note, the author of this recipe states that lamb can be substituted for the veal used here and prepared in the same way.

Ingredients (for 4 servings): 14 ounces shoulder of veal, cut into large cubes. 14 ounces ham, cut into large cubes. 6 tablespoons olive oil. 4 sprigs parsley, finely chopped. 3 tablespoons finely chopped chives. Dry white wine. Salt. Pepper.

The marinade: Place the veal and ham in a large bowl. Sprinkle with the oil. Add the parsley and chives. Stir. Marinate for two hours.

Cooking: Place the meat and the marinade in a saucepan. Pour in enough wine to cover. Add salt and pepper. Cover the saucepan, and cook over medium heat for one hour.

To Serve: Remove the meat with a slotted spoon, and place it on a serving platter. Keep hot. Boil the sauce over high heat until reduced by half; then pour it over the meat.

BREZOLLES

(Veal Stew with Shallots)

Alexandre Dumas gives a recipe for a dish similar to this one in his dictionary of cooking. He spells the name of this dish Bresolles and says it was invented by the cook to a certain Marquis de Bresolles. Dumas' recipe includes chopped mushrooms and a little garlic with the herbs listed below. Dumas also uses olive oil instead of butter, and he specifies that the meat should be served with chestnuts that have been cooked separately and added to the sauce in which the veal cooked just before serving. Both Menon and Dumas agree that other meats, especially lamb, can be cooked and served in the same way.

Ingredients (for 6 servings): 2 pounds round roast of veal. 6½ tablespoons butter. 4 sprigs parsley, finely chopped. 2 scallions, finely chopped. 10 shallots, peeled and finely chopped. Salt. Pepper. ½ pound thinly sliced fatback (for barding). 6 tablespoons dry white wine.

Preparation: Cut the veal into long, thin strips. Rub one and a half tablespoons of the butter around the sides and bottom of a cast-iron pot. Place one layer of the veal strips in the pot. Sprinkle with the chopped herbs. Top with two or three dots of butter and a little salt and pepper. Then make a new layer of veal, and repeat this procedure until all the veal, herbs, and butter are used up. Place the layer of fatback over the final layer of herbs. Arrange the fatback carefully, so that there are no open spaces left through which the juices of the meat could evaporate. Cover the pot.

Cooking: Place the pot on the stove over low heat, and simmer for thirty minutes. At the end of this time, add the wine. Cover, and continue cooking for one hour.

To Serve: Serve very hot in the pot in which the veal cooked. Accompany this dish with boiled potatoes or a vegetable of your choice.

COTELETTES DE VEAU A LA SINGARA

(Braised Veal Cutlets with Tongue)

This dish is typical of a kind of French cookery that appears wasteful to some people. Here lard, fatback, ham, and fresh bacon are used to impart flavor to veal cutlets larded with smoked tongue. All the first-named ingredients are eventually thrown away, since they are used only to flavor the veal and are strained out of the sauce served with the meat. Actually, since all the nutritive elements, as well as the flavor of these ingredients, have been transferred to the sauce, it is not really a waste.

Ingredients (for 4 servings): ¼ pound smoked tongue. 6½ tablespoons lard. Salt. Pepper. Nutmeg. 4 thick veal cutlets. 3½ tablespoons butter. 4 thin slices fatback (for barding). 1 sprig basil. 4 slices prosciutto or country-style ham. 4 thin slices fresh lean bacon (unsmoked and unsalted). 2 carrots, scraped and sliced. 4 medium onions, peeled and sliced. Bouillon.

Preparing the tongue: Cut the tongue into small strips, about one-eighth inch on each side and one and a half to two inches long. Melt the lard in a frying pan over low heat. Add the tongue, salt, pepper, and a little nutmeg. When the strips of tongue have browned, remove them from the fat, and let cool.

Cooking: Using a larding needle or small knife, insert the strips of tongue into the cutlets. Melt the butter in a frying pan, and add the cutlets. Brown the cutlets on both sides; then lift them out, and set them aside. In the same frying pan, place the slices of barding fat, the basil, and ham. Place the veal cutlets on top of these ingredients. Cover each cutlet with a slice of bacon. Add the carrots and onions. Pour in enough bouillon to cover the meat. Cover the pan, and simmer for two hours.

To Serve: Lift out the cutlets, and place them on a serving platter. Strain the cooking liquid through a sieve. Taste the sauce, and add salt, pepper, and nutmeg if necessary. Pour the sauce over the cutlets, and serve.

Stuffed veal scallops are usually called *paupiettes* in modern French recipes. They differ from those described here in that they are always surrounded with a piece of fatback (barding fat) and almost always braised with vegetables or simply cooked in a little bouillon. These stuffed scallops, which are cooked on skewers, could be barded with fatback, although the author of this recipe did not think it necessary. They would be delicious cooked over a charcoal fire instead of under the broiler.

INGREDIENTS

(for 8 servings)

2 sprigs parsley, finely chopped
1 scallion, finely chopped
2 pounds fresh button mushrooms, finely chopped
4 shallots, peeled and finely chopped
2 ounces truffle parings, finely chopped
2 tablespoons olive oil
Salt
Pepper
16 veal scallops (about 6 inches by 3½ inches each)

Preparing the vegetables

- Mix the parsley, scallion, mushrooms, shallots, and truffles together in a bowl.
- Add the oil along with a little salt and pepper.

Stuffing the veal scallops

- Pound the veal scallops with the flat side of a meat cleaver until they are very thin.
- Divide the vegetable mixture into sixteen equal parts. Place a portion of stuffing on each of the scallops; then roll them up. Tie them with a string so that they will not unfold.

Cooking

- Slide the stuffed scallops onto skewers (two scallops to a skewer).
- Cook under a medium broiler for thirty minutes. Turn the meat frequently so that it will cook evenly on all sides.

To Serve

- Serve the meat on the skewers.
- Accompany with a shallot sauce (see Poitrine de mouton, page 178) or lemon quarters.

"Jamin"

TENDRONS DE VEAU EN CHARTREUSE

(Veal Chartreuse)

Today the term *en chartreuse* usually means that the dish in question is served with cabbage. For centuries, however, the term simply meant that a dish was served with an elaborate (and copious) mixed vegetable garnish. This way of serving food is said to have originated with the Carthusian monks, who were supposed to be strict vegetarians. Apparently some of these religious men did not take their vows seriously and, the story goes, began concealing pieces of meat in the vegetable stews they were served. The following recipe does indeed contain meat buried between the thick layers of vegetables in typical *chartreuse* fashion.

Ingredients (for 8 servings): 2 pounds breast of veal. 6 tablespoons olive oil. 1 bay leaf. 1 sprig thyme. 2 medium onions, peeled and diced. 1 clove garlic, peeled and diced. Salt. Pepper. 40 small white onions, peeled. 6 carrots, scraped and sliced. 6 turnips, peeled and sliced. 1 pound string beans. 4 cups bouillon. 2 pounds fresh green peas, shelled. 2 heads leafy lettuce. 1 tablespoon butter.

The veal: Cut the veal into pieces about two inches square. Heat the oil in a large frying pan. Add the veal. Add the bay leaf, thyme, diced onions, and garlic. Sprinkle with salt and pepper. Cover, and cook slowly for two hours. Stir occasionally.

The vegetables: When the veal has cooked for one hour and twenty minutes, combine the small onions, carrots, turnips, and string beans in a pot. Add the bouillon, and bring to a boil. Cook for twenty-five minutes. Add the peas and lettuce. Cook fifteen minutes more. Drain carefully. Separate the lettuce from the other vegetables. Save the cooking liquid for later use.

The *chartreuse:* Butter a charlotte mold or any high-sided baking dish. Cover the bottom of the mold with half the vegetables; then place the lettuce on top of them. Drain the pieces of veal, and arrange them on top of the lettuce. Fill the baking dish with the remainder of the vegetables. Place the dish in a slow oven (300°) for as long as it takes to prepare the sauce.

The sauce: Add the vegetables' cooking liquid to the sauce remaining in the pan in which the veal was cooked. Boil this mixture over high heat until two-thirds has evaporated.

To Serve: Turn out the meat and vegetables from the baking dish onto a serving platter. Serve the sauce separately.

ESCALOPES DE VEAU AUX FINES HERBES

(Veal Scallops in Herb Sauce)

Gouffé's title for this recipe contains the term *aux fines herbes*, but he specifies the use of only parsley. Ordinarily, *fines herbes* means a mixture of several herbs. So it would be entirely permissible to add chopped chervil, tarragon, or chives to the sauce at the same time as the parsley; basil, mint, or sage could be added for those who like a more exotic taste.

Ingredients (for 4 servings): 3 tablespoons butter. 4 veal scallops (4 to 5 ounces each). Salt. Pepper. 1 tablespoon flour. ⅔ cup bouillon. 4 sprigs parsley, finely chopped.

Cooking the veal: Melt one and a half tablespoons of the butter in a frying pan over high heat. When the butter is hot, add the veal scallops to the pan, and cook for four minutes. Turn over, sprinkle with salt and pepper, and cook for four minutes more. Remove from the heat, and arrange the scallops on a serving platter. Keep hot.

The sauce: Sprinkle the flour into the pan, stirring constantly. Add the bouillon. Bring just to a boil, stirring constantly; then lower the heat and simmer for five minutes. Remove from the heat, and add whatever juice has drained from the veal scallops onto the serving platter, as well as the remaining butter and the parsley.

To Serve: Pour the sauce over the veal. Serve very hot.

LAMB AND MUTTON

Mutton is the meat of sheep over a year old, whereas lamb is the meat of sheep less than a year old. The two terms are confused today, since many butchers (and restaurants) label mutton as lamb with the notion that this makes the consumer believe the meat is more tender.

GALIMAFREE   Taillevent 1373
    (Lamb Gallimaufry)

Gallimaufry means a jumbled mixture or a hash. Today the term is rarely used in French or English, and when it does appear, it is usually in a pejorative sense, as an unappetizing mixture of ingredients. In Taillevent's day, gallimaufries were often prepared and widely appreciated. They were always made with leftover meat or fowl, and their seasoning depended largely on what was at hand and the taste of the chef. Some unscrupulous chefs would "pad" the dish with food that would otherwise be unpresentable, thus giving rise to the dish's bad reputation. The following is a recipe for a gallimaufry at its best.

Ingredients (for 4 servings): 5 tablespoons butter. 3 medium onions, peeled and diced. 2 tablespoons lemon juice. 1 pinch ground ginger. Salt. Pepper. 2½ cups chopped or ground leftover leg of lamb. Croutons.

Cooking: Melt the butter in a large frying pan. Add the onions, lemon juice, ginger, salt and pepper. Simmer slowly for thirty minutes. At the end of this time, add the lamb. Cook for fifteen minutes longer.

To Serve: Serve very hot, with croutons.

RATONS DE MOUTON
(Stuffed Lamb Steaks)

Both the word *raton* and this way of preparing lamb have disappeared from books on French cooking. *Ratons* are similar to what are called *paupiettes* today, but the latter is made with veal while the former is made with lamb. Unfortunately, La Chapelle does not specify what kind of meat stuffing to use in these *ratons*, so the chicken filling given below was borrowed from one of his contemporaries.

INGREDIENTS

(for 4 servings)

4 slices leg of lamb (4 to 5 ounces each)
3 sprigs parsley, finely chopped
1 scallion, finely chopped
1 clove garlic, peeled and finely chopped
Juice of 1 lemon
3½ tablespoons olive oil
Salt
Pepper
1½ tablespoons butter
⅔ cup diced cooked chicken (white meat)
Nutmeg
1 cup bread crumbs
6 tablespoons bouillon
4 thin slices fatback (for barding)
3½ tablespoons dry white wine
2 tablespoons heavy cream

Marinating the meat
- Flatten the lamb steaks with a cleaver.
- Place the lamb in a bowl with the parsley, scallion, garlic, lemon juice, and oil. Sprinkle with salt and pepper.
- Marinate the lamb for two hours, stirring occasionally.

The chicken stuffing
- Melt the butter in a frying pan. Add the chicken and a pinch of nutmeg. Sauté over low heat for fifteen minutes. Sprinkle in the bread crumbs. Add the bouillon, and stir. Simmer for ten minutes.
- Pour this mixture into a bowl. Stir vigorously or pound in a mortar, in order to make a smooth purée. Drain off any surplus bouillon.

Cooking
- Remove the lamb from the marinade, and place one-quarter of the chicken stuffing on each slice of lamb.
- Roll the slices lengthwise. Wrap each *raton* in fatback, and tie string around them in several places so they will keep their shape and prevent the stuffing from coming out. Put each *raton* on a separate skewer or together on one long skewer.
- Add the wine to the marinade.
- Cook the *ratons* under the broiler for ten minutes, basting them often with the marinade. (Cook for a few minutes longer if you prefer lamb well done.)

To Serve
- Remove the dripping pan from the oven to allow its contents to settle; then spoon off the fat that rises to the surface. Add the cream to the remaining drippings. Stir well.
- Serve the *ratons* on their skewers with the cream sauce offered separately in a sauceboat.

SELLE DE MOUTON A LA BARBERINE

(Braised Lamb à la Barberini)

Barberini was the name of an influential Italian family in the seventeenth century. Several cardinals and one Pope were Barberinis, and the recipe was no doubt named in honor of one of the members of this family. Since fresh uncooked foie gras is rarely, if ever, available, only a few lucky gourmets can ever sample this luxurious dish prepared according to the original recipe. However, fresh goose liver, if available, or chicken livers can be substituted.

INGREDIENTS

(for 10 servings)

½ pound fresh lean bacon (unsalted and unsmoked)
1 large onion, peeled and sliced
6 hard-cooked eggs, peeled
3 sprigs parsley, finely chopped
1 scallion, finely chopped
1 sprig basil, finely chopped
3 shallots, peeled and finely chopped
¼ pound lard
¼ pound bone marrow, finely chopped
Salt
Pepper
Nutmeg
3 raw egg yolks
1 sirloin roast of lamb (5 to 5½ pounds)
8 anchovy fillets in oil, cut in half lengthwise
6½ ounces fresh foie gras (uncooked), cut into strips
1 large pig's caul (lace fat)
¼ pound fresh pork rind
2 carrots, scraped and sliced
1 sprig thyme
1 bay leaf
¾ cup dry white wine
3 tablespoons bouillon

Preparing the ingredients

- Cut the bacon into thin strips one inch long.
- Cut the onion slices in half.
- Remove the yolks from the hard-cooked eggs. (Discard the whites, or use them in a salad.)
- Mix the parsley, scallion, basil, shallots, lard, bone marrow, and egg yolks. Stir all these ingredients together, or work them with the hands into a homogeneous mixture. Add salt, pepper, and a pinch of nutmeg. Mix thoroughly; then stir in the raw egg yolks.

Cooking

- Using a small sharp knife, make incisions in the lamb and insert the strips of bacon. Continue making incisions, and insert the anchovies, onion, and foie gras in the same way. Cover the meat with the mixed ingredients described above, and wrap the meat in the pig's caul.
- Place the pork rind, carrots, thyme, and bay leaf in a large cast-iron pot. Pour in the wine.
- Place the lamb in the pot. Cover the pot, and cook in a moderate oven (375°) for one hour and forty-five minutes.

To Serve

- Remove the lamb from the pot , and place on a serving platter.
- Allow the liquid in the pot to sit for a few minutes so that the fat will rise to the surface. Spoon off the fat.
- Add the bouillon to the sauce; then serve in a sauceboat at the same time as the meat.

"Rôtisserie Rivoli"

FILET D'AGNEAU A LA CONDE

(Roast Lamb with Lemon Butter à la Condé)

Many of the early recipes appearing in this book were named after princely families or powerful individuals who loved good food and banqueting. The Condé family became famous in the seventeenth century for the splendor and refinement that characterized the formal dinners they sponsored. Their name has since been linked with several now-classic French dishes that were no doubt served for the first time at one of the Condés' receptions. Both a dessert made with rice and apricots and a thick red bean soup are still called *à la Condé* in cookbooks today. Although this recipe was written almost fifty years after the family's influence began to dwindle, it was no doubt inspired by a similar dish once invented for this noble family or simply named in honor of these famous gourmets.

INGREDIENTS

(for 10 servings)

6 French vinegar pickles
   (cornichons)
20 anchovy fillets in oil
2 loin roasts of lamb, boned
2 hard-cooked eggs
¼ pound fresh button mushrooms,
   finely chopped
2 sprigs parsley, finely chopped
1 scallion, finely chopped
4 shallots, peeled and chopped
2 cups bread crumbs
2 tablespoons capers
Salt
Pepper
4 teaspoons olive oil
¾ cup soft butter
2 pig's cauls (lace fat)
Juice of 4 lemons
Nutmeg

Preparing the lamb

- Slice the pickles lengthwise into four pieces.
- Using a larding needle or a small knife, insert the pickles and the anchovy fillets into the lamb.
- Separate the yolks from the whites of the hard-cooked eggs.
- In a bowl, combine the mushrooms, parsley, scallion, shallots, one-half of the bread crumbs, the hard-cooked egg yolks, capers, salt, pepper, oil, and half the butter. Mix all the ingredients well until a homogeneous paste is formed.
- Spread this mixture over the lamb, and then wrap each roast in a pig's caul.

Cooking

- Cook the meat under a hot broiler, allowing eight minutes per pound of meat (longer if you prefer lamb well done).
- Turn the meat frequently as it cooks. When the roasts are almost done, sprinkle them with the remaining bread crumbs, and baste with their drippings. Continue cooking for another two minutes per pound before removing the lamb from the oven.

To Serve

- Mix the lemon juice with the remaining butter. Add a pinch of nutmeg. (If desired, the two hard-cooked egg whites can also be worked into the butter with the prongs of a fork.)
- Place the lamb on a serving platter, and cut it into slices. Top each slice with the lemon butter, and serve.

''Régence-Plazza''

The French name for this dish has led to a number of misconceptions about the ingredients used in this stew. Today *haricot* means bean, and it is common to find Haricot de mouton served in French restaurants as a white bean and lamb stew. Sometimes French cooks serve the meat with potatoes and onions instead of white beans, but it is rare to find this dish prepared, as it should be, in the traditional way—with turnips. Both white beans and potatoes were foods that were brought to Europe from South America, and both were only gradually admitted to French kitchens. The turnip, on the other hand, is a native European vegetable that was used in cooking for centuries before the discovery of America.

In the Middle Ages the word *halicoter* meant to cut things into small pieces. At that time a *haricot* was almost any stew made of chopped meat and vegetables. The term was finally applied to one of the more popular stews—lamb and turnip—and eventually was used to designate this dish. Unfortunately, when white beans were given the name *haricot* and the old verb *(halicoter)* disappeared from the language, the character of the dish changed. And when potatoes began to replace turnips as a common garden vegetable, the ingredients of the dish changed once more. The following recipe is for the authentic Haricot de mouton made with turnips—vastly superior to either of the counterfeit versions common today.

INGREDIENTS

(for 6 servings)

3 pounds breast of lamb
2 ounces beef suet
2 ounces bone marrow
3 sprigs parsley
1 scallion
1 sprig basil
1 clove garlic, peeled
1 sprig thyme
1 bay leaf
2 cloves
8 cups bouillon (approximately)
Salt
Pepper
1 pound turnips
1 tablespoon flour

The lamb

- Cut the lamb into pieces about two inches square. Melt the suet and the bone marrow in a cast-iron pot.
- Place the pieces of lamb in the hot fat, and brown on all sides.
- Make a bouquet garni by tying the parsley, scallion, basil, garlic, thyme, and bay leaf together. Stick the cloves into the scallion or garlic. (These ingredients can be tied in a small piece of cheesecloth instead of being tied together.)
- Add just enough bouillon to cover the meat. Season to taste with salt and pepper.
- Cover tightly, and cook over low heat for two hours.

The turnips

- When the lamb has cooked for one hour, peel the turnips; then cut them into quarters or thick slices. Cover with cold water, and boil for ten minutes. Drain.
- Take two cups of the cooking liquid from the pot in which the lamb is cooking, and spoon off the fat which rises to the surface.
- Add the turnips to this bouillon, and cook for thirty-five minutes.
- Mix the flour with a tablespoon of the lamb's cooking liquid; then stir this thickener into the pot with the turnips. Simmer for ten minutes more.

To Serve

- Place the pieces of lamb in a serving dish.
- Pour the turnips and their cooking liquid over the lamb, and serve immediately.

It is believed by some authorities that Ninon, a French playwright who died in 1706, invented this dish. It is possible that he did, although he probably never entered the kitchen. Gentlemen, at that time, usually "invented" dishes by giving new instructions to their cooks.

INGREDIENTS

(for 12 servings)

Salt
Nutmeg
Pepper
Cumin (optional)
Mint (optional)
¼ pound fatback with rind removed
1 leg of lamb (6½ pounds)
3 cloves garlic, peeled
4 shallots, peeled
3 sprigs parsley
1 scallion
Several small sprigs basil
3 cloves
1 sprig thyme
1 bay leaf
6 tablespoons olive oil
1½ cups dry white wine

Preparing the lamb

- On a platter, sprinkle a large pinch of salt, a pinch of nutmeg, a pinch of pepper, and any other seasoning that you like, such as cumin or mint. Mix well.
- Cut the fatback into long, thin strips, and roll them in the spices. Using a larding needle or small knife, insert the strips of fat into the lamb.

Marinating the lamb

- Cut each clove of garlic and each shallot into three or four pieces. Place in a deep earthenware platter with the parsley, scallion, basil, cloves, thyme, bay leaf, and oil.
- Place the lamb in this mixture, and marinate for twenty-four hours, turning often.

Cooking

- Add the wine to the marinade. (Be careful not to pour any of it directly onto the lamb, which must be coated only with oil if it is to brown properly.) Add salt and pepper.
- Place the platter in a very hot oven (475°). Cook for nine minutes per pound if you like your lamb rare, or ten minutes if you prefer it somewhat better done. Baste the meat with the marinade as it cooks.

To Serve

- Remove the leg of lamb from the platter in which it cooked, and place it on a serving platter.
- Spoon off the excess fat from the sauce remaining in the roasting platter.
- Pour the sauce into a bowl, and serve with the lamb.

"L'Espadon"

A leg of lamb, such as this one, was always roasted on a spit over an open fire. Today few people have the large fireplaces (or spits) that were once common in every kitchen. Good results can be obtained by roasting the meat in a hot oven; the waxed paper keeps the meat from drying out, and the juices that accumulate inside it should be added to the sauce.

INGREDIENTS

(for 12 servings)

1 leg of lamb (5½ to 6½ pounds)
4 cloves garlic, peeled and finely
    chopped
4 shallots, peeled and finely chopped
3 sprigs parsley, finely chopped
1 scallion, finely chopped
½ pound fresh button mushrooms,
    finely chopped
1 sprig thyme
1 bay leaf
Salt
Pepper
1 pinch ground basil

Preparing the lamb

- Detach the thin layer of skin that covers the outside of the meat. Pull it back toward the smaller end of the leg without tearing it.
- Cut the meat into very thin slices, but be very careful not to cut to the bone, for the slices must remain attached to the leg of lamb. Cut as many slices as you can—the original recipe calls for a hundred slices, but it is not necessary to count.

The stuffing

- Mix the garlic, shallots, parsley, scallion, and mushrooms together. Sprinkle in the leaves from the thyme and a crumbled bay leaf. Add salt, pepper, and the basil.

Cooking

- Place a little stuffing between each slice in the leg of lamb. Pull the skin back into place.
- Wrap the leg of lamb in a sheet of waxed paper. Grease the outside of the paper lightly, and place the meat on an open rack for roasting.
- Roast the lamb in a very hot oven (475°), allowing ten minutes per pound. Add an extra ten minutes to the total cooking time if you like lamb well done.
- Remove the waxed paper, reserving the juices collected inside to add to the sauce.

To Serve

- Serve the lamb on a large platter with a shallot sauce (see Poitrine de mouton, page 178) or a lemon sauce offered separately.

"Maxim's"

COUS DE MOUTON A LA PUREE DE LENTILLES

(Mutton Neck with Lentil Purée)

Lamb or mutton necks are rarely used in cooking in the United States. In Ireland, however, the neck is frequently cut into pieces and used in Irish stew, as well as many other dishes. Even in France mutton necks are usually sliced and stewed, but rarely served whole. This unusual recipe should encourage American cooks to experiment with this excellent cut of meat (generally inexpensive), and they will immediately discover why it is so popular in Europe.

INGREDIENTS

(for 4 servings)

4 carrots, scraped and sliced
4 medium onions, peeled and sliced
3 sprigs parsley
1 scallion
2 sprigs thyme
2 bay leaves
2 cloves
1½ pounds thinly sliced fatback
  (for barding)
2 necks of mutton or lamb
Bouillon (to cover the meat), plus 4
  cups for the lentils
½ pound lentils
1 medium onion, peeled and stuck
  with 1 clove
Salt
Pepper
6½ tablespoons butter
1 cup bread crumbs (approximately)
Dijon mustard

Preparing the mutton

- Place three-quarters of the carrots, the sliced onions, the parsley, and scallion in a pot along with one sprig of the thyme, one of the bay leaves, and cloves.
- Wrap enough barding fat around each of the necks to cover them. Tie the fat to the meat. Place the necks in the pot with the vegetables. Add bouillon to cover; then cover the pot, and simmer slowly for four hours.

The lentil purée

- If "young" lentils are used, they need not be soaked, but older lentils should be left in cold water for three to four hours before cooking. Wash the lentils; place in a pot with four cups of cold bouillon.
- Add the remaining carrot, thyme, and bay leaf, the onion stuck with a clove, salt, and pepper. Bring to a boil. Skim off the foam, and simmer for one hour, or until the lentils are soft.
- Remove the thyme, bay leaf, and onion with clove. Purée the lentils in a food mill or blender. Pour the purée into a bowl. Add half the butter and four tablespoons of the liquid from the pot in which the meat is cooking.

The final cooking

- Remove the necks from the pot. Discard the slices of barding fat. Sprinkle the meat with salt and pepper.
- Melt the remaining butter in a saucepan. Spread the melted butter over the necks. Roll the necks in the bread crumbs. Broil the necks for three to four minutes on each side.

To Serve

- Spread the lentil purée in a serving platter. Place the broiled necks on the purée.
- Serve with Dijon mustard.

"Le Bistrot de Paris"

COTELETTES DE MOUTON A LA SOUBISE

(Lamb Chops à la Soubise)

The Prince de Soubise (1715–1787) was very fond of onions, and several onion preparations bear his name—garniture Soubise, purée Soubise, etc. Beauvilliers (1754–1817) was the chef to the Count de Provence, and he no doubt invented this dish when the Prince de Soubise was an honored dinner guest at his patron's table. When Beauvilliers later opened a restaurant in the center of Paris, this dish became one of his most popular specialties. It has now become one of the standard preparations in classic French cooking.

INGREDIENTS

(for 6 servings)

¼ pound fatback (for larding)
¼ pound ham
6 two-rib lamb chops
3 pounds medium onions
¼ pound butter
2 carrots, scraped and finely chopped
3 sprigs parsley, finely chopped
1 scallion, finely chopped
Bouillon (to cover the meat), plus 2 cups for the onions
6 very thin slices fatback (for barding)
2 tablespoons flour
Salt
Pepper
6 tablespoons heavy cream

The chops

- Cut the fatback for larding into small strips (lardoons). Cut the ham into small cubes. Using a larding needle or small knife, insert both the fatback strips and the ham into the chops.
- Peel and chop four of the onions. Melt three tablespoons of the butter in a cast-iron pot. Add the chopped onions, carrots, parsley, and scallion. Place the lamb chops on top of the vegetables.
- Add enough bouillon to cover. Place the slices of barding fat on top of the meat.
- Cover the pot, and cook in a very hot oven (475°) for fifteen minutes. (The meat should be very rare. The vegetables are used only to give taste and will not be sufficiently cooked to be served.)
- Peel the remaining onions. Boil them for five minutes. Drain and cool. Slice the onions; then put them in a frying pan with the remaining butter. Cook over moderate heat, but do not brown the onions. Sprinkle in the flour, and stir. Then add two cups of bouillon. Stir; then cover the pan. Cook slowly for forty-five minutes.
- When the onions are soft, grind them through a sieve or food mill. Add salt and pepper to taste. Then, away from the heat, add the cream.

The glaze

- Remove the chops from the pot in which they cooked. Strain the cooking liquid, and reduce it quickly over high heat until it becomes a dark glaze. (The meat should be glazed only at the last minute, when the onion purée is ready to serve.)

To Serve

- Place the chops in the glaze, and cook them over low heat for two minutes per side (they should be dark and shiny).
- Place the onion purée on a platter, and arrange the chops around it. Serve immediately.

GIGOT DE MOUTON DE 7 HEURES
(Seven-Hour Lamb)

Long, slow cooking is essential to this dish. It is a favorite in the Auvergne region of France, and Durand no doubt based his recipe on one of the traditional versions of this dish still popular in many rural parts of the country.

INGREDIENTS
(for 12 servings)

6 ounces fatback (for larding)
6 ounces country-style ham or prosciutto (for larding)
5 French vinegar pickles (cornichons)
1¾ ounces whole truffles (optional)
Salt
Pepper
2 sprigs thyme
2 bay leaves
1 leg of lamb (6½ pounds)
4 anchovy fillets in oil, cut in half lengthwise
4 to 6 very thin slices fatback (for barding)
4 slices ham or bacon
½ pound veal (any stewing cut), thinly sliced
2 carrots, scraped and sliced
3 medium onions, peeled and sliced
3 sprigs parsley
2 cloves
6 tablespoons dry white wine
6 tablespoons bouillon
Flour and water (to seal the pot)

Preparing the leg of lamb

- Cut the fatback into thin strips (lardoons). Cut the ham into thin strips. Quarter the pickles lengthwise. Cut the truffles into slices.
- Mix a pinch of salt and a pinch of pepper with the crumbled leaves from one sprig of the thyme and one crumbled bay leaf.
- Insert the slices of truffles into the meat. Using a larding needle or small knife, insert the fatback strips, the ham strips, the pickles, and anchovy fillets. Distribute these ingredients evenly throughout the meat.
- Rub the surface of the meat with the mixture of salt, pepper, thyme, and bay leaf.

Cooking

- Cover the bottom of a large cast-iron pot with the barding fat. Add the four slices of ham or bacon and the veal.
- Add the carrots, onions, the remaining thyme and bay leaf, parsley, and cloves.
- Place the leg of lamb in the pot, and add the wine and bouillon.
- Seal the lid of the pot hermetically with moistened flour (see Boeuf mode, page 138). Place in a very slow oven (250–275°) for seven hours.

To Serve

- Remove the leg of lamb to a serving platter. Strain the cooking liquid.
- Pour the liquid over the lamb, and serve.

"Le Grand Véfour"

COTELETTES DE MOUTON PANEES ET GRILLEES
(Grilled Mutton Chops)

Gouffé 1867

Either mutton or lamb chops can be used in this recipe. If mutton chops are chosen, a single rib per chop will be sufficient. If lamb chops are used, each chop should be the thickness of two ribs.

Ingredients (for 4 servings): 4 mutton or lamb chops. Salt. Pepper. 2 tablespoons butter. 1½ cups bread crumbs (approximately).

Preparing the chops: Sprinkle each chop on both sides with salt and pepper. Melt the butter very slowly in a frying pan. Do not allow the butter to brown. Dip each chop into the melted butter. Roll each in the bread crumbs.

Cooking: Place the chops on a broiler rack, and broil for four minutes on each side.

To Serve: Serve with a *sauce piquante* or garnished simply with a slice of lemon. A green salad is an excellent accompaniment.

POITRINE DE MOUTON
(Grilled Breast of Lamb with Shallot Sauce)

Alexandre Dumas 1873

In this recipe, Dumas says that the breast of lamb should be breaded and grilled without being boned. But when the meat is cooked, it will come away from the bones, and this spoils the appearance of the dish. So, despite Dumas' instructions, one might consider removing the bones from the breast of lamb before it is cooked.

Ingredients (for 4 servings): 2 pounds breast of lamb. 3 quarts cold water. 1 large onion, peeled and stuck with 2 cloves. 1 carrot, scraped. 1 bay leaf. 1 sprig thyme. Salt. Pepper. 8 shallots, peeled and finely chopped. 4 sprigs parsley, finely chopped. 2 tablespoons vinegar. 2 tablespoons butter. 1½ cups bread crumbs (approximately).

The first cooking of the lamb: Tie the lamb as you would a roast. Place it in a pot with the cold water. Place the onion and the carrot in the pot. Add the bay leaf, the thyme, and salt and pepper to taste. Bring to a boil, and skim off the foam. Lower the heat. Cover, and cook slowly for two hours. Remove the meat, and drain. (Reserve the cooking liquid.)

The shallot sauce: Place the shallots and parsley in a saucepan with the vinegar and three-quarters cup of the lamb's cooking liquid. Salt and pepper to taste. Simmer gently until the shallots are soft.

The final cooking: Cut the cooked lamb into pieces. Melt the butter slowly in a small frying pan; it should not brown. Dip the pieces of lamb into the melted butter; then roll them in the bread crumbs. Place the pieces of meat on a rack, and broil for four minutes on each side.

To Serve: Serve the lamb on a platter. Serve the sauce separately in a sauceboat.

PORK

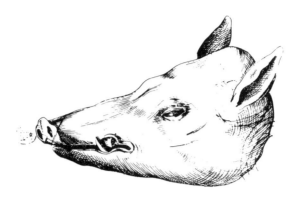

PORCELET FARCI
(Roast Suckling Pig with Chestnut Stuffing)

Ménagier de Paris 1392

Roast suckling pig was one of the most popular dishes in the Middle Ages. It is rarely prepared today except on festive occasions, and even then few cooks prepare it on a spit before an open fire. Pigs roasted in the oven never have the crisp, evenly browned skin which some consider the best part of the animal. In the days of the monarchy in France, some self-styled gourmets went so far as to say that the skin was the *only* part of the pig worth eating and patronizingly suggested giving the rest of the meat to the poor as charity! Few people today would agree—especially when the meat is prepared in the traditional manner described below.

Ingredients (for 20 servings): 1 suckling pig, 3 to 5 weeks old (11 to 15 pounds). ⅔ cup lard. 20 eggs. 50 chestnuts. ½ pound ham. ½ pound farmer's cheese or soft cream cheese. Salt. Pepper. Ground saffron. 1 teaspoon ground ginger. 6½ tablespoons butter. 6 tablespoons water.

Preparing the stuffing: (The pig should be prepared for cooking by the butcher, but save the liver, heart, and kidneys.) Clean the liver, heart, and kidneys thoroughly. Cut them into large cubes. Sauté them in a frying pan with one-third of the lard for three minutes. Remove from the heat. Boil the eggs for nine minutes. Cool them under running water, and peel. Separate the whites from the yolks. Use a sharp knife to peel off the outer skin of the chestnuts. Place the chestnuts in a pot. Cover them with cold water. Bring to a boil, and cook for ten seconds. Use a slotted spoon, and remove three or four hot chestnuts at a time. Rub each chestnut with a clean dish towel to remove the inner skin. Chop the egg yolks, chestnuts, and ham. Mix all these ingredients together with the cheese, then add them to the pan containing the fried viscera of the pig. Season with salt, pepper, a pinch or two of saffron, and the ginger.

Stuffing the pig: Stuff the pig, and sew it closed. Fold the hind legs under its thighs and its forelegs under its shoulders (it may be necessary to break the joints to do this). To hold the pig in this position, run skewers through the legs. Make light incisions in the skin of the head, shoulders, and thighs so that the skin will not burst during cooking. Run a large spit through the pig from head to tail.

Cooking: Rub the pig with the remaining lard. Place the butter and water in the dripping pan. Roast the pig over a medium fire for two hours, basting frequently. To test whether or not the meat is thoroughly cooked, insert a small skewer or long needle into one of the thighs. If the juice that flows from this cut is completely colorless, the meat is done. If it is even slightly pink, continue cooking. When the pig is done, the skin should be beautifully browned and crisp.

To Serve: Remove the pig from the spit. Separate the head from the body at the beginning of the shoulders. Next, remove the thighs and the shoulders, and cut them into pieces, leaving a section of skin with each piece. Then detach the ribs, cutting them at every second vertebra. Finally, cut off the ears, and split them in two. Arrange the meat on a large platter, and surround it with the stuffing. A sauce can be made from the drippings used to baste the pig. Add a little water to the drippings. Stir in any caramelized juices stuck to the dripping pan. Taste for seasoning. Bring to a boil, then serve the sauce in a sauceboat.

(Braised Ham in Wine)

Most hams sold today are precooked; they are never as flavorful as those you cook yourself. Unfortunately, "raw" hams (that is, hams that have been only cured and smoked) are often difficult to find and extremely expensive. Such hams are rarely cooked today because their price has become prohibitive, but once you have tasted a ham prepared as in the following recipe, you will certainly admit it was well worth the money.

INGREDIENTS

(for 15 servings)

1 country-style ham or prosciutto (8 to 11 pounds)
6 cups dry white wine
6 sprigs thyme
3 bay leaves
9 cloves
2 sprigs basil
½ calf's foot, cleaned (optional)
10 coriander seeds
10 peppercorns
½ lemon, quartered
Bouillon

Soaking the ham

- Place the ham in a large pot with cold water to cover. Soak the ham for twenty-four hours, changing the water frequently. This, obviously, is an average time. If the ham is old (ask the person who sells it), it is drier and saltier. In this event, an additional twelve or even twenty-four hours may be required to desalt it.
- When the soaking process has been completed, remove the ham from the water, and cut off the parts that are discolored or otherwise unsightly.

Preparations for cooking

- Place the ham in a large pot. Tie one end of a string around the narrow part of the ham, and attach the other end to the handle of the pot in such a way that the ham will not touch the bottom of the pot.
- Cover the ham with cold water. Add three cups of the wine, five sprigs of the thyme, two of the bay leaves, six of the cloves, and the basil. Bring just to a boil, then lower the heat, and simmer the meat slowly, allowing fifteen minutes cooking time per pound of ham.

Braising the ham

- Remove the ham from the pot. Cut off the rind. Place the calf's foot and half the rind from the ham on the bottom of an oval pot just large enough to hold the ham.
- Add the remaining thyme, bay leaf, and cloves, the coriander, peppercorns, and lemon. Place the ham in the pot. Pour in the remaining wine, then add enough bouillon to cover the ham. Place the remaining pieces of rind over the ham.
- Cover the pot, and cook in a moderate oven (350°), allowing six minutes cooking time per pound of ham. The ham is done when a long needle or skewer can be inserted into the thickest part, and withdrawn, without any resistance.

To Serve

- Remove the ham from the pot. Strain the cooking liquid, and pour it over the ham. Serve immediately if you prefer hot ham.
- If you want to serve the ham cold, let it remain in the pot with the strained liquid until it is barely warm. Remove it from the pot, and spoon the liquid over the ham frequently as it cools so that it will be evenly glazed when cold. (The ham can be decorated at this point, before the jelly sets.) Serve the ham and its jelly on an oval platter.

COCHON DE LAIT PAR QUARTIERS AU PÈRE DOUILLET
(Glazed Suckling Pig au Père Douillet)

This recipe appears in many seventeenth- and eighteenth-century cookbooks. It was probably invented by a priest (Père Douillet), as were many other then popular dishes that bear his name. Whatever its origin, this recipe demands both time and patience. It is typical of the elaborate ''centerpiece'' cookery that was popular in rich households 200 years ago.

INGREDIENTS

(for 20 servings)

4 carrots, scraped
1 turnip, peeled
4 leeks, cleaned
2 cloves garlic, peeled
1 medium onion, peeled and stuck
　　with 3 cloves
1 scallion
3 sprigs parsley
1 beef shank, crosscut
1 veal knuckle
2 calf's feet, split and cleaned
Salt
Pepper
Nutmeg
1 suckling pig (10 to 11 pounds)
2 cups dry white wine
4 large crayfish
6 egg whites (save the eggshells)
Juice of ½ lemon

The bouillon

- Place the carrots, turnip, leeks, garlic, onion, scallion, and two sprigs of the parsley in a large pot.
- Add the beef, veal, and calf's feet. Sprinkle in a little salt, pepper, and nutmeg. Add just enough water to cover the ingredients. Cover the pot, and simmer for four hours. Remove the vegetables and meat. Strain the bouillon.

Cooking the suckling pig

- Have the butcher cut the pig into five pieces (the head being one of the pieces). Put these pieces in a large pot, and pour the strained bouillon over them. Add the wine and a pinch of salt and pepper. Simmer for one hour and fifteen minutes.
- Wash the crayfish. Remove the intestines by pulling out the central fin of the tails. Add the crayfish to the pot, and cook for fifteen minutes longer.

The glaze

- Remove the pieces of pork and the crayfish from the pot. Allow the liquid to cool slightly so that the fat rises to the surface. Spoon off the fat, and put the pot back over low heat.
- Beat the egg whites and the shells together until stiff. (A blender will pulverize the shells very nicely.) Add the beaten egg whites and shells to the pot, along with the lemon juice. Cook for several minutes more, stirring constantly.
- Strain the contents of the pot through a clean cheesecloth.

Reconstituting the suckling pig

- Place two ladlefuls of the strained liquid on a platter large enough to hold the entire suckling pig. Let it cool and solidify. Chop the remaining parsley, and sprinkle it over this first layer of jelly. Place the five parts of the suckling pig onto the platter in such a way that the pig resumes its original shape. Arrange the crayfish on the pig's back.
- Spoon the rest of the glaze over the pig, and allow to cool for several hours.

To Serve

- Serve the pig on the platter, surrounded by the solidified jelly.

''Le Pactole''

The original recipe calls for the pot containing the meat to cook in cinders rather than in the oven as described here. It must be remembered that all eighteenth-century cooks worked over an open fire in a large fireplace. The hot ashes these large fires produced were often involved in cooking; a casserole would be literally buried in these ashes and left to cook slowly in their steady heat. This method of cooking disappeared only with the advent of "modern" stoves in the late nineteenth century.

INGREDIENTS

(for 4 servings)

3 tablespoons lard
3 sprigs parsley, finely chopped
1 scallion, finely chopped
¼ pound fresh button
    mushrooms, finely chopped
2 cloves garlic, peeled
    and finely chopped
4 top loin pork chops
4 slices country-style ham or
    prosciutto
¼ pound veal (any stewing
    cut), thinly sliced
Salt
Pepper
4 very thin slices fatback (for
    barding)
6 tablespoons dry white wine
Juice of 1 lemon
2 tablespoons heavy cream

Preparing the pork chops

- Melt the lard in a frying pan. Add the parsley, scallion, mushrooms, garlic, and pork chops.
- Cook all these ingredients quickly until they just begin to brown (the meat should not cook through).

Cooking

- Line a pot with the ham and veal. Add the pork chops and the herbs from the frying pan. Salt lightly, and add a little pepper.
- Place the strips of barding fat over the contents of the pot.
- Cover the pot, and cook in a moderate oven (375°) for twenty minutes. Remove the pot from the oven, and add the wine. Replace the lid, and continue cooking for another thirty minutes.

To Serve

- Remove the pork chops, and arrange them on a serving platter.
- Remove the strips of barding fat. Cut the slices of ham and veal into very small pieces, or remove them from the sauce as well. Away from the heat add the lemon juice and cream to the sauce.
- Pour the sauce over the meat, and serve immediately.

"Le Grand Véfour"

CARRES DE PORC EN COURONNE
(Stuffed Crown Pork Roast)

Onions are the traditional accompaniment to pork in French cooking. Usually, a sauce made with thinly sliced onions and seasoned with Dijon mustard is served with pork roast. Viard offers us a variation in his recipe which calls for small whole onions instead of the customary slices in the sauce. This makes for a prettier dish, especially when the roast is stuffed and crown-shaped as it is here.

INGREDIENTS

(for 12 servings)

1 ⅓ cups fresh bread crumbs
2 pounds sausage meat
4 eggs
Salt
Pepper
2 country-style pork rib roasts (6 ribs each)
6 ½ tablespoons butter
50 small white onions, peeled
2 tablespoons flour
⅔ cup dry white wine
6 tablespoons bouillon
1 tablespoon Dijon mustard

The stuffing

- Mix the bread crumbs with the sausage meat and eggs. Season with salt and pepper.

The meat

- Have the backbone removed from each rib roast. Cut between each of the ribs so that the roasts may be curved in a crown roast shape.
- Place the roasts in a baking dish or earthenware platter with the meaty side of each roast facing the other roast. Form a circle with the roasts; then tie string around this crown roast so it will not lose its shape.
- Place the stuffing in the center of the circle. Rub the pork all over with half the butter and some salt and pepper.
- Roast in a moderately hot oven (400°) for one hour and thirty minutes.

The onions

- Melt the remaining butter in a frying pan. Brown the onions lightly. Stir in the flour. Let the flour brown.
- Add the wine, and bring just to a boil, stirring constantly. Lower the heat, cover, and simmer the onions for one hour.
- Stir in the bouillon, and boil, uncovered, until the mixture thickens.

To Serve

- Just before serving, add the mustard to the onions, stirring until the sauce is well blended.
- Place the crown roast on a serving platter, or serve it in the dish in which it cooked. Serve some of the onions around the meat and the rest with their sauce in a bowl.

EMINCES DE COCHON A L'OIGNON

(Pork with Onions)

Viard's original recipe specified the use of madeira in the sauce. Sherry or any other sweet wine could be used just as well. In Viard's day, madeira was the only sweet dessert wine used to flavor sauces. Some extravagant cooks in the nineteenth century used several bottles of old madeira to prepare a single dish. Luckily for us, Viard was more prudent and calls for only one tablespoon of this expensive wine.

INGREDIENTS

(for 4 servings)

6 tablespoons vegetable oil
½ pound medium onions, peeled
   and thinly sliced
1 cup bouillon
1 teaspoon flour
1 tablespoon dry white madeira or
   sherry
Salt
Pepper
12 thin slices cooked pork roast
3 tablespoons butter
Several toasted croutons

Cooking

- Heat the oil in a frying pan. Add the onions, and cook until transparent. Drain.
- Place the onions in a pot with the bouillon, and simmer for ten minutes.
- Mix the flour with one tablespoon of the bouillon. Add this mixture to the pot with the onions, along with the madeira or sherry. Stir. Salt and pepper to taste. Simmer for ten minutes.
- Place the slices of pork in the pot, and continue to cook, over very low heat, for another ten minutes.

To Serve

- Before serving, add the butter to the pot, and stir in.
- Serve with toasted croutons.

COTELETTES DE COCHON EN CREPINETTES
(Pork Chops Wrapped in Onions)

As already noted, the French believe onions are the ideal accompaniment to fresh pork. One of the great beauties of French cuisine is that it can take an excellent combination like this and create recipe after recipe based on it—all of which are inventive and different. This particular recipe is a variant of the classic pork chop and onion sauce combination; the pig's caul (lace fat) gives a delicate, almost sweet taste to the onions, and the meat is all the tastier for having been cooked *wrapped* in the sauce.

INGREDIENTS

(for 6 servings)

¼ pound butter
30 small onions, peeled and
    thinly sliced
6 tablespoons bouillon
Salt
Pepper
6 pork chops
2 pig's cauls (lace fat), soaked for
    2 hours in warm water

The onions

- Melt 6 tablespoons of the butter in a large frying pan. Add the onions, and cook over low heat until soft. Do not let the onions brown.
- Add the bouillon, and boil rapidly until there is no liquid left. Grind the onions through a food mill, or mash them with a fork. Salt and pepper to taste. Set aside to cool.

The pork chops

- Melt the remaining butter in another frying pan. Add the pork chops. Brown them over moderate heat, six minutes on each side. Remove the pork chops from the pan. Set aside to cool.
- Remove the lace fat from the water, and squeeze as dry as possible. Carefully open them up, and spread them out on a clean table. Cut each one into three pieces.
- Place a layer of onions the size of a pork chop in the center of each piece of lace fat. Place a pork chop on each pile of onion. Cover each pork chop with a layer of onion.
- Wrap the pork chops in the lace fat, making sure that any holes are covered.

The final cooking

- Broil the pork chops (or fry them in a frying pan) three minutes on each side, or until the lace fat is nicely browned.

To Serve

- Serve very hot with a tomato sauce.

JAMBON A LA BROCHE
(Roast Ham with Wine Sauce)

A top-quality country-cured ham or a prosciutto ham is the only kind suitable for making this dish. You will have to start preparations two, three, or even four days ahead of time, depending on the age of the ham. In addition, two bottles of excellent red wine are crucial to the success of this dish. This may be enough to put off some cooks, but those who go ahead with this experiment will not regret it.

INGREDIENTS

(for 15 servings)

1 country-style ham or prosciutto (8 to 9 pounds)
6 cups dry red wine
1 large pig's caul (lace fat)
Pepper
Bread crumbs
1 medium carrot, scraped and diced
2 shallots, peeled and diced
1 small onion, peeled and diced
2 ounces fresh lean bacon (unsalted and unsmoked), diced
⅔ cup butter
3 tablespoons flour
1 cup bouillon
2 sprigs parsley
1 sprig thyme
½ bay leaf
3 juniper berries
6 peppercorns

Preparing the ham

- Remove the rind from the flat underside of the ham. Soak the ham in a large pot of cold water for twenty-four to forty-eight hours. During this period, change the water six or eight times. (Old hams need to be soaked longer—ask your butcher's advice.)
- After the ham has been soaked sufficiently, drain it, and put it in a large bowl. Pour the wine over the ham, and let it marinate another twenty-four hours, turning it over occasionally.

Cooking

- Wrap the ham in the lace fat. Place it on an open roasting tray, and cook in a hot oven (450°) for four hours.
- Add a little hot water and pepper to the drippings from the ham. Baste the ham frequently with this mixture.
- When the time is up, remove the ham from the oven. Take off the lace fat, and cut off the remaining rind. Rub the ham with bread crumbs, and return it to the oven until this crust begins to brown.

The sauce

- Place the carrot, shallots, onion, and bacon in a large saucepan with a third of the butter. Cook until the vegetables soften. Sprinkle in the flour, and stir. Add the bouillon, the wine used to marinate the ham, the parsley, thyme, and bay leaf. Simmer for forty minutes.
- Add the juniper berries and peppercorns. Simmer fifteen minutes longer. Remove the herbs, juniper berries, and peppercorns with a spoon. (The sauce can be ground through a sieve or in a food mill at this point, although this is not absolutely necessary.)
- Continue cooking over low heat for forty-five minutes, or until the remaining liquid equals approximately three cups. Taste for seasoning.
- Remove the saucepan from the heat, and add the remaining butter just before serving.

To Serve

- Serve the ham on a platter, and cut it into thin slices at the table.
- Serve the sauce in a separate dish.

''Le Taillevent''

ECHINE DE COCHON SAUCE POIVRADE

Viard 1820

(Pork Chops with Poivrade Sauce)

Although Viard's sauce is called a *poivrade* (pepper sauce), he does not say how much pepper it should contain. He simply says, "Add the pepper," perhaps assuming that his readers all knew the importance of this ingredient, given the sauce's name. In any case, freshly ground pepper is essential, or even better, whole peppercorns that have been coarsely crushed in a mortar can be used instead.

Ingredients (for 8 servings): 3 sprigs parsley. 10 scallions. 1 bay leaf. 1 sprig thyme. ¾ cup wine vinegar. 4 tablespoons butter. 1 large carrot, scraped and finely chopped. 1 large onion, peeled and finely chopped. 2 tablespoons flour. 2 cups bouillon. Salt. 2 pinches (or more) coarsely ground pepper. 8 pork chops. Vegetable oil.

The sauce: Put the parsley, scallions, bay leaf, and thyme in a pot with the vinegar and half the butter. Boil gently until half the liquid has evaporated. Strain out the seasonings. Melt the remaining butter in a saucepan. Add the carrot and onion. Cook over moderate heat for ten minutes, stirring occasionally. Sprinkle the flour over the onion and carrot, stirring constantly. Add the bouillon and the strained liquid prepared earlier. Cook slowly for one hour, stirring from time to time. Salt lightly, but add two large pinches (or more) of coarsely ground pepper just before serving the sauce.

The pork chops: Rub the pork chops with the oil. Broil them for a total of fifteen minutes, turning them over every five minutes. (If the chops are thick, add five minutes to the cooking time.)

To Serve: Arrange the pork chops on a platter, and cover with the sauce.

FILET DE PORC A LA SAUCE ROBERT

Gouffé 1867

(Braised Pork Roast with Onion Sauce)

Everything about this recipe is perfectly classic except for one thing—there is no Dijon mustard in the onion sauce. Gouffé adds a note to this recipe saying that he knew Sauce Robert *always* contained mustard, but since he knew that some people do not like mustard, he was not going to include it. He leaves the cook free to add it if "the guests" do not mind. The sauce is certainly good as described here, but if you "do not mind," adding a tablespoon of Dijon mustard just before serving could be considered an improvement.

Ingredients (for 10 servings): 1 boneless top loin pork roast (4 pounds). ½ pound coarse salt (approximately). 2 tablespoons butter. 4 cups bouillon. ¾ cup dry white wine. 1 bay leaf. 1 sprig thyme. 1 medium onion, peeled and stuck with 2 cloves. Pepper. 3 medium onions, peeled and diced. 2½ tablespoons flour. Salt.

Preparing the pork: Place the pork on a platter, and rub it all over with the coarse salt. Let it stand for two hours, turning it from time to time.

Cooking the pork: Remove the pork from the salt, and wipe it thoroughly. Melt one tablespoon of the butter in a pot. Add the pork, and brown on all sides. Add three-quarters cup of the bouillon, the wine, bay leaf, thyme, the onion stuck with cloves, and a little pepper. Cover the pot, and cook slowly for two hours. Turn the roast four times while cooking.

The sauce: Melt the remaining butter in a large pot. Add the diced onions. Cook slowly, stirring occasionally, until the onions begin to soften. Add the flour. Stir, and continue cooking for two minutes. Remove the pot from the heat, and add the remaining bouillon, a pinch of salt, and two pinches of pepper. Bring to a boil, stirring constantly. Lower the heat, and simmer for ten minutes. Keep warm until the pork is done. When the pork is cooked, add the liquid in which it cooked to the sauce. Cook the sauce five minutes, stirring frequently. Taste for seasoning.

To Serve: Pour the sauce into a deep platter, and place the pork in the sauce.

VARIETY MEATS AND CHARCUTERIE

FOIE DE VEAU FRICASSE
(Fricasseed Calf's Liver)

La Varenne 1651

Although capers are most frequently used today in fish cookery, they were once widely used in France to prepare meat and poultry dishes. The caper is the unopened bud of the caper plant *(Capparis spinosa)*. The plant grows in most tropical climates and some temperate countries, including France. The tiny buds are sorted according to size and pickled in strong vinegar. The smallest capers are generally considered the best. This recipe is an example of what was once the most common way of using capers—adding them to a sauce just before serving to impart a distinctive piquant flavor.

Ingredients (for 4 servings): 4 tablespoons butter. 2 medium onions, peeled and finely chopped. 4 slices calf's liver (4 ounces each). Salt. Pepper. 2 tablespoons wine vinegar. 1¼ cups bread crumbs. 2 tablespoons capers.

Cooking: Melt the butter in a large frying pan, and sauté the onions until golden brown. Push the onions toward the edges of the pan, and place the slices of liver in the pan. Cook the liver over low to medium heat for four minutes. Turn the slices, sprinkle with salt and pepper, and cook the second side for five minutes. (Do not cook the liver over too high a heat, or it will become tough.)

To Serve: Remove the liver from the frying pan, and arrange the slices on a platter. Return the onions to the center of the frying pan. Add the vinegar. Cook for two minutes. Add the bread crumbs and capers to the onions. Stir well. Pour over the liver, and serve.

CERVELLE DE VEAU AU PARMESAN ET A LA MOUTARDE

(Calf's Brain with Parmesan and Mustard)

The Greeks and Romans used mustard seeds in their stews and ground mustard on their roasts. Mustard seeds are never used in French cooking, and ground mustard is produced mainly in England. Prepared mustard, however, is a French specialty. Some people believe the secret of good French mustard is the high-quality wine vinegar employed in making it. The cities of Orléans and Dijon both claim to produce the finest mustard in France. In this recipe Dijon mustard is recommended, although any other hot French mustard would do as well.

Ingredients (for 6 servings): 2 calf's brains. 1 medium onion, peeled and stuck with 2 cloves. Juice of 1 lemon. Pinch of salt. 1 sprig thyme. 1 bay leaf. 4 cups cold water. 12 thin slices bread. 1⅔ cups freshly grated parmesan. ¼ pound butter. 3 tablespoons Dijon mustard.

The first cooking: Soak the calf's brains in a large bowl of cold water for two hours. Change the water five or six times. Place the onion, lemon juice, salt, thyme, and bay leaf in a pot. Add the water. Bring to a boil, and cook for thirty minutes. Remove the thyme and bay leaf, and allow the bouillon to cool. Place the brains in the cool bouillon. Bring back to a boil. As soon as the liquid begins to boil, remove the brains with a slotted spoon. Using a thin cloth, detach and carefully remove the membrane which covers the brains. Replace the brains in the bouillon, and simmer for twenty minutes. Drain carefully. Reserve the bouillon. Allow the brains to cool for ten minutes. Cut each brain into six slices of equal size.

The bread: Trim the slices of bread around the edges until they are approximately the same size as the slices of brain. Toast the bread under a medium broiler.

The final cooking: Crumble the bread trimmings, and add them to the cheese. Mix well. Melt the butter over low heat. Add the mustard and three tablespoons of the liquid in which the brains cooked. Place the toast on an ovenproof platter. Place a slice of brain on each slice of toast. Sprinkle with the butter and mustard mixture and then with the bread crumb and parmesan mixture. Place in a hot oven (450°) for ten minutes.

To Serve: Serve very hot with a mustard sauce and lemon wedges.

LANGUE DE BOEUF AUX CONCOMBRES

(Beef Tongue with Cucumbers)

Cucumbers are rarely cooked today, but they were frequently served in stews during the eighteenth century. European cucumbers are much longer than those grown in the United States, some reaching a length of almost two feet. (Recently this type of cucumber has been grown and marketed in the United States, although it is still not always available.) In France it is customary to remove the seeds from a cucumber before it is eaten in a salad or cooked because the seeds are particularly hard to digest. Sprinkling the cucumbers with salt an hour before cooking them is yet another way of making this vegetable more digestible.

Ingredients (for 10 servings): 1 beef tongue (4 to 4½ pounds). 4 medium onions, peeled. 4 cloves. 2 sprigs parsley. 1 sprig thyme. 1 bay leaf. ¼ pound fatback, with rind removed. 6 to 8 very thin slices fatback (for barding). 2 carrots, scraped and thinly sliced. 1 parsnip, peeled and thinly sliced. 1 sprig basil. Salt. Pepper. 3 pounds cucumbers. 3 tablespoons coarse salt. 2 tablespoons vinegar. 3 tablespoons lard. 2 tablespoons flour.

Preparing the tongue: Soak the tongue in a large bowl of cold water for two hours. Change the water three or four times. Remove the roots of the tongue if necessary. Insert one clove in two of the onions. Place the onions stuck with cloves in a pot with the parsley, thyme, bay leaf, and tongue. Cover with cold water. Bring to a boil. Skim off the foam, and cook for two hours. Remove the tongue from its bouillon, and strip away the white skin covering it. (Reserve the bouillon.) Cut the fatback into strips (lardoons) one-quarter inch on each side and two and a half to three inches long. With a larding needle or small knife, insert these strips into the tongue.

Braising: Finely chop the remaining onions. Line the bottom of an oblong pot with half the barding fat. Place the carrots and parsnip in the pot. Add the tongue, chopped onions, the remaining cloves, and basil. Sprinkle with salt and pepper. Cover with the remaining barding fat. Add one and two-thirds cups of the tongue's bouillon. Cover the pot tightly, and simmer for one hour.

The cucumbers: Peel the cucumbers, and cut them lengthwise into quarters. Remove the seeds; then cut the quarters into pieces two to three inches long. Sprinkle with the coarse salt and vinegar. Let stand for one hour. Drain carefully, and rinse. Pat dry with a cloth. Melt the lard in a saucepan or large frying pan. Add the cucumbers, and cook until they begin to brown. Sprinkle in the flour. Stir. Add three cups of the tongue's bouillon. Salt and pepper to taste. Cover, and cook over low heat for twenty-five minutes.

To Serve: Remove the tongue from the braising pot. Slice it, and arrange on a platter. Strain the braising liquid, and pour it over the tongue. Serve the cucumbers in a separate dish.

BOUDIN BLANC A LA BOURGEOISE
(Homemade White Sausage)

Menon 1746

The word *boudin* in French almost always refers to blood sausage, but *boudin blanc* is a completely different preparation made with milk, eggs, bread, and sometimes chicken or veal. The blood sausage is fatty, often hard to digest, and (in France) very inexpensive, while *boudin blanc* is delicate, light, and usually expensive when it contains chicken or veal. *Boudin blanc* is best simply grilled over hot coals, or under the broiler, and served with a fresh green vegetable like spinach or a salad.

Ingredients (for 8 servings): 2 cups milk. 8 cups fresh bread crumbs. 4 tablespoons butter. 12 small onions, peeled and finely chopped. ½ pound fatback, finely chopped. 6 egg yolks. 1 cup heavy cream. Salt. Pepper. Nutmeg. Sausage casings.

The stuffing: Bring the milk to a boil. Add the bread crumbs. Cook, stirring occasionally, until the bread has absorbed all the milk and the mixture is smooth. Let cool. Melt three tablespoons of the butter in a saucepan. Add the onions, and cook until soft. Do not allow the onions to brown. Add the fatback to the onions in the saucepan. When the onions are completely cooked and the fat has melted, add the bread and milk. Remove the saucepan from the heat. Mix the egg yolks with the cream, and add to the saucepan, along with salt, pepper, and a large pinch of nutmeg. Mix well.

The sausage: Cut the sausage casings into sections eight inches long. Tie off one end of each section. Using a funnel, fill each section three-quarters full of the stuffing. Tie the open end of the casing closed.

Cooking: Fill a large pot with water, and bring to a boil. Add the sausages. Lower the heat, and simmer for fifteen minutes. Remove the sausages with a slotted spoon. Cool under running water. Drain.

To Serve: Fry the sausages for about fifteen minutes in the remaining butter. They should be eaten very hot.

FROMAGE DE COCHON

Menon 1746

(Headcheese)

Headcheese is usually made by simply boiling a whole hog's head in highly aromatized water until the meat is completely cooked and comes easily away from the bones. The meat is then chopped and left to cool in a bowl with a little of the cooking liquid. Menon's version of this cold meat dish is more complicated since he bones and stuffs the head before cooking it. This requires both skill and luck because sewing the head back together is far from an easy task. Nevertheless, Menon's recipe gives beautiful results to cooks patient enough to follow it.

Ingredients (for 20 servings): 1 hog's head, cleaned (8½ pounds). 2 sprigs thyme. 2 bay leaves. 3 cloves. 10 coriander seeds. 10 white peppercorns. Salt. 2 cloves garlic, peeled and finely chopped. 4 shallots, peeled and finely chopped. 5 sprigs parsley, finely chopped. 5 basil leaves, finely chopped. ¼ nutmeg. 2 pounds lean country-style ham or prosciutto. 3 medium onions, peeled. 1 clove garlic, peeled. 4 cups dry white wine. Bouillon.

Preparing the head: Remove the ears, and put them aside. Bone the head, and cut all the meat off the skin. Be careful not to cut the skin while doing this. Sew the openings for the eyes closed, as well as any other holes. Cut the lean meat and ears into thin strips, and place them in a dish. Cut the fat into strips, and place it in a separate dish.

Preparing the cheese: Pound the leaves from one sprig of thyme, one bay leaf, the cloves, coriander seeds, and peppercorns in a mortar. Mix these ingredients with a pinch of salt and the chopped garlic, shallots, parsley, and basil leaves. Grate and add the nutmeg. Cut the ham into cubes. Place the skin from the head in a salad bowl. The inside of the skin should face upward. Arrange the meat and seasonings in layers on top of the skin in the following order: (1) the strips of lean meat and a few pieces of the ears; (2) the pieces of fat; (3) a few of the spices and ham cubes. Repeat until all the ingredients have been used. Sew the skin closed. Wrap it in cheesecloth. Tie the cheesecloth securely.

Cooking: Place the headcheese in a large pot. Add the onions, the whole clove of garlic, the remaining thyme and bay leaf, the wine, and enough bouillon to cover. Cover the pot with a tight-fitting lid, and cook over low heat for seven hours.

To Serve: Drain the headcheese, and remove the cheesecloth. Place the headcheese in a bowl. Cover it with a plate or board, and press under a heavy weight. Allow to cool for several hours. Remove the headcheese from the bowl. Place it on a serving platter, and cut it into slices.

FRAISE DE VEAU AU GRATIN DE GRUYERE

Cuisinière Républicaine 1795

(Calf's Ruffle with Gruyère)

The ruffle is the membrane which surrounds the intestines of a calf. Its name in both French and English reflects its resemblance to the large, stiffly pleated collar fashionable in the sixteenth century, which was called *fraise* in French and ruffle in English.

Ingredients (for 8 servings): 2 pounds calf's ruffle. 1 bay leaf. 2 sprigs thyme. Salt. 6 tablespoons flour. 6 medium onions, peeled and finely chopped. ⅔ cup butter. 1⅓ cups bouillon. 1 tablespoon vinegar. 3⅓ cups fresh bread crumbs. 1⅔ cups freshly grated gruyère. 2 eggs, beaten. Pepper. 8 slices bread.

Preparing the calf's ruffle: Place the ruffle in a large pot. Cover with cold water, and bring to a boil. Lower the heat, and poach for ten minutes. Drain, and cool under running water. Check to see that it is perfectly clean—remove any particles hidden between the folds. Put the ruffle in a pot with the bay leaf, thyme, and some salt. Cover with water. Mix four tablespoons of the flour with water until a smooth paste is formed, and pour into the pot. Bring to a boil, uncovered. Cook for two hours. Drain.

The cheese: Sauté the onions for ten minutes in a third of the butter. Do not allow the onions to brown. Sprinkle the remaining flour over the onions. Stir. Add the bouillon and vinegar. Simmer for ten minutes. Remove from the heat. Mix the onions, bread crumbs, cheese, and eggs. Add salt and pepper.

The final cooking: Butter an ovenproof dish. Cover the bottom of the dish with half of the cheese mixture. Cut the slices of bread into small strips. Fry in the remaining butter until brown on all sides. Cut the calf's ruffle into large pieces, and arrange on the cheese mixture in the dish. Place the fried bread around the ruffle. Cover with the remainder of the cheese mixture. Bake in a very hot oven (475°) for ten minutes.

To Serve: Serve piping hot on warm plates.

GRAS-DOUBLE EN CREPINETTES

(Honeycomb Tripe and Mushroom Patties)

Tripe is the inner muscular lining of the stomach of ruminant mammals. Honeycomb tripe, from the stomach of beef, is considered the best. If you cannot buy tripe precooked (it is often sold this way in France), simmer it slowly in water for four hours before using it in the following recipe.

Ingredients (for 6 servings): 1¾ pounds cooked honeycomb tripe, coarsely chopped. 1 pound fresh button mushrooms, coarsely chopped. 2 cloves garlic, peeled and coarsely chopped. ½ pound fatback (remove the rind), coarsely chopped. 3 cups fresh bread crumbs. 2 egg yolks. Salt. Pepper. Nutmeg. 1 pig's caul (lace fat).

The stuffing: Mix the tripe, mushrooms, garlic, and fatback with the bread crumbs and egg yolks. Season with salt and pepper to taste and a little nutmeg.

Cooking: Cut the lace fat into six equal pieces. Divide the stuffing into six portions, and place one portion on each piece of lace fat. Fold the lace fat over the stuffing, and flatten with the palm of the hand. Broil or grill the patties, allowing eight minutes per side.

To Serve: Serve very hot, accompanied by a sauce of your choice. Viard suggests a tomato sauce, but Poivrade Sauce (see Echine de cochon sauce poivrade, page 194) goes very well with this dish.

PIEDS DE MOUTON A LA POULETTE

(Lamb's Trotters with Mushroom Sauce)

We apparently live in an era when sheep are born without feet. At least it is difficult nowadays to buy lamb's trotters, although they can be obtained in some butcher shops on special order.

Ingredients (for 6 servings): 7 tablespoons flour. 1 medium onion, peeled and stuck with 1 clove. 3 sprigs parsley. Salt. 1 sprig thyme. 1 bay leaf. 3 tablespoons lard. 3 tablespoons vinegar. 12 lamb's trotters, scalded and boned. ½ pound fresh button mushrooms. 6 tablespoons water. Juice of 2 lemons. ¼ cup butter. 2 cups bouillon. Pepper. 3 egg yolks.

Cooking the trotters: Mix four tablespoons of the flour with water until a smooth, thin paste is formed. Pour into a large pot about half full of water. Bring the water to a boil, stirring constantly. Add the onion and one sprig of parsley to the pot. Add a pinch of salt, the thyme, bay leaf, lard, and vinegar. Put the trotters in the pot. Cover the pot, but leave a small opening for steam to escape. Simmer for four hours.

The sauce: Place the mushrooms, water, the juice of one lemon, and half the butter in a saucepan. Cook over high heat for five minutes, stirring occasionally. Melt the remaining butter in a separate saucepan. Add the remaining flour. Stir until smooth. Add the bouillon. Bring to a boil, stirring constantly; then simmer for ten minutes. Add salt and pepper. Chop the remaining parsley, and add to the sauce along with the juice of the remaining lemon. Add the mushrooms and their liquid as well. Remove the saucepan from the heat, and stir in the egg yolks.

To Serve: Drain the trotters, and arrange them on a serving platter. Cover with the sauce.

SAUTE DE RIS DE VEAU

(Sautéed Calf's Sweetbread)

Viard 1820

Sweetbread is the soft, milky thymus gland usually from a calf, lamb, or young pig. Calf's sweetbread is highly prized and has long been considered a delicacy in Europe. Sweetbreads were often used in stuffings for fowl or mixed with a cream sauce to stuff pastry shells in the eighteenth century. Today they are usually served alone, as in this recipe, but since fresh sweetbreads are expensive, the portions tend to be small. By the end of their cooking time the sweetbreads should be extremely soft—in France they are traditionally eaten with a spoon.

Ingredients (for 8 servings): 2 pounds calf's sweetbreads. 6½ tablespoons butter. Salt. Pepper.

Preparing the sweetbreads: Soak the sweetbreads for several hours in a large bowl of cold water. Change the water four or five times. Place the sweetbreads in a saucepan. Add enough water to cover. Bring to a boil, and cook for five minutes. Remove the sweetbreads with a slotted spoon. Rinse them under cold running water; then drain thoroughly. Remove any fat or skin.

Sautéing: Slowly melt the butter in a frying pan. Cut the sweetbreads into slices about one-half inch thick. Salt and pepper each slice. Brown the sweetbreads ten minutes on each side.

To Serve: Arrange the sweetbread slices around the edge of a platter. Place a stewed vegetable of your choice in the center of the platter. Serve immediately.

TETE DE VEAU A LA TORTUE

(Mock Turtle Stew)

Viard 1820

This elaborate preparation is a French version of an English specialty. Anything British, even certain foods, was considered fashionable in France during the nineteenth century. For many years a mock turtle stew was considered *the* dish to serve at formal banquets. Today calf's head is still popular in France, but recipes like this one have all but been forgotten—a fact lamented by many gourmets.

Ingredients (for 12 servings): ½ calf's head, with tongue and brain. 1 lemon, cut in half. 6½ tablespoons flour. 2 carrots, scraped and thinly sliced. 2 medium onions, peeled and coarsely chopped. 2 lemons, peeled, seeded, and quartered. 6 peppercorns. 1 bay leaf. 2 sprigs thyme. 1 clove. Salt. ⅔ cup butter. 1 medium onion, peeled and stuck with 1 clove. 3 tablespoons lard. 3 cups dry madeira. 12 very thin slices fatback (for barding). ½ pound small fresh button mushrooms. 8 French vinegar pickles (cornichons), sliced into rounds. 10 capers. 12 crayfish. 12 hard-cooked eggs, peeled and quartered.

Preparing the calf's head: Soak the calf's head for two hours in cold water. Change the water three or four times. Remove the brain, and set aside. Place the tongue and the calf's head in a large pot. Pour in enough cold water to cover, and bring to a boil. Skim off the foam. After six minutes, drain the head and rinse under cold water. Wipe dry; then rub with the cut lemon. Mix three and a half tablespoons of the flour with cold water until a smooth, thin paste is formed. Pour into the emptied and rinsed pot. Add three quarts cold water, half the carrots, half the chopped onions, half the quartered lemons, the peppercorns, one-half bay leaf, one sprig of thyme, the clove, and some salt. Bring to a boil. When the water begins to boil, add one-third of the butter; then put the tongue in the water. Cover the pot, but leave an opening at one side of the lid. Cook for one hour. Add the head, and continue cooking for thirty minutes longer. While the head is cooking, clean the brain. Place the onion stuck with a clove in a pot with two cups of water, one-quarter bay leaf, one-half sprig thyme, and a pinch of salt. Bring to a boil. Lower the heat, and put the brain into the water. Cover, and simmer for twenty minutes.

Cooking: In a third pot, melt the lard over low heat, along with half the remaining butter, one-quarter bay leaf, several thyme leaves, the remaining carrots, chopped onions, and lemon quarters. Brown lightly; then add one-quarter of the madeira and one cup of the liquid in which the tongue and head were cooked. Lift the calf's head out of its pot, and cut into pieces. Place six slices of barding fat on a piece of cheesecloth. Lay the pieces of calf's head on the barding fat; then cover the head with the rest of the barding fat. Close the cheesecloth, and tie both ends with string. Place this package in the pot. Cover and simmer for one hour to one and a half hours.

The stew: Melt the remaining butter in another pot. Add the remaining flour, three-quarters cup of the liquid in which the head and tongue were cooked, and the remaining madeira. Add the mushrooms, pickles, and capers. Simmer for twenty-five minutes. Remove the intestines from the crayfish by pulling out the central fin of their tails. Add the crayfish to the stew. Drain the tongue, skin it, and cut it into slices. Cut the brain in two. Place the tongue, brain, and eggs in the stew, and cook for eight minutes.

To Serve: Remove the calf's head from its pot. Remove the cheesecloth and the barding fat. Arrange the pieces of calf's head on a platter, and cover with the stew.

ANDOUILLE A LA BECHAMEL
Viard 1820
(Pork Sausage Béchamel)

Chitterlings, the small intestine of the pig, are normally the main ingredient in *andouille* sausages. This recipe is a variant of the traditional preparation, since calf's ruffle (see page 198) is used instead of chitterlings and a white sauce is mixed with the meat before the sausages are formed. This is completely unorthodox, but delicious nevertheless.

Ingredients (for 8 servings): 1½ tablespoons butter. 3 shallots, peeled and coarsely chopped. 1 clove garlic, peeled and coarsely chopped. 4 sprigs parsley. 1 sprig basil. 1 slice prosciutto or 2 slices bacon. 2 sprigs thyme. 2 bay leaves. 4 cups heavy cream. 4 cups crumbled stale bread. 1 pound calf's ruffle, precooked. 2 pounds lean pork. ½ pound fatback. ½ pound fresh lean bacon (unsalted and unsmoked). 6 egg yolks. Salt. Pepper. Nutmeg. Sausage casings, cut into 8-inch pieces. 4 cups milk. 4 cups bouillon.

The Béchamel: Melt the butter in a saucepan. Add the shallots, garlic, parsley, basil, prosciutto or bacon, one sprig of thyme, and one bay leaf. Cook, without browning, for fifteen minutes. Add the cream. Let half of the mixture evaporate without bringing it to a full boil. Remove the thyme and bay leaf; then grind the rest of the ingredients through a food mill. Add the bread to the mixture. Return to the saucepan. Simmer, stirring occasionally, until the bread has absorbed all the liquid.

The meats: Cut the calf's ruffle, pork, fatback, and fresh bacon into small, very thin strips. Stir these ingredients into the Béchamel. Away from the heat, stir in the egg yolks. Add salt, pepper, and a pinch of nutmeg.

Cooking: Tie off one end of each of the pieces of sausage casing; then stuff them with the meat mixture. (If the skins are very thin, use two for each sausage, one inside the other.) Tie off the open end. In a saucepan, mix the milk with the bouillon. Add the remaining thyme and bay leaf. Bring to a boil. Add the sausages, and simmer for two hours. Remove from the heat, and let the sausages cool in the liquid.

To Serve: Prick each of the sausages in several places with a pin or small skewer; then broil or grill them eight minutes per side. Serve very hot.

PATE DE JAMBON
(Ham Pâté)

French cooks still mix black pepper, nutmeg, cloves, and ginger to make their own *quatre-épice* (four-spice mixture). This mixture is now prepared commercially and is often confused with allspice (the dried berry of the allspice tree). The allspice berry gets its name from the fact that its taste does indeed resemble that of the four-spice mixture, but it is not the same thing. To make your own four-spice mixture, combine one tablespoon ground pepper, one-quarter teaspoon ground clove, three-quarters teaspoon ground ginger, and one teaspoon grated nutmeg. Use it in stews and pâtés such as the one described here.

Ingredients (for 10 servings): 1¼ pounds cooked ham. 1 pound fatback. 1½ pounds round roast of veal. 4 sprigs parsley, finely chopped. 2 eggs. Salt. Pepper. 1 large pinch four-spice mixture (see above). Truffle parings. 1 pound very thinly sliced fatback (for barding). 1 sprig thyme. 1 bay leaf. Flour.

Preparing the ham: Remove the rind from the ham, and discard. Remove the fat, and cut it into thin strips. Cut the lean part of the ham into slices, each about one-quarter inch thick.

Preparing the veal: Cut a third of the fatback into strips about the size of the little finger. Using a larding needle or small knife, insert these lardoons into the veal. Cut the veal into scallops about the same thickness as the slices of ham.

The stuffing: Finely chop a little less than half of the veal and the remaining fatback, or run them through a meat grinder. Mix with the parsley, eggs, salt, pepper, mixed spices, and truffle parings. If the parings are canned, add some of the juice from the can to the stuffing.

The pâté: Line the bottom and sides of an earthenware pâté mold (terrine) with strips of barding fat. Make a layer of stuffing, then a layer of veal with a little ham fat, then a layer of ham. Begin again with the stuffing, veal, and so on, ending with a layer of stuffing. Cover with strips of barding fat. Crumble the thyme and bay leaf over the top of the pâté.

Cooking: Cover the terrine and seal hermetically with a paste made of flour and water. (see Boeuf mode, page 138.) Bake in a moderate oven (350°) for three hours.

To Serve: As soon as the pâté comes from the oven, remove the top, and cover the pâté with a plate or board which fits inside the opening of the mold. Place a clean two-pound weight on the plate, and leave until the pâté is cold. Remove the weight, plate, and excess fat. Cover and chill the pâté before serving.

ROGNONS DE BOEUF SAUTES
(Sautéed Beef Kidneys)

Beef, veal, lamb, and pork kidneys all are marketed in France. Veal and lamb kidneys are generally considered the best, but both beef and pork kidneys have their admirers. Although beef kidneys tend to be tough, Gouffé's method of cooking them in wine helps make them tender and more appetizing. For those who prefer, any of the other kidneys mentioned can be substituted for beef kidneys and prepared in the same way.

Ingredients (for 4 servings): 1¾ pounds beef kidneys. 7 tablespoons butter. Salt. Pepper. 1⅓ cups dry white wine. 2½ tablespoons flour. 6 tablespoons bouillon. 6 tablespoons water. 4 sprigs parsley, chopped.

Preparing the kidneys: Cut the kidneys in half, lengthwise. With a small, sharp knife, remove all the white interior parts. Melt the butter in a frying pan. Place the kidneys in the pan, and sprinkle with salt and pepper. Cook over medium heat for six minutes, turning three or four times. Remove from the frying pan.

The sauce: Pour the wine into a saucepan. Add salt and pepper. Bring to a boil, and cook until half the liquid has evaporated. Put the kidneys back in the frying pan. Sprinkle the flour over them, and sauté for twelve minutes on each side. Pour the wine over the kidneys. Add the bouillon and water. Simmer, without boiling, for one minute.

To Serve: Place the kidney halves on a serving platter. Add the parsley to the sauce. Pour the sauce over the kidneys, and serve.

TERRINE DE FOIES DE CANARDS

Cuisinier Durand 1830

(Duck Liver Terrine)

This terrine will keep for several days (actually, it is often better the day after it is made). However, if it is to be eaten immediately, spoon off as much fat as you can as soon as it comes from the oven and replace the fat by several tablespoons of chicken consommé. Allow the consommé to gel before serving. If duck livers are unavailable, chicken livers will do as well.

Ingredients (for 12 servings): 1½ pounds duck livers. 1½ pounds fresh bacon (unsalted and unsmoked). 1½ pounds cooked ham. 3 sprigs parsley, chopped. 3 tablespoons butter. 2 egg yolks. Salt. Pepper. Four-spice mixture (see introduction to Pâté de jambon, page 202) or allspice. 1 truffle (3 ounces). 1 pound very thinly sliced fatback (for barding). Flour.

Preparing the livers: Wash and trim the livers. Place them in a saucepan of cold water, and heat over low heat. Just before the water comes to a boil, remove the livers with a slotted spoon. Cool the livers under running water. Drain them, and chop.

Preparing the stuffing: Cut the fresh bacon and ham into slices; then chop. Mix with the parsley. Melt the butter in a frying pan. Sauté the meat and parsley mixture over high heat for two minutes. Remove from the heat. Add the egg yolks, salt, pepper, and a pinch of four-spice mixture or allspice.

Cooking: If you have a fresh truffle, brush it clean under running water. Cut the truffle into thin slices. Line the bottom and sides of an earthenware pâté mold (terrine) with strips of barding fat. Place a few slices of truffle at the bottom of the terrine. Make a layer of stuffing, then a layer of liver. Begin again with the truffle, making successive layers until about one inch from the top of the mold. Cover with strips of barding fat. Seal the lid hermetically by using a paste made of flour and water (see Boeuf mode, page 138). Bake in a hot oven (425°) for one hour.

To Serve: As soon as the terrine comes from the oven, remove the top, and place a clean plate or board directly on top of the pâté. Set a clean two-pound weight on the plate, and leave the terrine for several hours to cool completely. Remove the plate, weight, and excess fat. Chill the terrine before serving.

SAUCISSES AU VIN BLANC

Gouffé 1867

(Sausages in White Wine Sauce)

Gouffé does not specify what kind of sausage to use in this recipe, but any top-quality boiling sausage is acceptable. Most French boiling sausages are unsmoked and relatively mild (like breakfast sausages). A mild sausage is preferable, so that its flavor will not overpower that of the wine sauce.

Ingredients (for 4 servings): 4 pork sausages. ¾ cup dry white wine. Pepper. 4 teaspoons butter. 1 tablespoon flour. 6 tablespoons bouillon. 1 egg yolk. 4 sprigs parsley, finely chopped.

Cooking the sausages: Place the sausages in a frying pan with the wine and two pinches of pepper. Cover, and cook for eight minutes. Keep hot.

The sauce: Melt two teaspoons of the butter in a saucepan. Add the flour. Stir over low heat for two minutes. Add the bouillon, and continue cooking for ten minutes, stirring frequently. Away from the heat, add the remaining butter and the egg yolk. Remove the sausages from the frying pan, and arrange them on a serving platter. Pour the sausages' cooking liquid into the saucepan. Place over low heat for four minutes. Do not boil. Away from the heat, add the chopped parsley.

To Serve: Pour the sauce over the sausages, and serve.

Poultry and Game

The history of poultry and game on French tables reflects both changing taste and changing situations. In the Middle Ages, for example, game was abundant, but not everyone could eat it. Most of what was called "noble game" was limited to the large estates of the rich, and animals such as deer, boar, and grouse were exclusively reserved for the upper classes. On the other hand, "small game," such as hares, rabbits, partridges, etc., were available to almost everyone—provided that he had skill enough to kill one. Pigeons (squabs) were bred especially for the rich, and birds such as herons, storks, swans, and peacocks were favored by cooks preparing sumptuous banquets. Peacocks were especially in demand, since it was customary (with other birds as well) to remove all the feathers before the bird was cooked and replace them over the cooked meat so that the bird would appear in all its spectacular plumage when brought to the table.

During the Renaissance several "new" foods made their first appearance on French tables. Poulardes and capons (specially fattened, desexed chickens) were bred for the rich, and turkeys, imported from America, were introduced into France, where they were enthusiastically received but were so expensive that only the very rich could afford them. The guinea hen (which had been eaten by the ancient Romans but never served in France) was imported from its native Africa, and such oddities as crow stew or roast raven were popular in Renaissance households. The porcupine, dormouse, and bear were not disdained, and a famous pâté made of badger was considered a great delicacy.

The poultry industry in France began to flourish in the seventeenth century. The cities of Bresse, Le Mans, Caen, and Rouen became famous for the chickens and ducks raised there. Chicken became cheaper and consequently lost much of its appeal for the rich gourmets of the period, who believed that only expensive and exotic birds were fit for their elaborate feasts. Of course, the poorer classes welcomed this situation, and chicken fricassee became the emblem of family cooking for generations to follow. Turkey (perhaps because of its continued rarity) was more popular than ever, and rabbits suddenly surpassed both geese and ducks in popularity. Wild boar and deer (mostly made into pâtés) continued to be reserved for the rich, and pheasants, peacocks, and swans continued to ornament richly served tables.

When the eighteenth century began, new trends were established that have come down to us today. The decorative peacock disappeared from the table (it was never considered a particularly tasty bird); ducks, pheasants, quail, and doves became the most popular game birds; and turkeys were bred on a larger scale. Oddities such as badger, porcupine, stork, and dormouse disappeared forever, and large game, though still food of the upper classes, began to lose its once important place on banquet menus.

The French Revolution in 1789 marked the beginning of the modern era, and the private game reserves of the rich were finally opened to all who wished to hunt them. During the nineteenth century, game of all kinds were sold for the first time in open markets throughout France, and chicken, turkey, ducks, and geese were found on almost every table.

It must be remembered that most of the cookbooks written before the nineteenth century were intended for well-to-do households, and many of the preparations that follow were tasted only by the rich landowners of the past. Nevertheless, such "homely" dishes as chicken fricassee were to appear in almost every old cookbook, perhaps because their appeal was universal.

Among the recipes that follow, a few, for example those that call for songbirds, are merely culinary curiosities for Americans (it is illegal to kill these birds). Others use game that is virtually impossible to obtain in the United States. However, they are included not only for their historical interest, but because they are still representative of a certain kind of French cooking. Cooks today are generally in a better position to execute most of these recipes than cooks in the past. Frozen foods and fast transport have made previously "exotic" products widely available. It is no longer a question of who has the right to certain foods, but a question of who has the talent and skill to prepare them. These recipes give us a glimpse of how past masters of French cuisine handled the preparation of poultry and game.

FOIE GRAS CUIT DANS LES CENDRES

La Varenne 1651

(Baked Foie Gras)

Foie gras is the name for the specially fattened liver of either a duck or a goose. The bird is force-fed for several months before it is slaughtered with the result that its liver swells to three or four times the normal size. This process has been employed since Roman times and is periodically denounced by animal lovers and defended by gourmets. Foie gras de oie (fattened goose liver) is extremely expensive, even in France, and La Varenne's recipe was no doubt devised for one of the princely households in which he worked since few ordinary people then, or now, could afford the amount of fresh foie gras he calls for here.

Ingredients (for 8 servings): 1 fresh foie gras (approximately 1¾ pounds). 4 or 5 sheets waxed paper. Lard. 1 clove. ¼ bay leaf. 5 or 6 thyme leaves. 5 to 6 peppercorns. Salt. 1 pound very thinly sliced fatback (for barding).

Cleaning the foie gras: Remove any parts of the liver which may have been stained green by the gallbladder, as well as any fibers or skin.

The waxed paper: Generously grease the waxed paper on both sides with lard.

Cooking: Pound the clove, bay leaf, thyme, peppercorns, and one pinch of salt in a mortar until reduced to a fine powder. Sprinkle half this mixture over the goose liver; then wrap the liver in the strips of barding fat. Sprinkle the remaining spices over the liver. Wrap the liver in the sheets of waxed paper. In order to keep the juices from leaking out, alternate the directions of the paper, wrapping the first sheet lengthwise, the second crosswise, and so on. Bury the package in very hot cinders of a fireplace, or bake in a hot oven (425°) for one hour.

To Serve: Remove the package from the cinders. Remove the first sheet of waxed paper. Place the foie gras, still wrapped in the other sheets of paper, on a dish. Then gently remove two or three more sheets, leaving only one sheet around the foie gras. Open the final sheet, but do not remove it, when serving.

FRICASSEE DE POULET

Bonnefons 1654

(Chicken Fricassee)

Chicken fricassee was once so popular in France that distinguished chefs refused to prepare it in the belief that the dish was too ''common'' for refined taste. The popularity of this dish started to decline in the nineteenth century, and it seldom appears on restaurant menus today. Nevertheless, it continues to be popular outside France, where it is often transformed to suit foreign taste and rarely prepared in the traditional manner described in this recipe.

Ingredients (for 6 servings): 6½ tablespoons lard. 1 chicken (3 pounds). 1⅔ cups water. ¾ cup dry white wine. 6 sprigs parsley. 3 scallions. Peel of ½ lemon. Salt. Pepper. 1½ tablespoons butter. ½ pound small fresh button mushrooms. ¾ cup heavy cream.

Cooking: Melt the lard in a frying pan over low heat. Cut the chicken into twelve pieces: two wings, two thighs, two drumsticks, two breasts, four sections of back. Brown on all sides in the melted lard for ten minutes. Add the water and wine. Tie three sprigs of the parsley, the scallions, and the lemon peel together, making a bouquet garni. Add this bouquet to the chicken. Salt and pepper to taste; then cover and simmer for forty-five minutes. Melt the butter in another frying pan over medium heat. Add the mushrooms, and sauté for seven to eight minutes, or until all the water given out has evaporated and the mushrooms begin to brown. Fifteen minutes before the chicken is done, add the mushrooms.

To Serve: Remove the pieces of chicken from the saucepan, and arrange them on a serving platter. Remove the bouquet garni from the sauce, and discard. Away from the heat, stir the cream into the sauce. Chop the remaining parsley. Pour the sauce over the chicken, and sprinkle with the chopped parsley. Serve piping hot.

CANARD EN RAGOUT

(Duck Stew)

Bonnefons 1654

A ragout is a stew, and duck stews are still popular in France, although they are seldom prepared like this one created by Bonnefons more than 300 years ago. The sweetbread, artichokes, and mushrooms he calls for are a far more interesting accompaniment for duck than the turnips or green peas that so frequently appear with duck stews in France today.

Ingredients (for 6 servings): 1 calf's sweetbread (1¾ to 2 pounds). 6 medium artichokes. 1 lemon, cut in half. Juice of 1 lemon. ¼ pound fatback with the rind removed. 10½ ounces fresh button mushrooms. 1 bouquet of herbs: parsley, scallion, chervil, and tarragon. 1 duck (3 to 4 pounds), with liver, heart, and gizzard. 1⅓ cups dry white wine. Salt. Pepper. 6 ½ tablespoons butter. 1 tablespoon vinegar.

The stew: Soak the sweetbread for three hours in a large bowl of cold water. Change the water five or six times. Drain the sweetbread, and place it in a large pot. Pour in enough water to cover. Bring to a boil over low heat. Boil for two minutes; then drain. Cool the sweetbread under running water. Remove all the skin and bits of fat on the sweetbread; then cut it into slices about two inches thick. Remove the stems from the artichokes. Cut off all the leaves around the meaty part of the base. Lay each artichoke on its side, and cut the leaves off, about one and a half inches from the base. Rub the artichoke bottoms with half a lemon. Scoop out the choke with a spoon. Fill a pot with cold water, and add the lemon juice and artichoke bottoms. Bring to a boil; then lower the heat, and simmer for thirty minutes. Drain and cut each bottom into eight sections. Cut the fatback into small strips. Place the fatback, the slices of sweetbread, the mushrooms, artichoke bottoms, herbs, and the liver, heart, and gizzard of the duck in a saucepan. Cook over very low heat for ten minutes, stirring occasionally. Add the wine, salt, and pepper. Cover the saucepan, and simmer for thirty-five minutes.

The duck: Cover the entire duck with five tablespoons of the butter. Sprinkle with salt and pepper. Place on a rack in an open roasting pan, and cook in a hot oven (450°) for fifteen to twenty minutes per pound. Melt the remaining butter in a small saucepan, and add the vinegar. Baste the duck frequently with this mixture and with the pan juices. Do not overcook the duck—the meat should be slightly pink when served.

To Serve: The duck may be served in either of two ways: (1) Place the duck on a serving platter. Pour the stew around it and serve. (2) Place the duck on a platter, and cut it into eight to ten pieces. Add it to the stew, along with any juices left in the platter. Boil gently, uncovered, for five minutes; then serve.

CHEVREUIL

(Venison in Wine Sauce)

Pierre de Lune 1656

Chevreuil is a roe deer, a small, graceful species of deer common in Europe. Since it is not available in the United States, except on occasion in frozen form at gourmet markets, venison may be substituted. Traditionally, venison is hung for a week, then marinated before it is cooked. In this recipe, the meat is not marinated; it might therefore be preferable to limit the aging process to no more than three or four days.

Ingredients (for 6 servings): 3 ounces fatback. 2 pounds boned shoulder of venison. 5 tablespoons lard. 3 sprigs parsley. 2 sprigs chervil. 1 sprig thyme. Several chives. 1 bay leaf. 2 cloves. Salt. Pepper. Nutmeg. ¼ lime. 6 tablespoons bouillon. 6 tablespoons dry white wine. 1 tablespoon flour. Juice of 1 lemon. 1 tablespoon capers.

Preparing the venison: Cut one thin slice from the fatback, and reserve. Lard the venison with the rest of the fatback cut into strips (lardoons) one-quarter inch on each side and one and a half inches long. Melt three tablespoons of the lard in a large pot. Brown the venison eight minutes on each side over medium heat. Remove the meat from the pot.

The sauce: Wrap the parsley, chervil, thyme, chives, and bay leaf in the strip of fatback reserved earlier. Tie with string, and stick the cloves into the fatback. Place in the pot in which the meat browned. Add some salt and pepper, a little nutmeg, and the lime. Pour in the bouillon and wine. Cook for ten minutes. Remove the bouquet of herbs and the lime.

Cooking: Melt the remaining lard in a frying pan. Stir in the flour. Add several tablespoons of the sauce; then pour this mixture into the pot, stirring constantly. Place the venison back in the pot. Cover, and simmer for one hour, or until done.

To Serve: Slice the venison, and arrange on a serving platter. Away from the heat, add the lemon juice and capers to the sauce. Pour the sauce over the venison, and serve.

INGREDIENTS

(for 10 to 12 servings)

6 cups flour
2 ½ teaspoons salt
1 pound soft butter in pieces (for
 dough)
¾ cup cold water (approximately)
1 pheasant (1 ¾ to 2 pounds)
1 chicken (2 ½ pounds)
1 calf's sweetbread (1 ¼ pounds)
1 bouquet of herbs (parsley, chervil,
 chives, tarragon)
1 ¼ pounds fresh button
 mushrooms
6 tablespoons butter
2 lemons
½ pound round roast of veal
6 ½ ounces ham
1 pound fatback
Salt
Pepper
1 egg, lightly beaten
1 shallot, peeled and chopped
¾ cup dry white wine
1 tablespoon flour
2 tablespoons heavy cream

The pastry dough

- Mix the flour and salt in a bowl. Add the soft butter, mixing it in with the tips of the fingers. Add the water, little by little. The dough should be soft but not sticky. Divide the dough into pieces, and flatten each one with the palm of the hand. Press the pieces together into a ball. Repeat this procedure. Place the dough in a bowl. Cover with a cloth, and let stand for twelve hours in a cool place.

Preparing the stuffing

- Lightly butter the skins of the pheasant and chicken. Roast them in a hot oven (425°) for twenty-five minutes. (The birds should not be completely cooked.)
- Soak and poach the sweetbread as described in the recipe for Canard en ragoût, page 207. Remove the skin and any fat.
- Simmer the herbs and half the mushrooms over low heat for five minutes, with two tablespoons of the butter and the juice of one lemon.

The stuffing

- Remove all the meat from the pheasant and chicken. Chop, along with the veal, ham, fatback, sweetbread, herbs, and mushrooms. Add some salt and pepper.

Cooking

- Roll out the dough into a rectangle about one-half inch thick, with the edges slightly thinner. Arrange the stuffing lengthwise in the center of the dough. Then fold the dough over the stuffing. Dampen and pinch the edges of the dough to seal them.
- Using a basting brush, paint the surface of the dough with the beaten egg to glaze it. With an apple corer or knife, make a small hole in the upper surface of the dough, and insert a hollow two-inch-high cylinder (''chimney'') of aluminum foil into the hole.
- Butter a cookie sheet, and place the pâté on it.
- Bake in a moderate oven (375°) for one hour and thirty minutes.

The sauce

- Pound the carcass of the pheasant in a mortar. Place the carcass in a pot with the shallot and wine. Simmer for one hour.
- Simmer the remaining mushrooms for ten minutes, with three tablespoons of the butter and the juice of one lemon. Purée the mushrooms.
- Strain the wine. Measure—there should be one-half cup. If not, add water to it.
- In a small saucepan, over low heat, make a roux using the remaining butter and one tablespoon of flour. Add the wine, and salt and pepper to taste.
- Add the puréed mushrooms. Remove from the heat, and stir in the cream.

To Serve

- As soon as you take the pâté from the oven, remove the ''chimney,'' and pour the sauce into the hole in the crust—gradually, so that it does not overflow.
- Serve very hot.

''Le Clos du Moulin''

POULARDE AUX OLIVES

(Chicken Stewed with Olives)

A poularde is a spayed hen, the female counterpart of the capon. Like the capon, its flesh is considered tastier than that of ordinary chickens, but few producers go to the trouble to raise birds this way today. (An ordinary chicken can be used in this recipe if a poularde is unavailable.) This dish is typical of seventeenth- and eighteenth-century taste. At that time olives, anchovies, and capers were often served with meat as well as fish. The quantity of olives used in this particular recipe can be increased (even tripled) without detracting from the taste of the chicken.

INGREDIENTS

(for 8 servings)

1 poularde or chicken (3 to 3½ pounds, with heart, liver, and gizzard
½ pound thinly sliced fatback (for barding)
¼ pound fresh bacon (unsalted and unsmoked), diced
4 sprigs parsley
3 scallions
4 anchovy fillets in oil
1 tablespoon capers
24 green olives, pitted
1 sprig thyme
½ bay leaf
1 tablespoon olive oil
1 tablespoon flour
2 tablespoons bouillon
¾ cup dry white wine
Juice of 1 orange

Roasting the chicken

- Truss the fowl, and cover the breast with strips of barding fat. Tie them on with string.
- Roast for one hour in a hot oven (425°).

The stew

- Melt the fresh bacon over low heat in a saucepan.
- Chop the parsley, scallions, anchovies, capers, olives, and the heart, liver, and gizzard of the chicken together.
- Add all these ingredients, along with the thyme, bay leaf, and olive oil, to the bacon. Sauté over medium heat for ten minutes.
- Sprinkle in the flour. Stir. Add the bouillon and wine. Simmer covered, until the chicken is done.

The final cooking

- Remove the chicken from the oven, and cut it into ten pieces: two drumsticks, two thighs, two breasts, two wings, and the back cut into two pieces.
- Place the chicken pieces in the stew, and cook for ten minutes. Turn the pieces, and cook for ten minutes more.

To Serve

- Remove the chicken from the stew, and arrange on a serving dish.
- Stir the orange juice into the stew; then pour the stew over the chicken.
- Serve very hot.

The thrush was the most popular bird eaten in ancient Greece, but young people were not allowed to eat it for fear that its exquisite flavor might give birth to premature greediness! These birds were equally popular in ancient Rome, where patrician ladies raised them as a hobby and some Roman gourmets ate themselves into bankruptcy because of their inordinate love for the taste of this particular bird. To this day thrush is a favorite food in both France and Italy. The birds are often stuffed and roasted, as in La Chapelle's recipe, or made into pâtés which are considered great delicacies in France. Although many species of thrush occur in the United States, it is illegal to trap, net, or kill them, and thus, this dish cannot be savored by Americans. However, small, young pigeons can be substituted, though the flavor of the dish would then, of course, be different.

INGREDIENTS

(for 4 servings)

1 carrot, scraped and sliced
1 parsnip or small rutabaga, peeled and sliced
1 medium onion, peeled and sliced
1 slice ham, diced
10 ½ ounces veal knuckle, diced
2 cups bouillon
4 hard-cooked egg yolks
1 cup chopped cooked chicken breasts
10 blanched almonds, chopped
3 ½ cups fresh bread crumbs
1 pinch ground coriander seeds
4 thrushes
16 juniper berries
6 ½ tablespoons butter
4 thin strips fatback (for barding)
Juice of 1 lemon
Salt
Pepper

The sauce

- Place the carrot, parsnip or rutabaga, onion, ham, and veal in a saucepan. Add six tablespoons of the bouillon. Cover, and cook over very low heat for thirty minutes. Do not allow to brown.
- Add the remaining bouillon; then replace the lid, and simmer gently for one hour.
- Mix the egg yolks, chicken, almonds, and bread crumbs. Stir vigorously until the mixture is homogeneous.
- When the bouillon has finished cooking, remove the saucepan from the heat. Strain out the meat and vegetables, and discard. To the bouillon add the coriander seeds and the mixture of chicken, almonds, and bread crumbs. Stir well.

The birds

- Pluck and clean the birds if necessary. Remove the gallbladder and any greenish parts from the liver. Replace the livers inside the birds.
- Parboil the juniper berries for five minutes. Mash four of the berries; then mix with the butter. Stuff each of the birds with a quarter of this mixture. Cross the legs of each bird, and stick its beak into its breast. Wrap each bird in a strip of barding fat.
- String all four birds on a long skewer, going through them sidewise. Wrap the birds and skewer in greased waxed paper, allowing only the ends of the skewer to protrude.

Cooking

- Place the skewer on a spit or under a hot broiler. Cook for ten to fifteen minutes, turning frequently.
- Place the sauce over low heat. Add the lemon juice and the remaining juniper berries. Salt and pepper to taste.
- Unwrap the birds. Remove them from the skewer, and remove the barding fat. Simmer the birds in the sauce for five minutes.

To Serve

- Arrange the birds on a platter.
- Serve the sauce in a sauceboat.

''Lucas-Carton''

POULARDE EN MOUSSELINE
(Stuffed Chicken Casserole)

The simplicity and refinement of this dish would make it appear that no improvements could be made in it. Nevertheless, a famous chef (Alexandre Dumaine) who was a contemporary of Marin's prepared a very similar dish (he changed the stuffing) based on the principles employed here but with one difference. Before putting the chicken in to cook for eight hours, he placed a small tripod in the casserole so that the chicken would cook entirely in the steam of the bouillon rather than in the bouillon itself. The result was, of course, delicious, but Marin's method is excellent as well. What is most important is that the casserole be well sealed so that none of the juices escape and that the bird cooks slowly to ensure a perfect result.

INGREDIENTS
(for 10 servings)

1 chicken (3 ½ to 4 pounds), with
    heart, liver, and gizzard
4 sprigs parsley, chopped
2 scallions, chopped
8 shallots, peeled and chopped
6 ounces fresh foie gras
6 ounces bone marrow
2 egg yolks
Salt
Pepper
6 tablespoons chicken bouillon
Flour

The stuffing

- Chop the heart, liver, and gizzard of the chicken. Mix with the parsley, scallions, and shallots. Add the foie gras, bone marrow, egg yolks, salt, and pepper. Mix well.

Cooking

- Sew the opening at the neck of the chicken closed. Stuff the chicken. Sew the opening at the tail closed.
- Wrap the chicken in a piece of buttered cheesecloth.
- Place the chicken in an earthenware or cast-iron casserole. Add the bouillon. Seal the lid shut with a mixture of flour and water (see Boeuf mode, page 138).
- Cook in a slow oven (275°) for eight hours.

To Serve

- Lift the chicken out of the casserole.
- Carefully remove the cheesecloth. Replace the chicken in the casserole, and serve.

"Taillevent"

The author of this recipe specified that the juice of a bigarade orange was to be used in this dish. The bigarade, or Seville orange, is sometimes called the sour or bitter orange because its taste is so different from that of sweet oranges. It was, up until the sixteenth century, the only orange known to Europeans and was extensively used in cooking because of its pleasantly acid flavor. If bigarade oranges are not available, add the juice of half a lemon to the juice of half a sweet orange, and use this mixture instead.

INGREDIENTS

(for 8 servings)

2 young rabbits (2 pounds each),
   skinned and cleaned
6 sprigs parsley, chopped
3 scallions, chopped
½ pound fresh bacon (unsalted and
   unsmoked), chopped
½ pound bone marrow, chopped
Leaves from 2 sprigs savory
2 egg yolks
Salt
Pepper
6 ½ tablespoons butter
Several large, very thin slices
   prosciutto or country-style ham
Several thin slices bread
2 large pig's cauls (lace fat)
Juice of 1 bigarade (Seville orange)
   or juice of ½ sweet orange, plus
   juice of ½ lemon

The stuffing

- Chop the livers of the rabbits, and mix with the parsley, scallions, fresh bacon, and bone marrow.
- Add the savory and egg yolks. Salt and pepper generously. Mix well.

Cooking the rabbits

- Stuff each rabbit with half the stuffing mixture. Place the forepaws into the opening at the breast, and sew the rabbit closed. Sew the hind paws along the length of the body.
- Melt the butter in a frying pan, and brown the rabbits on all sides.
- Wrap each rabbit in slices of ham—only the heads should protrude.
- Arrange the slices of bread around the rabbits so that they form a layer over the ham. Hold the bread in place by wrapping each rabbit entirely in lace fat.
- Place the rabbits on a broiler rack, and broil under medium heat for one hour, turning frequently.

To Serve

- Remove the lace fat. Cut the rabbits into pieces, along with the ham and bread.
- Sprinkle the orange juice over the rabbits, and serve.

"Le Pactole"

There is a widespread misconception that hares are not available in the United States. Actually, however, most undomesticated American rabbits (such as the jackrabbit) are hares. Obtaining a hare is not therefore an overwhelming problem for American cooks. The problem lies in obtaining the hare's blood, one of the basic ingredients of this stew. Once rabbits (or hares) were sold alive in city markets. In those days rabbit blood obviously came with the rabbit, but now (unless you trap your own rabbit) the animal is sold skinned and cleaned, and the blood (which thickens and flavors the sauce) is almost impossible to procure. This recipe is ideal for those occasions when a freshly killed rabbit (more specifically a hare) is to be had and can be cooked, blood and all, in this traditional manner.

INGREDIENTS

(for 8 servings)

1 hare, skinned (3½ pounds), with
    blood and liver
3 cups dry red wine
Vegetable oil
1 sprig basil
2 medium onions, peeled and sliced
1 cup wine vinegar
4 cloves
2 bay leaves
2 sprigs thyme
6 tablespoons olive oil
½ pound fresh slab bacon (unsalted
    and unsmoked)
3 ½ tablespoons butter
12 small onions, peeled
Salt
Pepper
1 medium onion, peeled and stuck
    with 2 cloves
4 tablespoons flour
1 cup bouillon
Fried croutons

The hare

- Clean the hare, and reserve the blood in a bowl. Add three tablespoons of the wine to the blood.
- Place the liver of the hare in another bowl, and pour in enough vegetable oil to cover.

The marinade

- Place the basil and sliced onions in a bowl. Add the vinegar, cloves, one bay leaf, one sprig thyme, and the olive oil. Marinate the hare in this mixture for several hours, turning occasionally.

Browning the hare

- Remove the hare from the marinade, and wipe dry. Place on an open rack, and roast in a very hot oven (475°) for ten to fifteen minutes, or until golden brown. The purpose is not to cook the animal, but simply to brown it lightly on the surface.

Cooking the hare

- Remove the rind from the fresh bacon, and cut it into three or four pieces. Cut the bacon itself into large cubes.
- Melt the butter in a large pot. Add the pieces of rind and the cubes of bacon. Brown over low heat.
- Remove the bacon from the pot, and reserve. Place the small onions in the pot in which the bacon cooked.
- Remove the hare from the oven, and cut it into ten to twelve pieces. As soon as the onions have become transparent, place the pieces of hare in the pot. Add the reserved bacon, along with the remaining bay leaf and thyme, salt and pepper to taste, and the onion stuck with cloves.
- Sprinkle in the flour, and stir. When the flour browns, stir in the remaining wine and the bouillon.
- Cover the pot, and place in a slow oven (325°) to cook for two hours.

To Serve

- Remove the pieces of hare from the pot, and arrange them in a serving dish. Keep hot.
- Cut the liver into slices, and put them in the pot in which the hare cooked. Poach for three minutes; then add to the hare.
- Remove the thyme, bay leaf, and onion stuck with cloves from the pot. Away from the heat, pour the reserved blood into the sauce, stirring vigorously with a whisk.
- Pour the sauce over the hare, and serve with fried croutons.

POULET AU PERSIL

Marin 1739

(Roast Chicken with Herb Butter)

Marin says to remove the entire skin from the chicken, to spread herb butter over the meat, and then to replace the skin. This laborious process can be replaced by a traditional Chinese method (used in preparing duck), which consists of blowing air between the skin and the meat, then placing the herb butter into the opening. Admittedly, either approach requires skill and patience, but the result is well worth the effort.

Ingredients (for 4 servings): 8 sprigs parsley, finely chopped (for the stuffing). 1 small bunch chives, finely chopped. 8 shallots, peeled and chopped. ⅔ cup soft butter. Salt. Pepper. 1 egg yolk. 1 chicken (3 to 3½ pounds). 1 tablespoon flour. 3 sprigs parsley, chopped (for the sauce). ½ cup water (approximately).

The herb butter: Mix the parsley for stuffing, chives, and shallots with two-thirds of the butter, salt, pepper, and egg yolk. Mix well until a homogeneous paste is formed.

Preparing the chicken: With a small sharp knife, make a narrow incision in the skin of the back, another in the breast, and one in each drumstick. Insert a drinking straw into these incisions; then blow to loosen the skin from the meat. With a long, narrow utensil—a chopstick, for example, or a lobster fork—smear the herb butter between the skin and the meat of the chicken. Try to apply the butter evenly over the entire inner surface of the bird.

Cooking: Place the chicken on a rack in an open roasting pan, and roast in a hot oven (425° to 450°) for one hour and fifteen minutes.

To Serve: Place the chicken on a serving platter. Keep hot. Mix the remaining butter with the flour, and stir into the pan juices. Add the parsley. Stir; then add the water. Bring to a boil, stirring constantly. If the sauce is too thick, add more water. Taste for seasoning. Serve the chicken on the platter and the sauce in a sauceboat.

POULET A L'OREILLE

Cuisinier Gascon 1740

(Roast Chicken Stuffed with Oysters)

The French name for this dish literally means ''eared'' chicken. Eared? The name makes no more sense in French than it does in English, and since the author of this eighteenth-century book is noted for the odd names he gave to dishes, it may have no meaning at all. But could the ''ears'' be a reference to the shape of the oysters that are used to stuff the chicken? In any event, it does not matter, since this dish is delicious, whatever you choose to call it.

Ingredients (for 4 servings): 24 oysters. Pepper. 1 chicken (3 to 3½ pounds). ½ pound thinly sliced fatback (for barding). 4 sprigs parsley, chopped. Juice of 1 lemon. 3½ tablespoons butter.

The oysters: Open the oysters over a saucepan to catch all their juice. Place the oysters in the saucepan along with their juice. Sprinkle with pepper. Bring just to a boil over low heat. Remove the saucepan from the heat.

The chicken: Stuff the chicken with the oysters, and sew it closed. (Reserve the juice of the oysters.) Wrap the chicken in strips of barding fat. Then wrap it in greased waxed paper or a thin sheet of aluminum foil. Place the chicken on a rack in an open roasting pan. Roast in a hot oven (425° to 450°) for one hour.

The sauce: Heat the juice from the oysters without allowing it to boil. Stir in the parsley, lemon juice, and butter. Unwrap the chicken carefully so as not to lose the drippings contained in the wrapping. Stir these drippings into the sauce.

To Serve: Serve the chicken on a platter and the sauce in a sauceboat.

MARINADE DE PIGEONS AU CITRON

Menon 1746

(Marinated Pigeons with Lemon Sauce)

Although many varieties of pigeon are eaten in Europe, only young birds, squabs, are sold in the United States. If the birds are small, you may have to count one per serving. Otherwise, prepare them in the way described for pigeons below.

Ingredients (for 4 servings): Juice of 4 lemons. 4 medium onions, peeled and finely chopped. 1 sprig basil, chopped. 1 pinch ground cloves. ¾ cup bouillon. Pepper. 2 pigeons or 4 squabs, cleaned, with hearts and livers. 2 egg whites. Salt. Flour. 6½ tablespoons butter. 3 sprigs parsley, chopped.

The marinade: In a deep platter, mix the lemon juice, onions, basil, cloves, bouillon, and a large pinch of pepper. Cut the birds in half, lengthwise. Chop the hearts and livers, and set them aside. Marinate the birds for four or five hours, turning often.

Cooking: Sprinkle the egg whites with salt and pepper. Beat lightly. Dip each of the bird halves into the egg whites, and roll in flour. Melt the butter in a large, deep frying pan over medium heat. When the butter is very hot, place the birds in the pan, and fry for twenty-five minutes, turning occasionally.

To Serve: Arrange the birds on a serving platter. Keep hot. Sprinkle the parsley into the frying pan in which the birds cooked, along with the hearts, livers, and marinade. Simmer for ten minutes. Serve the birds on the platter and the sauce in a sauceboat.

OIE A LA MOUTARDE

Menon 1746

(Roast Goose with Mustard)

From a culinary standpoint, the word "goose" is used to designate both the male (gander) and female of the species and their young (gosling). Only birds less than a year old are considered fit for the table. The age of a bird can be tested by pressing the thumb against the upper part of the bill. If it bends or curves in the middle, the bird is young and tender, but if it is hard and inflexible, the bird is too old and probably tough. The firmer the bill, the older (and less desirable) the bird.

Ingredients (for 10 servings): 1 goose, cleaned (5 to 6 pounds), with heart, liver, and gizzard. 3 sprigs parsley, chopped. 2 scallions, chopped. 1 sprig basil, chopped. 2 shallots, peeled and chopped. ½ clove garlic, peeled and chopped. ¼ bay leaf, crumbled. 1 pinch thyme. Salt. Pepper. ⅔ cup soft butter. 2 tablespoons Dijon mustard. 3 cups bread crumbs. 4 tablespoons flour. 1 teaspoon wine vinegar. 6 tablespoons bouillon. Watercress or leafy lettuce.

The goose: Sew the opening at the neck of the goose closed. Chop the heart, liver, and gizzard, and set aside.

The stuffing: In a bowl mix the parsley, scallions, basil, shallots, garlic, bay leaf, and thyme. Add the heart, liver, and gizzard of the goose. Sprinkle with salt and pepper. Add two-thirds of the butter. Beat vigorously until well blended. Stuff the goose, and sew it closed. Truss the bird, and prick the skin in several places with a skewer.

Cooking: Place the goose on a spit over a dripping pan, and roast in front of an open fire, if possible. If not, place it on a rack over a shallow roasting pan in a hot oven (450°), turning occasionally. In either case, roast for one hour. At the end of this time, add a heaping tablespoon of mustard to the contents of the dripping pan. With a small ladle or baster, cover the goose with the mixture from the dripping pan; then immediately sprinkle it with bread crumbs. Repeat this procedure several times, until you have used all the crumbs and the goose is well breaded. Continue roasting for about thirty minutes, or until the goose is golden brown. The total cooking time should not exceed one hour and thirty minutes. (Count a little more time if roasting in the oven to allow for heat loss while opening and closing the oven door.)

The sauce: Melt the remaining butter in a small saucepan over low heat. Stir in the flour. Add the remaining mustard, the vinegar, and bouillon. Add pepper, and taste to see if more salt is needed.

To Serve: Serve the goose on a platter, on a bed of watercress or lettuce. Spoon off the fat from the dripping pan; then add the remaining juices to the sauce, and stir. Serve the sauce in a sauceboat.

Split peas have always been the poor man's substitute for green peas. The latter, expensive and sought after when they are fresh from the garden, are considered the finest of vegetables by many gourmets, while split peas are too often frowned on because they no longer have the delicate flavor associated with the fresh vegetable. Because split peas are cheaper, more nourishing, and more plentiful than their fresh counterparts, it would be foolish to neglect them simply because their taste is different from that of fresh green peas. Since split peas are known also to counteract the effects of fatty foods and aid in their digestion, they are frequently served with pork, sausages, goose, and (as in this recipe) duck. The "younger" the split peas, the faster they cook. Peas that have been sitting on a shelf for years may have to be soaked overnight and cooked like white beans, while "young" split peas can be cooked like rice.

INGREDIENTS

(for 4 servings)

1 pound split peas
6 cups chicken bouillon
　(approximately)
4 sprigs parsley
2 scallions
1 sprig basil
1 duck, cleaned (2 to 2½ pounds),
　with heart, gizzard, and liver
6 ounces fresh lean bacon (unsalted
　and unsmoked)
½ clove garlic, peeled and stuck
　with 2 cloves
1 sprig thyme
Pepper
Salt

Cooking the split peas

- Place the split peas in a pot with four cups of cold chicken bouillon. Bring to a boil.
- Add two sprigs parsley, one scallion, and one-half sprig of basil to the peas, and cook, at a slow boil, for two hours. If too much of the bouillon evaporates while cooking, add a few spoonfuls more of hot bouillon.

Cooking the duck

- Place the heart and gizzard back inside the duck. Set the liver aside.
- Cut the bacon into small strips. Cook the strips in a cast-iron pot, over low heat, for ten minutes.
- Place the duck in the pot, and brown on all sides. Tie the remaining parsley, scallion, and basil together with garlic and thyme to make a bouquet garni. Add to the duck along with the remaining bouillon. Pepper to taste.
- Cover, and simmer very gently for twenty-five minutes.
- Add the liver, and cook for two minutes longer. Remove from the heat, and remove the bouquet garni.

The split pea purée

- Drain the peas. Remove the herbs. Grind the peas through a food mill; then place them in a saucepan over high heat to thicken. Stir constantly with a wooden spoon so that the purée will not stick to the saucepan.
- When the purée is quite stiff, stir in three-quarters of the sauce from the pot in which the duck cooked. Add salt and pepper to taste.

To Serve

- Spread the purée in the serving platter.
- Carve the duck, and arrange the pieces, including the liver, over the purée.
- Pour what remains of the sauce over the duck, and serve.

"La Tour d'Argent"

POULET AU FROMAGE
(Chicken au Gratin)

Menon 1746

Despite the hundreds of cheeses that have always been produced in France, only a few are ever used in cooking. In the eighteenth century an Italian cheese, parmesan, was even more popular than any of its French rivals. In general, only hard cheeses, of the Swiss cheese type, are used in French cooking. This particular recipe calls for gruyère, but parmesan could be used as well—or for that matter, Dutch or German hard cheese could be tried if you are in an experimental mood.

INGREDIENTS
(for 6 servings)

1 chicken (2½ pounds)
3 tablespoons butter
6 tablespoons dry white wine
6 tablespoons bouillon
3 sprigs parsley
1 scallion
1 clove garlic, peeled
2 cloves
½ bay leaf
1 sprig thyme
2 or 3 basil leaves
Salt
Pepper
2 cups freshly grated gruyère

The chicken
- Place the chicken on its breast, and whack the back, lengthwise, with the blunt edge of a meat cleaver. Lean on the bird to flatten it.
- Melt the butter in a frying pan over medium heat. Add the chicken, and brown it on both sides.
- Add the wine and bouillon.
- Add the parsley, scallion, garlic, cloves, bay leaf, thyme, and basil all tied together in a bouquet garni. Sprinkle with salt and pepper.
- Cook over low heat for one hour.

The cheese
- Remove the chicken from the pan, and discard the bouquet garni.
- Pour half the liquid from the pan into an ovenproof serving dish. Sprinkle half the cheese into the liquid; then place the chicken in the dish.
- Pour in the rest of the sauce from the pan in which the chicken cooked. Sprinkle in the remaining cheese.
- Cover the dish with a lid or with a piece of aluminum foil.
- Bake in a very hot oven (475°) for ten minutes.
- Remove the lid or foil. Raise the heat to 500°. Bake for about five minutes more—just long enough to brown the cheese.

To Serve
- Remove from the oven, and serve immediately.

"Ambassade d'Auvergne et du Rouergue"

Quail, or partridges, are delicious prepared this way. This recipe is best suited for the gourmet hunter who has time (and knowledge enough) to collect the wild mushrooms used to flavor the birds he has shot and then to cook them slowly in the embers of a woodfire in the open air. Few modern sportsmen think of making a dish like this one while still in the field—too bad, since the pleasures of the hunt cannot rival the pleasures of the table (at least in cases like this). This dish, of course, can also be prepared in an indoor fireplace or in a backyard barbecue pit—or even in the kitchen oven.

INGREDIENTS

(for 4 servings)

4 plump quail, cleaned, with hearts and livers
3 sprigs parsley, finely chopped
1 scallion, finely chopped
¼ pound wild mushrooms (morels, chanterelles, etc.), finely chopped
1 shallot, peeled and finely chopped
½ bay leaf, crumbled
Salt
Pepper
½ pound thinly sliced fatback (for barding)
¼ pound thinly sliced prosciutto or country-style ham
¼ pound thinly sliced lean veal (any cut)
⅔ cup dry white wine
⅔ cup bouillon
Juice of 1 lemon

The quail

- Chop the hearts and livers of the birds. Mix them with the parsley, scallion, mushrooms, shallot, and bay leaf. Salt and pepper lightly.
- Divide the stuffing into four equal parts. Stuff each of the birds.
- Wrap a strip of barding fat around each bird.

Cooking

- Cover the bottom of an earthenware or cast-iron pot just large enough to hold the four birds with additional strips of barding fat. Arrange the birds over the fat, breast down.
- Cover the birds with the ham, then with the veal, and finally with more strips of barding fat.
- Cover the pot tightly.
- Place the pot in a bed of very hot cinders so that it is entirely buried in the cinders. Cook for one hour. (Or bake in a slow oven—325°—for one hour.)

The sauce

- Remove the birds from the pot. Keep hot.
- Add the wine and bouillon to the liquid in the pot.
- Simmer over low heat for thirty minutes.
- Spoon off the excess fat.

To Serve

- Place the birds in the sauce for five minutes over very low heat.
- Remove the birds from the sauce, and arrange them on a serving platter.
- Strain the sauce, and add the lemon juice and pepper to taste.
- Pour the sauce over the birds, and serve immediately.

"Le Clos du Moulin"

LAPIN EN GATEAU
(Rabbit Loaf)

Menon 1746

Menon suggests serving this dish hot, in which case it becomes a main dish which should be served with a hot vegetable. It is also possible, however, as soon as the rabbit is removed from the oven, to pour the sauce in the casserole and then allow it to cool. In this case you have an excellent pâté which should be served cold as an entrée or eaten with a green salad as a light lunch.

Ingredients (for 8 servings): 1 rabbit, skinned and cleaned (4 to 4½ pounds), with heart and liver. 2 tablespoons chopped parsley. 1 tablespoon chopped chives. 2 basil leaves, chopped. 2 shallots, peeled and chopped. ¼ pound fatback, chopped. Salt. Pepper. 3 egg yolks. ½ pound thinly sliced fatback (for barding). 1 cup dry white wine. 6 tablespoons bouillon.

Preparing the rabbit: Remove the meat from the saddle and hind legs of the rabbit, and cut it into thin slices. Remove the rest of the meat with a small knife. Reserve all the bones. Chop this meat with the heart and liver of the rabbit; then mix with the parsley, chives, basil, shallots, and chopped fatback. Add salt and pepper. Mix with the egg yolks, stirring vigorously, until the mixture is homogeneous.

Cooking: Cover the bottom of an earthenware casserole with strips of barding fat. Over the fat, place a layer of the sliced rabbit meat, then a layer of the stuffing. Repeat this procedure, ending with a layer of sliced meat. Cover this layer with strips of barding fat. Cover, and cook in a moderate oven (350°), allowing thirty-five minutes per pound of meat. Test to see if the pâté is done by inserting a metal knitting needle or long skewer into its center. Leave it there for two seconds; then withdraw it. Feel all along the part of the needle which was inside the pâté. If it is very hot at all points, the pâté is done. If the tip of the needle is cooler than the rest, the pâté must cook longer. If the cooking liquid is clear rather than milky, it is another sign that the pâté is done.

The sauce: Place the rabbit's bones in a saucepan with the wine and bouillon. Cover, and simmer over low heat until all but about six tablespoons of the liquid has evaporated.

To Serve: Take the casserole from the oven, and remove the strips of barding fat. Turn the pâté out onto a serving platter, and remove the remaining strips of barding fat. Pour the sauce over the pâté, and serve.

PERDREAUX A LA COIGNY
(Partridge in Wine Sauce)

Menon 1746

Although the term "partridge" is used in the United States, it often incorrectly designates native American birds rather than the true European partridges which have been imported to this country. Partridge is often used synonymously with squab to designate young pigeons, or else (in the South) it is another name for the bobwhite, while in other sections of the country a "partridge" is in fact a ruffed grouse. Happily, any one of these birds will make an acceptable substitute for the true European partridge originally called for in this recipe.

Ingredients (for 6 servings): 3 partridges, cleaned, with livers. 2 tablespoons chopped parsley. 1 tablespoon chopped chives. 3 shallots, peeled and chopped. 6 tablespoons olive oil. Salt. Pepper. 6 tablespoons bouillon. 6 tablespoons dry white wine. Juice of 1 lemon.

The birds:: Using the blunt edge of a meat cleaver, whack the back of each bird lengthwise. Lean on the birds to flatten them.

The marinade: Chop the livers of the birds. Place in a small bowl with the parsley, chives, and shallots. Add the oil and salt and pepper to taste. Marinate the birds for three hours, turning occasionally.

Cooking: Place each bird on a square of aluminum foil. Turn the edges of the foil up, forming a "dish" around each bird. Pour one-third of the marinade over each bird. Seal the aluminum foil as tightly as possible. Bake in a hot oven (425°) for twenty minutes. (The meat of partridges is eaten rare.)

The sauce: Pour the bouillon and wine into a saucepan. Boil for ten minutes. Add the lemon juice.

To Serve: Unwrap the birds carefully so as not to lose any of the juice or herbs. Place the birds on a serving dish, and stir the juice and herbs into the sauce. Cover the birds with the sauce, and serve.

POULARDE EN BALLON
(Chicken Stuffed en Ballon)

Dictionnaire Portatif 1765

Chefs today completely ignore certain old tricks that cooks in former times devised for improving the taste of certain dishes. In this recipe, for example, chicken is stuffed, then placed inside a beef bladder before being boiled in water. The bladder sealed in all the juices of the bird and helped it keep its shape during the long, slow cooking. The bird was tastier and easier to serve. Of course, it can be argued that beef bladders are hard to come by today, but even in their absence a cook who understands the principle used here can wrap barding fat around the chicken, then enclose it in cheesecloth and achieve a similar result. (Note: If other mushrooms are not available, fresh button mushrooms can be used alone.)

Ingredients (for 8 servings): 2 medium artichokes. 1 calf's sweetbread (1¾ pounds, approximately). 1 whole fresh truffle or 1 canned truffle. 3½ tablespoons butter. 1 pound mixed mushrooms (wild mushrooms, small fresh button mushrooms, and morels). Salt. Pepper. 2 egg yolks. 1 lemon. 1 chicken (3½ to 4 pounds), with heart, liver, and gizzard. 1 beef bladder (or thinly sliced fatback for barding—see introduction above).

The stew: Prepare the artichoke bottoms and soak the sweetbread as described in the recipe for Canard en ragoût, page 207. Cook the artichoke bottoms in boiling salted water for fifteen minutes; then cut each into eight pieces. Place the sweetbread in a pot of cold water. Bring the water almost to a boil; then immediately drain the sweetbread, and cool it under running water. Remove the fat and bits of skin; then cut into thick slices. If the truffle is fresh, clean it by scrubbing it under cold running water. Cut the truffle into twelve slices. Melt the butter in a saucepan over low heat. Add the artichoke bottoms, sweetbread, mushrooms, salt, and pepper. Simmer gently, uncovered, for ten minutes. Remove from the heat. Add the truffle and egg yolks.

Preparing the chicken: Cut the lemon in half, and rub the outside of the chicken with it. With the dull edge of a meat cleaver, give the chicken a hard blow on the breastbone to break it. Then, working from inside the bird, remove the breastbone. Sew the hole at the neck of the chicken closed. Cut the liver and the heart of the chicken into thin slices. Cut the gizzard into even thinner slices. Stir into the stew. Spoon the stew into the chicken. Sew the chicken closed, and truss it. Place the chicken inside the beef bladder, neck first, so that the bird's tail is at the opening of the bladder. Tie the bladder shut, leaving a fairly long piece of string hanging loose with which to attach the bladder to the handle of the pot in which it cooks.

Cooking the chicken: Bring a large pot of salted water to a boil. Place the bladder in the water, tying the string to the handle of the pot so that the bladder does not touch the bottom. Cover, and simmer for four to five hours.

To Serve: Remove the chicken from the bladder. Place on a platter, and serve.

CUISSES DE DINDON REVEILLANTES
(Braised Turkey Legs)

The turkey is of American origin—from Mexico, to be precise. It was unknown in France until the marriage of Charles IX to the daughter of the Emperor Maximilian II, at Mézières, on November 26, 1570. The bride was so delighted by the new delicacy that it was decided to breed turkeys in France. The first turkey farm was established at Bourges, by the Jesuits, and for many years, country folk referred to turkeys simply as "jesuits." This recipe is a way of using leftovers after roasting the now familiar bird. In France it was at one time customary not to serve the legs of a roast turkey, since they were considered too tough for most people's taste. The legs were put aside for use in dishes such as this one. It is certainly worth depriving yourself of the roasted drumsticks one night when you can look forward to preparing this delicious dish with the "leftovers" the next evening.

INGREDIENTS

(for 4 servings)

2 roasted turkey legs
1 cup dry white wine
1⅓ cups bouillon
1 clove garlic, peeled and stuck with 2 cloves
2 bouquets with 3 sprigs parsley and 1 scallion each.
Salt
Pepper
10½ ounces calf's sweetbread
½ pound fresh button mushrooms
3 tablespoons butter
1 tablespoon flour
2 anchovy fillets in oil, chopped
1 tablespoon capers, chopped
1 handful pitted green olives, chopped

Braising the turkey legs

- Place the turkey legs in a pot with two-thirds cup of the wine and half the bouillon.
- Add the garlic to the pot along with one bouquet of parsley and scallion, salt, and pepper.
- Place over low heat, and simmer for one hour. If properly cooked, the turkey legs should absorb all the liquid.

The sauce

- Place the sweetbread in a pot of cold water, and bring almost to a boil. Drain, and cool under running water. Remove the fatty matter and the skin; then dice the sweetbread.
- Chop the mushrooms together with the second bouquet of parsley and scallion.
- Melt the butter in a frying pan over medium heat, and sauté the sweetbread, chopped mushrooms, and herbs. Sprinkle in the flour. Stir.
- Add the remaining wine and bouillon. Simmer for one hour, stirring occasionally.
- Remove the pan from the heat. Add the anchovies, capers, and olives.

To Serve

- Cut each leg in half at the joint, making two drumsticks and two thighs. Arrange on a platter.
- Pour the sauce over the turkey, and serve.

It is generally agreed that a pheasant should be "hung" (aged) for four or five days after being killed so that it is at its best when cooked. This rule is usually observed in France, although some impatient hunters roast the bird immediately after it is taken (an unfortunate mistake). As noted in an earlier recipe, bigarades, or Seville oranges, were often used in cooking, and it is preferable to use this kind of "bitter" orange, rather than the sweet orange, in the following recipe.

INGREDIENTS

(for 4 servings)

1 carrot, scraped and chopped
1 leek, chopped
1 stalk celery, chopped
1 medium onion, peeled and
   chopped
6 ounces veal knuckle, chopped
1 cup water
1 sprig thyme
½ bay leaf
Salt
1 pheasant (2½ to 3 pounds before
   plucking)
3 cups dry white wine
Pepper
6½ tablespoons butter
1 tablespoon each chopped parsley,
   chervil, and chives
Juice of 1 bigarade (Seville orange)

Preparing the ingredients for the sauce

- Place the carrot, leek, celery, onion, and veal in a saucepan. Add the water, thyme, bay leaf, and a pinch of salt.
- Cover, and simmer over low heat for one hour. Strain the bouillon, and discard the veal and vegetables after pressing them to remove as much liquid as possible.

The sauce

- Pluck and clean the bird, reserving the heart, liver, and gizzard. (Remove the gallbladder from the liver and the grain pouch from the gizzard.)
- Cut all the meat off the bird.
- Crush and grind the carcass, and place it in the saucepan with the veal bouillon. Add the wine. Salt and pepper to taste.
- Cook, uncovered, over low heat for approximately forty-five minutes.
- Strain the liquid; then replace it in the saucepan over low heat.
- Chop the heart, liver, and gizzard of the pheasant. Add to the sauce. Simmer for ten minutes more. Keep hot.

The pheasant fillets

- Cut the meat of the pheasant into long, thin strips.
- Melt the butter in a deep frying pan. Add the parsley, chervil, chives, and meat. Cook for ten minutes over low to medium heat. At the end of this time the meat should be nicely browned.

To Serve

- Arrange the fillets on a platter.
- Add the orange juice to the sauce, along with the liquid and herbs from the pan in which the pheasant cooked. Stir.
- Pour the sauce over the meat, and serve very hot.

"Le Clos du Moulin"

KARI DE LAPEREAUX
(Rabbit Curry)

Despite the name of this dish, it is not a true curry even though turmeric is included as one of the ingredients. Turmeric belongs to the same family as ginger and figures, in varying proportions, in many true curry preparations. It gives the characteristic yellow color to the dish and the slightly sweet taste that is common to most commercial curry powders. Viard's curry is a Frenchman's interpretation of this Indian specialty, and although it lacks authenticity, it has a distinctive character all its own.

INGREDIENTS

(for 10 servings)

30 small white onions, peeled
½ pound butter
8 cups bouillon (approximately)
2 young rabbits, skinned and cleaned
    (2½ pounds each), with livers
6½ ounces fresh button mushrooms
    (or wild mushrooms if available)
5 artichokes
Juice of 1 lemon
5 very small eggplants or 2 large
    eggplants
5 cucumbers
1 small cauliflower
5 medium tomatoes, peeled
1 pound string beans
6½ ounces fresh bacon (unsalted
    and unsmoked), diced
2 tablespoons turmeric
10 chili peppers
2 bay leaves
2 cloves
Salt
⅓ cup flour
3 eggs

Preparing the ingredients

- Place the onions in a saucepan with one tablespoon of the butter and six tablespoons of the bouillon. Cover, and simmer for one hour.
- Cut the rabbits into serving pieces. Set the livers aside.
- In a frying pan, sauté the mushrooms in two tablespoons of the butter over high heat for five minutes. Remove from the heat, and set aside.
- Prepare the artichoke bottoms as described in the recipe for Canard en ragoût, page 207. Place them in a large bowl of cold water laced with the lemon juice.
- Peel the eggplants and cucumbers. Add them to the artichoke bottoms.
- Add the cauliflower, tomatoes, and string beans to the lemon water as well.

Cooking the rabbits

- Place the remaining butter and the bacon in a large pot. Melt over low heat. Add the turmeric, chili peppers, bay leaves, and cloves. Stir. Sprinkle with salt.
- Add the rabbit pieces, and brown on all sides. Stir in the flour.
- Pour in enough bouillon to cover the rabbit pieces by about an inch.
- Cover, and cook over high heat for forty-five minutes—some of the bouillon should evaporate.
- Drain the vegetables. Cut the artichoke bottoms and tomatoes into quarters, as well as the mushrooms if they are large. Slice the eggplants and cucumbers. Divide the cauliflower into flowerets. Leave the string beans whole.
- Remove the chili peppers, bay leaves, and cloves from the pot with the rabbit. Add all the vegetables (including the onions) to the pot. Cover, and cook over low heat for another thirty minutes.

To Serve

- Remove the pot from the heat.
- Remove the rabbit pieces and vegetables. Place them in a serving dish.
- Using a fork, crush the rabbits' livers. Beat them into the eggs. Slowly add the livers and eggs—stirring constantly—to the contents of the pot. Pour over the rabbit and vegetables.
- Serve with rice.

"Les Copains"

SALMIS DE PERDREAUX
(Partridge Salmi)

Most authorities agree that partridges should be aged, unplucked, for at least twenty-four hours and preferably for two days before being cooked. However, one must not confuse aging with putrefaction. If the birds have been shot and contain lead pellets in their bodies, they should be cooked and eaten without delay.

INGREDIENTS

(for 4 servings)

5 ounces fresh button mushrooms or
   wild mushrooms if available
7 tablespoons butter
1 carrot, scraped and chopped
4 or 5 sprigs parsley, chopped
2 shallots, peeled and chopped
1 sprig thyme
1 bay leaf
2 tablespoons flour
1⅔ cups bouillon
Juice of 1 lemon
2½ tablespoons water
¾ cup dry white wine
2 partridges
4 vine leaves
½ pound thinly sliced fatback (for
   barding)
Salt
Pepper
8 large croutons fried in butter

The sauce

- Chop four of the mushrooms. Melt two tablespoons of the butter in a frying pan. Add the chopped mushrooms, carrot, parsley, shallots, thyme, and bay leaf. Cook over low heat until the mushrooms are browned.
- In a saucepan, make a roux by melting one tablespoon of the butter over low heat and stirring in the flour. Add the bouillon, and bring to a boil, stirring constantly.
- Pour the contents of the frying pan into the saucepan. Simmer.
- Cook the remaining mushrooms in two tablespoons of the butter, the lemon juice, and the water over high heat for five minutes. Drain. Reserve the cooking liquid. Set the mushrooms aside.
- Add the mushrooms' cooking liquid to the sauce, along with the wine. Simmer for one hour.

The partridges

- Pluck the partridges. Clean and truss them. Reserve the livers.
- Wrap each of the partridges in two vine leaves. Hold the leaves in place with strips of barding fat tied on with string.
- Place the birds on a rack in an open roasting pan. Roast in a hot oven (425°) for twenty minutes.

The salmi

- Remove the barding fat and vine leaves. Carve the birds. Arrange them on a serving platter. Keep hot.
- Pound the carcasses and the livers of the birds in a mortar. Add to the sauce, along with salt and pepper.
- Increase the heat slightly, and allow the sauce to boil, uncovered, for twenty minutes.

To Serve

- Strain the sauce. Return it to the saucepan, and add the pieces of partridge. Simmer for five minutes.
- Remove the partridge, and arrange on a serving platter.
- Remove the sauce from the heat, and stir in the remaining butter and the reserved mushrooms.
- Pour the sauce over the pieces of partridge.
- Arrange the croutons around the platter, and serve very hot.

''Lucas-Carton''

COTELETTES DE SANGLIER SAUTEES

(Sautéed Chops of Wild Boar)

Wild boars were once plentiful in forests throughout France. Now there are fewer and fewer, and the boar has become an endangered species in some parts of France. What is called for in this recipe is a young wild boar. The meat of the adult animal is tough and has to be marinated before cooking. Despite the shrinking population of wild boars in France, the animals are still seen hanging in front of Parisian butcher shops, especially in the fall and winter, and are often prepared in the way described by Viard in this recipe. In the United States wild boars are hunted in Tennessee and North Carolina, but they are generally unknown to people living in other parts of the country. Although the taste would not be the same, this dish can be prepared with ordinary pork chops.

INGREDIENTS

(for 4 servings)

¼ cup butter
8 boar chops
Salt
Pepper
1 tablespoon flour
¾ cup dry white wine
1 pinch four-spice mixture (see introduction to Pâté de jambon, page 202)

Cooking the chops

- Melt the butter in a frying pan over high heat. Add the chops.
- After four minutes, turn the meat over. Sprinkle with salt and pepper. Cook until the chops are well done. (Although boar meat is eaten slightly rare in France, it is not advisable to eat rare pork in the United States.)
- Remove the chops from the pan, and keep hot.

The sauce

- Lower the heat, and stir the flour into the pan juices. Gradually add the wine.
- Taste for salt and pepper. Add the four-spice mixture. Stirring constantly, bring to a boil; then immediately remove from the heat.

To Serve

- Pour the sauce over the chops, and serve.

"Rôtisserie Rivoli"

BECASSES BRULEES AU RHUM A LA BACQUAISE
(Spit-Roasted Woodcocks with Rum)

This recipe was included by Brillat-Savarin in his famous book on food, *La Physiologie du goût*. Legend has it that Brillat-Savarin always carried a dead woodcock in his coat pocket to age properly before he cooked it. This is no doubt an exaggeration, for although this gourmet insisted that game birds had to be hung before cooking them, it is doubtful that he inconvenienced himself (and his acquaintances) by carrying the birds on his person. Today some cooks believe woodcocks should not be aged at all, but many still agree with Brillat-Savarin and age the bird for a day or two before preparing it. As was customary in the early nineteenth century, the birds were spit-roasted over an open fire. Brillat-Savarin's original instructions for roasting are given here, but cooks today might be tempted to cook the birds in a broiler if they cannot take the time to follow the old method described below.

INGREDIENTS

(for 8 servings)

4 woodcocks
Several thin slices fatback (for barding)
4 thin slices country-style bread
2 cloves garlic, peeled and crushed
Salt
Pepper
4 tablespoons rum

Preparing the woodcocks

- Choose four whole woodcocks which have been aged slightly after killing. Pluck the birds. Split the skin at the neck, and remove the crop and the gizzard. Leave the other viscera in the birds.
- Turn the legs of each bird so that one is clasped within the other. Insert the beak into the body, through the thighs.
- Wrap each bird in thin strips of barding fat. (It is important that the strips be *thin*. If they are too thick, the melting fat will spoil the taste of the bird.) Tie a piece of string around the bird to hold the fat in place. Put the birds on a spit.

The bread

- Toast the slices of bread very lightly—just enough to give them a little color. Spread them with the crushed garlic.
- Place the toast in the dripping pan, one slice under each bird.

Cooking

- Cook the birds over an open fire or hot coals for twenty minutes. (Woodcocks are eaten slightly rare.)

To Serve

- Remove the barding fat. Cut each bird in half. Salt lightly. Remove the viscera with a small spoon—gently, so as not to break the gallbladder. Remove the gallbladder, and discard. Using a fork, crush the rest of the viscera. Add salt and pepper to taste.
- Spread this mixture on the slices of toast; then cut the slices in half. Place half a woodcock on each half slice of toast. Sprinkle with three tablespoons of flaming rum.
- Put the remaining rum into the dripping pan to thin the liquid. Serve this sauce with the birds.

DINDE EN DAUBE
   (Stewed Turkey)

Too many American cooks do not realize that turkey does not always have to be stuffed and roasted and served with cranberry sauce. This particular stew is a good way to prepare a tough bird (an old turkey hen, for instance), but a tender young turkey could be stewed this way as well. Since stews like this often improve when they are reheated, leftovers are no problem.

Ingredients (for 8 servings): 1 sprig thyme. 1 small bouquet parsley and chives, finely chopped for lardoons. Salt. Pepper. ½ pound fatback (for larding). 1 turkey (8½ pounds), with liver, heart, and gizzard. 1 large bouquet parsley and chives, finely chopped for stuffing. 1 pound thinly sliced fatback (for barding). 6 slices veal knuckle. 3 slices country-style ham, cut into strips. 3½ ounces fatback, diced. 2 bay leaves. 2 cloves garlic, peeled and finely chopped. 5 medium onions, peeled and finely chopped. 4 carrots, scraped and thinly sliced. 2 cloves. ¾ cup brandy. Bouillon.

Preparing the turkey: Crumble the thyme leaves into a bowl. Add the small bouquet of parsley and chives and salt and pepper to taste. Cut the fatback into long, thin strips (lardoons) for larding. Roll them in the seasonings, and then, with a larding needle or small knife, insert them into the turkey. Chop the liver, heart, and gizzard of the turkey. Mix with the large bouquet of parsley and chives, and place inside the bird. Sew the turkey closed and truss it.

Cooking: Cover the bottom of a large cast-iron pot with strips of barding fat. Add the veal knuckle, ham, the diced fatback, bay leaves, garlic, onions, carrots, and cloves. Place the turkey on these ingredients. Add the brandy and just enough bouillon to cover. Cover the bird with strips of barding fat. Over the whole, place a sheet of greased waxed paper. Cover the pot, and cook in a moderate oven (350°) for two hours. After two hours, remove the paper and barding fat. Turn the turkey, and taste for seasoning, adding salt and pepper if necessary. Replace the fat, paper, and lid. Cook for two hours longer.

To Serve: Remove the paper and barding fat. Remove the turkey from the pot, and place on a platter. Boil four cups of the cooking liquid until reduced by half. Strain the liquid into a sauceboat, and serve with the turkey.

CANARD AUX NAVETS A LA BOURGEOISE
   (Duck with Turnips)

Turnips are the traditional accompaniment to fatty meats. Both lamb and duck are stewed in identical ways with turnips, since this vegetable not only complements the flavor of the meat but makes it easier to digest. Some gourmets even think the taste of the turnips in this stew is superior to that of the duck and have suggested renaming the dish "Turnips with Duck."

Ingredients (for 4 servings): 3½ tablespoons butter. 1 duck (3½ pounds), cleaned and trussed. 2 pounds young turnips, peeled. 2 tablespoons flour. 2 cups bouillon. 3 sprigs parsley, several chives, and 1 bay leaf tied together. ½ clove garlic, peeled and crushed. Salt. Pepper.

The duck: Heat two tablespoons of the butter in a large cast-iron pot. Add the duck, and brown on all sides. Remove the duck from the pot, and place on a platter.

The turnips: Add the turnips to the fat in which the duck was browned. Cook until they brown. Remove the turnips with a slotted spoon, and place on the platter with the duck.

Cooking: Melt the remaining butter in the same pot. With a wooden spoon, stir in the flour to make a roux. Then add the bouillon, the bouquet of herbs, and the garlic. Salt and pepper to taste. Replace the duck in this sauce, and cook, covered, for twenty-five minutes. Add the turnips. Cook for forty minutes longer over medium heat.

To Serve: Remove the herb bouquet. Place the duck on a platter. Serve the turnips and sauce in a vegetable dish.

SOUFFLE DE VOLAILLE

Carême 1833

(Chicken Soufflé)

Soufflés have never been as popular in France as they have been in French restaurants abroad. Carême's recipe is one of the earliest references to soufflés, and even he (who tended to elaborate on most things) devotes only a few pages to their preparation. Soufflés are simply an ingenious way of using leftovers. That is the way Carême saw them, and that is the way they are still regarded in France today.

Ingredients (for 4 servings): 1⅓ cups diced leftover fowl (*e.g.*, chicken breasts, etc.). 3 tablespoons milk (approximately). 6 eggs, separated. 2 teaspoons butter (for the molds).

Preparing the soufflé: Pound the fowl in a mortar until it forms a smooth paste. Stir in the milk to obtain a thin purée. (If necessary, increase the quantity of milk.) Place this mixture in a pot, and heat gently, stirring constantly, without bringing to a boil. Remove from the heat, and stir in the egg yolks one by one. Beat the egg whites until stiff; then fold them carefully into the other ingredients.

Cooking the soufflé: Butter four individual soufflé molds. Divide the purée among the four molds. Do not fill the molds more than one inch from the top. Bake in a moderate oven (375°) for twenty minutes.

To Serve: A soufflé waits for no one. It must be served immediately upon removal from the oven.

SALADE DE POULET

Alexandre Dumas 1873

(Chicken Salad)

Alexandre Dumas was one of the rare French gastronomes to experiment with different kinds of salads. The French are basically conservative when it comes to salads and rarely mix anything with their lettuce. Dumas, on the other hand, loved to try new combinations in salad, and his cookbook contains a surprising number of inventive mixtures. This particular salad may seem tame to American palates, but the subtle taste of the ingredients employed here are perfectly balanced, and Dumas' instructions should be respected.

Ingredients (for 4 servings): 1 boiled or roasted chicken (3½ pounds). 1 large bouquet mixed herbs (parsley, chervil, tarragon, chives, etc.), finely chopped. 8 French vinegar pickles (cornichons), thinly sliced. 8 anchovy fillets in oil, finely chopped. 2 tablespoons capers. 6 tablespoons olive oil. 2 tablespoons wine vinegar. 4 hard-cooked eggs. 1 head leafy lettuce.

Making the salad: Cut the breast of the chicken into strips, but leave the wings and legs whole. Remove all the meat from the carcass, and cut into strips as well. Place the strips of chicken in a large salad bowl with the mixed herbs, pickles, anchovies, and capers. Add the oil and vinegar. Mix well, and allow to stand for a few minutes.

To Serve: Peel and cut each egg in half. Wash and drain the lettuce. Arrange the lettuce leaves on a long platter. Place the wings and legs of the chicken and the eggs around the edges of the lettuce. Place the contents of the salad bowl in a mound on top of the lettuce leaves, and serve.

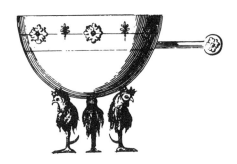

Vegetables

During the Middle Ages a great variety of vegetables were for sale in the streets of Paris: parsnips, carrots, sorrels, chervils, leeks, turnips, beets, green peas, broad beans, lentils, cabbages, watercress, onions, asparagus, cucumbers, garlic, and many more. In fact, more vegetables were available then than now. Some historians have misinterpreted an often-repeated description of the medieval serfs' food. At the time serfs were said to live on "roots and herbs"—poor fare, until one learns that until the eighteenth century anything that grew underground was called a root, and everything that grew aboveground was called an herb! Thus, a poor peasant eating tender cooked turnips or young carrots and a green salad would have been described as eating "roots and herbs."

During the Renaissance new foods appeared on French tables, and improved varieties of popular vegetables were developed. For instance, there were seventeen kinds of spinach available at the time, and red cabbage, broccoli, artichokes, and pumpkins are only a few of the vegetables that were being grown for the first time in France.

About this time an unexpected source of new foods was discovered—America. Then such "exotic" vegetables as the white bean, tomato, Jerusalem artichoke, and potato were imported to Europe from the New World. It took awhile for the potato and the tomato to catch on in France, but the white bean was quickly accepted and soon replaced the European broad bean in many traditional dishes. For example, a famous French dish, *cassoulet*—a stew made of goose, mutton, pork, and white beans—was undoubtedly made with broad beans before the white bean was imported from America.

It is impossible to discuss the history of vegetables in France without mentioning La Quintinie, the gardener to King Louis XIV at Versailles. He developed methods of fertilizing, sheltering, and crossbreeding that are still employed. Thanks to his work, cauliflowers and several new varieties of lentils were grown for the first time on a large scale, and hothouse vegetables made their first appearance in France.

Today vegetables are regarded as accompaniments to main dishes. In the past vegetables were usually served alone, after the main course. This tradition is still found in France, although it is limited to strictly formal occasions. It was customary at one time to have a vegetable course, during which three or four vegetables were brought to the table. However they are served, it is important that vegetables be carefully prepared and varied. The following recipes from old French cookbooks illustrate a number of creative uses of standard vegetables as well as some surprising new vegetable ideas that should relieve the monotony of many modern dinners in which vegetable cooking has become routine and boring.

CRETONNEE DE POIS NOUVEAUX

(Green Pea Purée with Chicken)

Taillevent 1373

This very old recipe is perfect for making use of leftover chicken or turkey. The saffron and ginger mixture used here is characteristic of the use of spices in the Middle Ages.

Ingredients (for 4 servings): 3 pounds unshelled green peas. 6 tablespoons cold water. 1½ cups crumbled stale bread. 6 tablespoons milk. 1 pinch ground ginger. 1 pinch saffron. 2 large cooked chicken breasts. 3 tablespoons lard. Salt. Pepper. 4 egg yolks.

Preparing the ingredients: Shell the peas. Place them in a pot with the water. Cover the pot with a soup bowl, and fill the bowl with cold water (this prevents any steam from escaping). Bring the peas to a boil; then lower the heat, and cook for thirty minutes. Place the bread in a bowl, and add the milk, ginger, and saffron. Cut the chicken into strips. Heat half the lard in a frying pan. Add the chicken, and brown.

Making the purée: When the peas are cooked, grind them through a food mill. Place the purée in a saucepan with the remaining lard. Cook over medium heat, stirring constantly. Add all the ingredients prepared earlier to the peas. Salt and pepper to taste. Bring just to a boil; then immediately remove from the heat. Away from the heat, stir in the egg yolks.

To Serve: Serve very hot.

EPINARDS A LA CREME

(Creamed Spinach)

La Varenne 1651

In La Varenne's time there were more than a dozen kinds of spinach. Today there are very few. During the Middle Ages spinach already cooked, chopped, and pressed into balls was sold in the streets. These spinach balls were prescribed by the physicians of the time as a cure for intestinal disorders. La Varenne notes that spinach is at its best if one adds a bit of sorrel to it. This practice was common until the nineteenth century in France, and it may be worth trying, although the acidity the sorrel adds is not to everyone's taste.

Ingredients (for 4 servings): 2 pounds fresh spinach. 3 scallions. 1 large onion, peeled and stuck with 2 cloves. ½ teaspoon salt. 1 pinch pepper. 6½ tablespoons butter. ¾ cup heavy cream. Nutmeg.

Cleaning the spinach: If large-leafed spinach is used, remove the tough midrib of each leaf (small leaves can be left as they are). Wash the leaves thoroughly in cold water. Place in a colander to drain.

Cooking the spinach: Place the scallions and onion in a large pot. Add the salt, pepper, and butter. Add the spinach. Cover the pot. Simmer over low heat for fifteen minutes, stirring two or three times.

To Serve: Remove the scallions and onion. Just before serving, stir in the cream and a little nutmeg.

CONCOMBRES FARCIS

(Stuffed Cucumbers)

Cucumbers are seldom cooked nowadays, but in the past they were rarely served any other way. Since they are not very nourishing by themselves, they were often stuffed with either cooked meat or poultry. Bonnefons suggests in a preface to this recipe that chicken or fish could be used instead of veal in the stuffing. In fact, you can invent your own stuffing and include anything you like, since the mild taste of the cucumbers makes a perfect background taste for any number of stuffing combinations.

Ingredients (for 4 servings): 4 sprigs parsley. 6 ounces veal (any stewing cut). 6 ounces fatback. 2 eggs. Salt. Pepper. Nutmeg. 4 medium cucumbers. Several thin slices fatback (for barding). Bouillon. Butter.

The stuffing: Finely chop the parsley, veal, and fatback together. Add the eggs, a dash of salt and pepper, and a little nutmeg to the chopped meat mixture.

The cucumbers: Peel the cucumbers, and cut them in half lengthwise. Using a small spoon, remove the seeds. Stuff each cucumber half with the chopped meat mixture.

Cooking the cucumbers: Cover the bottom of an ovenproof dish with slices of barding fat. Arrange the cucumbers in the dish. Add just enough bouillon to cover the cucumbers but not to cover the stuffing. Cover with aluminum foil, and bake in a moderate oven (375°) for one hour.

To Serve: Drain any juice that remains in the dish. Dot the cucumbers with butter, and serve hot.

CARDES D'ARTICHAUTS A LA MOELLE

(Cardoons with Bone Marrow)

Both the artichoke and the cardoon have, as a common ancestor, a thorny, thistlelike plant native to the Mediterranean basin: the wild cardoon. Cardoons are taller and more prickly than artichoke plants, and their greenish gray leaves are often three to four feet long. Cardoons are chiefly grown for the leafy midribs of the young plants, which are thick, fleshy, tender, yet crisp. The most popular way of cooking cardoons in France has always been with bone marrow. The following recipe is still found in many modern French cookbooks virtually unchanged after 300 years.

Ingredients (for 6 servings): 2 quarts water. 2 tablespoons flour. Salt. Juice of 1 lemon. 1 sprig thyme. 1 bay leaf. 3 tablespoons suet. 6 pounds cardoons. 1 lemon, cut in half. 6 ounces fresh bacon (unsalted and unsmoked). 2 shallots, peeled and finely chopped. 1⅔ cups bouillon. Pepper. 6 ounces bone marrow. ¾ cup water. 1 teaspoon arrowroot. 3 tablespoons butter. 1 tablespoon madeira.

The cooking liquid: Bring the two quarts of water to a boil in a pot. In a bowl, mix the flour with a pinch of salt and the lemon juice. Gradually add this mixture to the water, stirring constantly. Add the thyme, bay leaf, and suet to the pot. Simmer.

Preparing the cardoons: Remove the leaves and any hollow parts of the cardoon stalks. Wash the cardoons in cold water. Cut the stalks off about one and a half inches from the base of the cardoons. Reserve the base. Cut the stalks into sections. Peel each section to remove the stringlike fibers, and immediately rub each section with a piece of lemon. Remove any discolored parts from the base. Cut it into six sections, and rub with the lemon as well. Place all the pieces of cardoon in the cooking liquid, and cook slowly for one hour.

The final cooking: When the cardoons are done, drain them thoroughly. Form several small bunches containing three or four pieces of cardoon each, and tie each bunch together with string. Dice the bacon, and place it in a pot with the shallots. Put the cardoons into the same pot. Add the bouillon and pepper. Simmer for fifteen minutes.

The bone marrow: Cut the bone marrow into slices one-quarter inch thick (this can be done easily if the blade of a knife is first dipped into boiling water). Put the bone marrow into three-quarters cup boiling salted water, and poach for ten minutes.

To Serve: Remove the cardoons from the bouillon. Cut the strings, and arrange the pieces of cardoon on a serving platter, along with the rounds of bone marrow. Away from the heat, add the arrowroot, butter, and madeira to the bouillon. Taste for seasoning. Pour the sauce over the cardoons, and serve very hot.

ASPERGES EN POIS VERTS
(Green Pea Style Asparagus)

Today white asparagus is the rule in France, but once all French asparagus was green. The whiteness is produced by piling earth around the young asparagus so it is protected from the light; the chlorophyll is never allowed to develop and color the plant green. White asparagus is generally more tender than green asparagus, but green asparagus is preferable for stewing, as in the following recipe. It is believed that this recipe was invented as a substitute for green peas. Since green peas, once more popular than asparagus in France, were expensive and asparagus was cheap, some clever chef devised the following preparation.

Ingredients (for 4 servings): 4½ pounds green asparagus. 2 tablespoons lard. 2 tablespoons butter. Salt. Pepper. ½ sprig thyme. 2 tablespoons chives, finely chopped. 6 tablespoons bouillon. 2 tablespoons heavy cream.

Preparing the ingredients: Break off the very end of each asparagus; then peel the asparagus with a potato peeler, being careful not to damage the tips. Cut the asparagus into one-half-inch pieces.

Cooking: Melt the lard in a frying pan with the butter. Add the asparagus, and sauté quickly over high heat for one minute. Add salt, pepper, the thyme, and the chives. Pour in the bouillon. Lower the heat, and simmer for eight minutes. Remove the thyme. Away from the heat, stir in the cream.

To Serve: Serve piping hot.

CHOU FARCI
(Stuffed Cabbage)

The cabbage was known and esteemed in remotest antiquity. It was not only popular as a food, but was also considered a cure for hangovers and stomachaches. Cabbage leaves were used in home remedies up until the nineteenth century. In almost every country where cabbage is grown there is a stuffed cabbage recipe. The French version of this dish calls for placing the stuffing between the leaves of the cabbage without detaching the leaves from the head. Stuffed cabbage was apparently more popular in the seventeenth and eighteenth centuries than it is today since recipes like this one appeared in all the old books but are rarely seen in modern books on French cooking.

Ingredients (for 6 servings): 1 large white cabbage (about 2 pounds). ¼ pound fresh button mushrooms, finely chopped. 4 sprigs parsley, finely chopped. 1 scallion, finely chopped. 1 clove garlic, peeled and finely chopped. ½ cup finely chopped chicken breast. ¼ pound round roast of veal, finely chopped. ¼ pound sausage meat. ¼ pound fatback, finely chopped. 2 cups fresh bread crumbs. Salt. Pepper. 2 eggs. 2 egg yolks. 3 tablespoons butter. 4 medium onions, peeled and sliced. 14 ounces veal knuckle, cut into slices. 1 tablespoon flour. 4 cups bouillon.

The cabbage: Using a small knife, remove as much of the hard central core of the cabbage as possible without detaching the leaves. Place the cabbage in a large pot of cold water, and bring to a boil. As soon as the water boils, remove the cabbage, and drain it.

The stuffing: In a large bowl, mix the mushrooms, parsley, scallion, garlic, chicken, chopped veal, sausage meat, fatback, and bread crumbs. Stir well. Add salt and pepper. Add the eggs and the egg yolks. Continue stirring until all the ingredients are homogeneously mixed.

Stuffing the cabbage: Carefully open the leaves of the cabbage, one by one, working from the outside in toward the center. Cut away the small leaves in the center. In the opening thus created, place some of the stuffing. Then fold the leaves closest to the center over the stuffing. Place a layer of stuffing on top of these leaves; then cover the stuffing with another layer of cabbage leaves. Continue stuffing the cabbage in this way until all the stuffing has been used up and the cabbage has resumed its original form. To keep the cabbage from losing its shape during cooking, wrap it in cheesecloth, and tie a string around it.

Cooking the cabbage: Melt the butter in a pot large enough to hold the cabbage. Add the onions, and sauté until they become transparent. Add the veal knuckle. Brown the veal. Sprinkle in the flour. Stir; then add the bouillon. Cover, and simmer for thirty minutes. At the end of this time, put the stuffed cabbage in the pot. Cover, and cook over low heat for three hours and thirty minutes.

To Serve: Remove the cabbage from the pot, and untie it. Serve whole, or slice in the kitchen before serving. Strain the cooking liquid, and serve as a sauce.

CASSEROLE AU RIZ
(Rice Casserole)

This dish has a misleading name since the rice it contains is insignificant compared to the rich meat and vegetables which are essential to its preparation. This is truly a dish for a special occasion, for not only should the best and freshest ingredients be employed, but great care must be taken when cooking and serving this dish with the deceptively simple title.

Ingredients (for 6 servings): 3 large artichokes. Juice of 1 lemon. 1 calf's sweetbread (1¼ pounds). ½ pound small fresh morels. 1⅔ ounces truffles. ¾ cup butter. ½ pound small fresh button mushrooms. Salt. Pepper. 3 cloves garlic, peeled. 6 basil leaves. 6 tablespoons dry white wine. ¾ cup rice. Boiled or roasted white meat of 1 chicken.

Preparing the ragout: Cut off the stems of the artichokes, and remove the leaves and choke (see Canard en ragoût, page 207). Place the artichoke bottoms in a pot of water. Add the lemon juice, and bring to a boil. Cook for thirty minutes. Drain, and cut each bottom into eight pieces. Soak the sweetbread, and poach according to the instructions given in Canard en ragoût, page 207. Drain, and cool the sweetbread under cold running water. Remove the skin and fat; then cut the sweetbread into cubes. Remove the sandy ends of the morel stems; then soak the morels in a small amount of water. Stir them around until they are clean. Remove the morels, and strain the water through a cheesecloth. Place the morels and their water in a saucepan, and cook for five minutes. Remove from the heat. Lift out the morels, and save them and their cooking liquid for later use. Mince the truffles. Melt half the butter in a frying pan. Add the pieces of artichoke, sweetbread, morels, and mushrooms. Salt and pepper, and simmer gently for fifteen minutes, uncovered. Stir occasionally. Remove from the heat, and add the truffles. In another saucepan, place the morels' cooking liquid, the garlic, basil, and wine. Bring to a boil, and reduce by half. Strain, and add this liquid to the pan containing the other ingredients.

The rice: Cook the rice in a large pot of salted water for fifteen to twenty minutes. Drain.

The casserole: Cut the chicken into thin slices. Place the slices in an ovenproof dish. Cover with the mushroom and artichoke mixture; then cover this with the rice. Dot the rice with the remaining butter. Bake in a hot oven (425°) for ten minutes.

To Serve: Serve steaming hot as soon as it comes from the oven.

HARICOTS EN ALLUMETTES
(Deep-Fried String Beans)

Only fresh young string beans should be used in this recipe. The beans should be crisp when broken, and the seeds barely visible inside them. The batter described here could be used to fry other vegetables cut into thin strips and precooked like the beans. This type of batter improves if it is allowed to "age." It can be prepared as much as twenty-four hours in advance, but most cooks make it two to three hours ahead of time and leave it in a warm place until it is needed.

Ingredients (for 4 servings): 1 cup flour. Salt. 1 teaspoon vegetable oil. 1 egg. 6 tablespoons beer. 10½ ounces very thin string beans. 1 medium onion, peeled and stuck with 2 cloves. 2 slices lemon. 1 slice fatback. Bouillon. Oil for deep frying.

The batter: Mix the flour and a pinch of salt in a bowl. Make a well in the center. Place the oil, egg, and beer in the well. Mix together, incorporating the flour little by little, stirring vigorously. The batter should be rather thick and smooth. Let stand for at least thirty minutes before using.

The string beans: Cut off the ends and remove the strings from the beans. Place the onion, lemon, fatback, and beans in a saucepan. Add bouillon to cover. Bring to a boil, and simmer for fifteen minutes. Drain thoroughly.

Frying the beans: Dry the beans with a clean cloth (any dampness will prevent the batter from adhering properly). Dip the beans one by one into the batter; then place them in a deep fryer containing very hot oil. When the beans rise to the surface of the oil, turn them with a slotted spoon. When the beans are golden brown, remove and drain.

To Serve: Serve very hot as an accompaniment for roast meat or fowl.

LAITUES A LA DAME SIMONNE

(Stuffed Lettuce in Cream Sauce)

In the United States lettuce, like cucumbers, is regarded as a salad and is rarely cooked. In France, however, lettuce is cooked like spinach, and on special occasions stuffed lettuce is still prepared as described in Marin's recipe. This particular recipe could be considered a main dish at a luncheon or other light meal.

Ingredients (for 4 servings): 2 leeks. 1 stalk celery. 4 cups water. 4 chicken breasts, uncooked, cut into strips. ½ cup rice. Salt. Pepper. 2 eggs, separated. 3 tablespoons heavy cream. Nutmeg. 4 heads leafy lettuce. 2½ ounces fresh bacon (unsalted and unsmoked), diced. 2 small onions, peeled and finely chopped.

Preparing the sauce: Place the leeks and celery in a pot with the water. Put the chicken in the pot. Cook for fifteen minutes. Add the rice. Cook for eighteen minutes more, or until the rice is soft. Then, using a slotted spoon, remove half the rice and half the chicken. Pour off two cups of the cooking liquid, and reserve for later use. Grind the ingredients remaining in the pot through a food mill to obtain a thin purée. Add salt and pepper to taste. Mix the egg yolks and two tablespoons of the cream together. Stir the egg yolk and cream mixture and a little nutmeg into the purée.

The stuffing: Place the reserved chicken and rice in a mortar. Add a little salt and pepper, the egg whites, and the remaining cream. Pound these ingredients until a paste is formed.

The lettuce: Wash the lettuce carefully, without detaching the leaves. This can be done easily by holding the heads of lettuce by the stem and swirling them back and forth in a large container of water. (Change the water for each head of lettuce.) Place the lettuce in a pot of boiling water. Cook for two minutes, and drain. Squeeze the heads of lettuce to remove excess water. Arrange the heads of lettuce, base downward, and gently separate the leaves one by one. Place some of the stuffing between each of the leaves. When each head has been stuffed, tie it with a piece of string so that it will not lose its shape (or its stuffing) while cooking.

Cooking the lettuce: Place the bacon in a pot large enough to hold the stuffed lettuce. Heat until the bacon begins to melt. Add the onions, and cook until they become transparent. Add the heads of lettuce. Cover, and simmer for ten minutes. Add the two cups of the reserved cooking liquid. Cover, and simmer slowly for ninety minutes.

To Serve: Remove the lettuce from the pot, and untie the string. Carefully arrange the lettuce on a serving platter. Away from the heat, pour the sauce into the pot in which the lettuce cooked. Heat this mixture until it is warm—do not let it boil. Then pour it over the lettuce, and serve immediately.

ARTICHAUTS A LA GALERIENNE

(Artichokes with Wine and Mushrooms)

Artichokes were frequently used in stews (both meat and fish) in the eighteenth century. They were seldom boiled whole, as they are today, but were cut into pieces and sautéed like potatoes or carrots. The following recipe is similar to one still popular in the South of France called Artichauts à la barigoule (not the one in this book)—the difference being that the southern recipe uses whole baby artichokes that are extremely tender and this one uses fully grown artichokes pared and cut into quarters.

Ingredients (for 4 servings): 4 large artichokes. 6 tablespoons olive oil. 1 bouquet parsley and chives. 8 fresh button mushrooms. 2 shallots, peeled and finely chopped. 2 cloves garlic, peeled. 2 slices lemon. ¾ cup dry white wine. ¾ cup bouillon. Juice of 1½ lemons.

Preparing the artichokes: Remove the stem of each artichoke by tearing it off, thus removing the tough fibers from the base at the same time. Cut each artichoke into quarters. Remove all but one leaf from each artichoke quarter. The remaining leaf should be stiff and firmly attached to the bottom. Also remove the choke. Cook the artichoke quarters for five minutes in boiling salted water. Drain.

Cooking: Heat the oil in a frying pan. Add the parsley, chives, mushrooms, shallots, garlic, and lemon. Put the artichoke quarters in the pan. Add the wine and bouillon. Cook for thirty minutes. (The single leaf remaining on each quarter should remain firmly anchored.)

To Serve: Lift the artichoke quarters out of the cooking liquid. Arrange them on a serving platter, with the leaves upward. Remove and discard the herbs, garlic, and lemon. Let the cooking liquid stand for a few minutes so that the fat may rise. Spoon off the fat. Add the lemon juice to the sauce, and pour it over the artichokes. Serve immediately. (The artichokes are eaten by hand, using the leaf as a handle.)

TRUFFES EN PUITS

   (Fresh Truffles with Stuffing)

This recipe has to have come from the Périgord region of France, where its two main ingredients (fresh truffles and fresh foie gras) have long been local specialties. It would be difficult to prepare this dish outside France—in fact, even in Paris fresh truffles *and* fresh foie gras are hard to come by (and expensive). In any event, this recipe illustrates how these two ingredients can be combined in a dish whose simplicity highlights the subtle taste of both the truffles and the foie gras—a rare culinary achievement.

Ingredients (for 2 servings): 2 large fresh truffles (about 3 ounces each). 3 or 4 sprigs parsley. 3 or 4 scallions. Salt. Pepper. 2 ounces fresh foie gras. ½ egg yolk. 2 thin slices fatback. 1 small slice lean veal, minced. 1 very thin slice country-style ham or prosciutto. ⅔ cup dry white wine. Juice of ½ lemon. 2 tablespoons butter.

Preparing the truffles: Scrub the truffles vigorously under cold running water. Make sure no dirt remains. Wipe dry with a clean cloth. Remove and reserve a small slice from each truffle. Using the handle of a very small spoon, scoop out the interior of the truffles—carefully, so as not to break them.

The stuffing: Chop half the parsley and half the scallions with the scooped-out interior of the truffles. Add salt and pepper to taste. Place in a bowl with the foie gras and egg yolk. Mix all the ingredients until a homogeneous mixture is formed. Carefully fill the truffles with this mixture. Replace the slice, taken earlier from each truffle.

Cooking the truffles: In a small pot (just large enough to hold the truffles), place the fatback, veal, ham, and the remaining parsley and scallions. Add the wine. Cover, and simmer for fifteen minutes. Place the truffles in the pot. Cover, and continue cooking, over very low heat, for twenty minutes.

To Serve: Place each truffle in its own tiny casserole for serving. Strain the liquid in which the truffles cooked, and away from the heat, add the lemon juice and butter. Stir well. Pour the sauce over the truffles, and serve very hot.

ARTICHAUTS A LA BARIGOULE

   (Artichokes with Vinaigrette)

Although the French name of this dish is the same as that of a famous Provençale recipe still popular today, the two have little in common. As pointed out in the introduction to an earlier recipe (Artichauts à la galérienne, page 250), the southern dish is composed of tiny young artichokes that are sautéed with olive oil and garlic, then eaten whole with their sauce. Here the artichokes are stewed, then broiled before being served with an oil and vinegar dressing. It is essential that the artichokes used in this recipe be extremely fresh. The leaves should be tight around the head and uniformly colored. Pointed leaves indicate that an artichoke is probably old and stringy and should therefore be rejected.

Ingredients (for 4 servings): 4 large artichokes or 12 very small artichokes. 1 tablespoon wine vinegar (for washing). 1 carrot, scraped and finely sliced. 1 parsnip or turnip, peeled and finely sliced. 1 medium onion, peeled and thinly sliced. 2 cups bouillon. 2 tablespoons olive oil (for cooking). 1 bay leaf. 1 sprig thyme. Salt. Pepper. 6 tablespoons olive oil and 2 tablespoons wine vinegar (for vinaigrette).

Preparing the artichokes: Remove the stems, and cut off the tough leaves around the base of each artichoke. Then cut off the top third of the remaining leaves. Wash each artichoke thoroughly in a mixture of one tablespoon vinegar and water.

The first cooking: Place the carrot, parsnip or turnip, and onion in a flameproof casserole. Add the bouillon, two tablespoons oil, bay leaf, thyme, salt, and pepper. Place the artichokes in the casserole. Cook over medium heat until the liquid has almost entirely evaporated.

The final step: With the handle of a small spoon, remove the choke from each artichoke. Put the artichokes back in the casserole. Place under a very hot broiler to brown the leaves.

To Serve: Prepare an oil and vinegar dressing by combining the six tablespoons oil, two tablespoons vinegar, a pinch of salt, and a pinch of pepper. Serve with the artichokes as soon as they come from the oven.

PETITS POIS A LA DEMI-BOURGEOISE
(Green Peas with Lettuce)

Menon 1746

It is impossible to say when this recipe was invented, but it has been followed, with few changes, for centuries in France. It is by far the best way to prepare fresh green peas, and probably one of the simplest. The peas are cooked without any water other than that which they and the lettuce emit when heated. None of this liquid should be allowed to escape, and so the peas must be cooked in a pot which has a concave lid, or else a soup plate can be used to cover the pot. In either case, the top is filled with water or ice which immediately condenses the steam rising from the vegetables and prevents the loss of flavor.

Ingredients (for 8 servings): 6½ pounds unshelled green peas. 2 heads leafy lettuce. 5 tablespoons butter. 3 sprigs parsley and 1 scallion, tied together. 1 pinch sugar. Salt. Pepper. 2 egg yolks. 2 tablespoons heavy cream.

Preparing the ingredients: Shell the green peas. Remove the outer leaves of the lettuce, and discard. Wash each head, and cut it into quarters.

Cooking: Place the peas in a pot with the butter, parsley, scallion, and lettuce. Cover the pot with a soup plate or concave lid, and pour some water into it to keep the vegetable juices from evaporating. Simmer for thirty minutes. Add the sugar. Sprinkle with salt and pepper. Simmer for ten minutes longer.

To Serve: Remove the lettuce, and keep it hot. Remove and discard the parsley and scallion. Beat the egg yolks with the cream. Away from the heat, stir them into the peas. Pour the peas into a serving bowl. Arrange the lettuce on top of the peas. Serve very hot.

CHAMPIGNONS AU FOUR
(Stuffed Mushrooms)

Buc'hoz 1771

This recipe is a mushroom lover's delight. Whenever possible, wild mushrooms should be used; otherwise, fresh button mushrooms are acceptable.

Ingredients (for 8 servings): 2 pounds wild mushrooms (*e.g.*, morels or chanterelles) or fresh button mushrooms. Juice of 1 lemon. 3 sprigs parsley, finely chopped. 1 scallion, finely chopped. 1 clove garlic, peeled and finely chopped. 1 tablespoon olive oil. 1¼ cups bread crumbs. Salt. Pepper.

The first step: Separate the caps from the stems of the mushrooms. As you do so, place the caps in a container of water laced with the lemon juice. Peel the stems, and place them in the lemon water. Rub the mushrooms gently to remove any sand. Remove the stems, and chop them very finely. Mix the chopped stems with the parsley, scallion, and garlic. Add all the chopped ingredients and the drained mushroom caps to a pan containing the oil. Cook gently for four minutes.

The second step: Remove the caps from the pan. Arrange them on a greased ovenproof platter. Away from the heat, mix the bread crumbs with the ingredients remaining in the pan. Add salt and pepper to taste. Then stuff each mushroom cap with some of this mixture. Bake in a hot oven (450°) for fifteen minutes.

To Serve: Serve very hot.

POMMES DE TERRE A L'ECONOME

(Potato Patties)

Although potatoes could have been grown in France earlier, it was not until the French Revolution in 1789 that this precious vegetable was accepted by the French. The French accepted it only because famine, and the economic exigencies of the Revolution, forced it on them. The potato had long been considered poisonous in France, but once the French tried it and survived, they showed a surprising amount of enthusiasm for this "new" food. The following recipe is taken from one of the first postrevolutionary French cookbooks and is one of the earliest French recipes using potatoes.

Ingredients (for 4 servings): 3 sprigs parsley, finely chopped. 1 scallion, finely chopped. 4 shallots, peeled and finely chopped. 2 cups chopped cooked meat (leftover meat or poultry). 2 pounds potatoes. 3½ tablespoons butter. 1 egg. 1 egg, separated. Salt. Pepper. Flour. Oil for frying. Chopped parsley (to garnish).

The herbs and meat: Mix the finely chopped parsley, scallion, and shallots with the chopped meat.

The potatoes: Boil the potatoes in their jackets for thirty minutes in lightly salted water. Peel while still hot; then mash with a fork.

The patties: Combine the mashed potatoes and the chopped ingredients. Add the butter, egg, and egg yolk. Salt and pepper to taste. Shape into medium patties . (If they are too small, they will be too crunchy, and if too large, the centers will not cook thoroughly.) Beat the egg white until it begins to stiffen. Dip the patties into the egg white; then roll them in flour.

Cooking the patties: Place the patties in a frying pan with very hot oil. Turn so that they will brown on all sides.

To Serve: Drain well, and serve garnished with parsley.

MACEDOINE A LA BECHAMEL

(Mixed Vegetables in Béchamel Sauce)

This dish is a perfect way to serve a variety of vegetables in a combination that is both pleasing to the eye and the palate. Any number of fresh vegetables can be incorporated into this dish, but it is important that they all be extremely fresh.

Ingredients (for 8 servings): 4 artichokes. 1 pound unshelled green peas. 1¼ pounds unshelled lima beans. 1 small cauliflower. 6½ tablespoons butter. ½ pound small white onions, peeled. ½ pound carrots, scraped and diced. ½ pound turnips, peeled and diced. ½ pound eggplant, peeled and diced. ½ pound cucumbers, peeled and diced. ½ pound string beans, diced. Salt. Pepper. 4 tablespoons flour. 3 cups bouillon. 4 sprigs parsley. 6 tablespoons heavy cream. Nutmeg.

Preparing the vegetables: Remove the stems from the artichokes. Cut off the leaves, and remove the choke. Cut the artichoke bottoms into quarters. Shell the green peas and lima beans. Separate the flowerets from the cauliflower.

Cooking the vegetables: Melt three and a half tablespoons of the butter in a large frying pan. Add all the vegetables mentioned above, as well as the onions, carrots, turnips, eggplant, cucumbers, and string beans. Sprinkle with salt and pepper. Cook for thirty minutes (no water need be added since the vegetables give off water as they cook).

The Béchamel sauce: Melt the remaining butter in a saucepan. Stir in the flour, and keep stirring until smooth. Add the bouillon. Stir constantly for ten minutes. Add the parsley. Continue to cook slowly for twenty minutes, stirring occasionally to keep the sauce from sticking to the pan. Remove from the heat. discard the parsley. Stir in the cream. Add a pinch of nutmeg.

To Serve: Combine the vegetables and the sauce. Taste for seasoning, and adjust if necessary. Serve with veal, lamb, mutton, or pork.

RAGOUT DE FEVES EN GRAINS

(Lima Bean Stew)

The original recipe for this dish specifies the use of the broad bean (*Vicia faba*), one of the oldest cultivated vegetables, which have been found in Iron Age sites in Europe and were one of the favorite vegetables in ancient Egypt. Broad beans, however, were never widely planted in the United States, for when the New World was discovered, a large number of native American beans were found that eventually replaced the broad bean in popularity even in Europe. Fresh lima beans are similar in taste, size, and consistency to broad beans and have therefore been used as a substitute in this recipe.

Ingredients (for 4 servings): 5½ pounds unshelled lima beans, 5½ tablespoons butter. 1 slice country-style ham or prosciutto. 1 tablespoon flour. Bouillon. 1 head leafy lettuce. 2 sprigs marjoram or savory. Salt. Pepper. Hot milk (if necessary). 3 egg yolks.

Preparing the beans: Shell the lima beans. Place the beans in a saucepan. Cover with cold water, and bring to a boil. Cook for five minutes. Drain.

The ragout: Melt the butter in a large frying pan. Add the beans and ham. Sprinkle with the flour. Stir. Add bouillon to cover. Wash the lettuce without separating the leaves. Place the lettuce in the pan with the beans. Add the marjoram or savory. Sprinkle with salt and pepper. Simmer for thirty minutes. If the liquid evaporates too quickly, add a bit of hot milk.

To Serve: Remove the ham, lettuce, and marjoram or savory. Away from the heat, stir in the egg yolks. Serve immediately.

FRITURE DE SALSIFIS

(Deep-Fried Salsify)

Salsify is also known as oyster plant, a name deriving from the fact that it was once believed that the taste of raw salsify resembled that of the oyster—an opinion not shared by many gourmets today. It is available in the United States in some gourmet stores and shops catering to people of Mediterranean background but is still not widely marketed. In Europe, however, it is a popular vegetable, its taste most often compared to that of asparagus. Actually, the plant has a delicate flavor all its own and is an excellent accompaniment to such meats as lamb or pork.

Ingredients (for 4 servings): 1 cup flour (for the batter). 1 egg, separated. 1 tablespoon olive oil. ⅔ cup beer. Salt. Pepper. 1 pound salsify. Vinegar. 3 tablespoons flour. 2 tablespoons soft butter. 2 quarts water. 1 medium onion, peeled and stuck with 2 cloves. ½ lemon. Oil for deep frying.

The batter: Place the cup of flour in a deep bowl, and make a well in the center. Place the egg yolk, olive oil, beer, and a little salt and pepper in the well. Stir these ingredients, incorporating the flour as you do so. Continue stirring until all the flour has been mixed in and a smooth batter is formed. Let the batter sit, undisturbed, for at least two hours before using it. Just before using the batter, beat the egg white until stiff, and fold it in.

The salsify: Use a paring knife to peel the salsify. Cut each salsify into three- or three-and-a-half-inch sections. Place the sections in a bowl of water mixed with some vinegar. Combine the three tablespoons flour and the butter to form a paste. Place this mixture in a large pot containing two quarts of water. Add the onion to the water, along with the lemon and a pinch of salt. Place over low heat. Drain the salsify sections, and drop them into the water. Cook gently for about one hour and thirty minutes. Remove the salsify sections with a slotted spoon, and dry them with a clean towel.

Frying the salsify. Dip the salsify sections in the batter. Place them, seven or eight at a time, in a deep fryer containing very hot oil. Fry them quickly. When the sections rise to the top of the oil, turn them. When they are golden brown on all sides, remove and drain thoroughly.

To Serve: Cover a serving platter with a white napkin, and place the salsify on the napkin. Sprinkle with salt and pepper, and serve immediately.

FEUILLES DE CELERI A LA MENAGERE

(Celery Casserole)

For centuries celery leaves were used in combination with other herbs as a seasoning, while the stalks were cooked separately as a vegetable. White celery (which has been blanched by piling soil around the plant to protect it from the light) is generally preferable to green celery, although either can be used in this recipe.

Ingredients (for 4 servings): 1 large bunch celery, cleaned and trimmed. Salt. 4 cups fresh bread crumbs. 3 cups milk or bouillon. 3½ tablespoons butter. 2 anchovy fillets in oil, finely chopped. Pepper. 2 eggs, separated. 1 cup freshly grated gruyère.

Preparing the celery: Cut each celery stalk lengthwise into four parts. Place the celery in a pot of boiling salted water. Cook for one hour. Drain and chop.

The bread crumbs: Add the bread crumbs to a pot containing the milk or bouillon. Bring to a boil.

Cooking: Melt the butter in a frying pan. Add the chopped celery, and simmer. Add the anchovies and a little pepper. Stir in the bread-crumb mixture little by little. Cook over low heat until most of the liquid has evaporated. Remove from the heat, and stir in the egg yolks.

To Serve: Beat the egg whites until very stiff. Mix almost all the cheese into the celery; then fold in the egg whites. Pour into a well-buttered baking dish. Sprinkle the remaining cheese over the top. Bake in a very hot oven (500°) for five minutes. Serve hot from the oven in the baking dish.

POMMES D'AMOUR AU GRATIN

(Baked Stuffed Tomatoes)

Until the French Revolution in 1789 the tomato was virtually unknown in Europe outside of a small area along the Mediterranean. Then, in 1790, a battalion of volunteers from Marseilles arrived in Paris, bringing with them the hymn which became the national anthem of France—and tomatoes. Durand called tomatoes *pommes d'amour* (love apples), and they were known by this name for many years in both French and English. The most popular way to prepare them at that time was to stuff them with leftover meat (preferably veal or chicken). This was not only a convenient way to use leftovers, but, since tomatoes were expensive, the most economical way of serving this versatile and delectable food.

Ingredients (for 4 servings): **For the spice salt:** 1 clove. 1 nutmeg. 3 bay leaves. 2 sticks cinnamon, each 6 inches long. 2 tablespoons peppercorns. 2 teaspoons dried basil. 2 teaspoons coriander seeds. ¾ cup salt. **For the recipe:** 8 medium tomatoes. Salt. 4 sprigs parsley, finely chopped. 1 shallot, peeled and finely chopped. ⅔ cup cooked meat (leftover chicken or veal), finely chopped. 5 ounces fatback, finely chopped. 1½ ounces bone marrow, finely chopped. 2 egg yolks. Bread crumbs.

The spice salt: (Note: The specific spices in Durand's recipes are rarely indicated. The reason is that he made a mixture of various spices and used the mixture in almost all his dishes. The following is his recipe for spice salt. Far more is made here than will be used in this particular recipe, but the mixture keeps well in a tightly stoppered bottle and can be used in other dishes.) Using a mortar and pestle, finely grind the clove, nutmeg, bay leaves, cinnamon, peppercorns, basil, and coriander. When all these ingredients have been ground into a fine powder, sift, and mix with the salt.

Preparing the tomatoes: Cut the tomatoes in half. Carefully squeeze out the juice, and remove the seeds. Using a small spoon, hollow out each tomato half, being careful not to damage the skin. Reserve the pulp removed from inside the tomatoes. Sprinkle a small pinch of salt in each tomato half. Place the tomato halves upside down on a plate to drain.

The stuffing: Mix the parsley and shallot with the meat, fatback, bone marrow, and the pulp from inside the tomatoes. Add one teaspoon of the spice salt and the egg yolks. Stir until everything is well mixed.

Cooking the tomatoes: Stuff each tomato half, and place in an ovenproof dish. Sprinkle each stuffed tomato with bread crumbs. Bake in a moderately hot oven (400°) for fifteen to twenty minutes.

To Serve: Serve very hot as soon as the tomatoes come from the oven.

CROQUETTES DE POMMES DE TERRE

(Potato Croquettes)

Carême 1833

Few vegetables are used so often with so little imagination as the potato. Boiled, fried, and mashed potatoes have almost worn out their welcome on many tables. Unfortunately, habit and perhaps lack of imagination keep many cooks from discovering varied and interesting uses for the potato that would enliven any meal. Carême did not lack imagination or taste when he devised this version of potato croquettes.

Ingredients (for 4 servings): 2 pounds potatoes. Bouillon. 2½ tablespoons butter. 1 pinch nutmeg. 1 pinch sugar. Salt. Pepper. 2 eggs, separated. 3 tablespoons heavy cream. 2½ cups bread crumbs. 1½ cups freshly grated parmesan. 2 eggs. Oil for deep frying.

Cooking the potatoes. Peel the potatoes, and quarter them. Place the potatoes in a pot, and add bouillon to cover. Add the butter, nutmeg, sugar, and salt and pepper to taste. Cover, and bring to a boil. Cook for twenty minutes. The potatoes, when cooked, should have absorbed all the bouillon.

Preparing the croquette mix: Grind the potatoes through a food mill. Place the mashed potatoes in a frying pan. Cook over low heat, stirring briskly with a wooden spoon to complete the evaporation of the cooking liquid. Remove the pan from the heat. Stir in the egg yolks and cream.

The croquettes: Place half the bread crumbs in a shallow dish. Mix the remaining bread crumbs with the cheese, and place in a similar dish. In a bowl, vigorously beat the eggs and the egg whites. Take a little croquette mix (it should have cooled off but not be cold), and use the hands to shape it into a ball about the size of a small egg.

Cooking the croquettes: Roll the croquettes first in the bread crumbs, then in the beaten eggs, and finally in the mixture of bread crumbs and cheese. Place the croquettes immediately in hot oil in a deep fryer, and cook for five to six minutes. Drain on a napkin.

To Serve: Serve very hot with roasted or braised meat.

CAROTTES A LA FLAMANDE

(Glazed Carrots with Cream)

Gouffé 1867

Gouffé specified that only young, tender carrots were to be used in this recipe, and his advice should be followed today. This dish is best in spring and early summer, when carrots are always tastier.

Ingredients (for 4 servings): 10 medium carrots. 3 tablespoons water. 3 tablespoons butter. Salt. 1 teaspoon sugar. 2 sprigs parsley, finely chopped. 2 egg yolks. 3 tablespoons heavy cream.

Cooking the carrots: Cook the carrots for five minutes in boiling water. Drain, and hold them under cold running water; then wipe vigorously with a cloth to peel them. Cut the carrots into slices about one-half inch thick. Place the slices in a large frying pan. Add the water, two tablespoons of the butter, a pinch of salt, and the sugar. Cover the pan. Simmer for twenty minutes, stirring every five minutes or so.

The cream: Remove the carrots from the heat. Add the parsley, along with the egg yolks, the remaining butter, and the cream.

To Serve: Stir well, and serve immediately.

HARICOTS BLANCS A LA MAITRE D'HOTEL

Gouffé 1867

(White Beans à la Maître d'Hôtel)

This recipe is truly outstanding when fresh white beans are used, but dried white beans can be substituted. If dried beans are used, they have to be soaked overnight, then placed in cold salted water and cooked for two and a half to three hours (fresh beans cook much more quickly). Fresh lima beans can be used instead of fresh white beans and are delicious prepared this way.

Ingredients (for 4 servings): 2 pounds unshelled fresh white beans. 3 quarts water. 2 teaspoons salt. 2 tablespoons butter. 1 tablespoon flour. 4 sprigs parsley, finely chopped. Juice of ½ lemon. Salt and pepper (to season).

Cooking the beans: Shell the beans. Place the water in a pot. Add the salt, and bring to a boil. Place the beans in the boiling water, and cook at a slow boil until you can easily crush the beans with your fingers (about twenty-five minutes). Drain, and reserve three tablespoons of the water in which the beans cooked.

The final preparation: Use a fork to mix the butter and flour together to form a paste. Separate the mixture into pea-sized pieces. Place the drained beans in a vegetable dish. While stirring, add the butter and flour mixture little by little. Pour in the water reserved earlier. Add the parsley and lemon juice. Salt and pepper to taste.

To Serve: Serve very hot.

CHOU-FLEUR AU GRATIN

Gouffé 1867

(Cauliflower au Gratin)

Cauliflower should be perfectly white, and the flowerets that compose the head should be tight against each other and unblemished. In France it is customary to sell cauliflower with the leaves still attached as proof of freshness. It should be noted that Gouffé uses more parmesan than gruyère in this recipe. Up until this century parmesan was the cheese most often used in French cooking.

Ingredients (for 4 servings): 1 medium cauliflower. 3 tablespoons vinegar. 4 quarts, plus 2¾ cups, water. 1½ teaspoons salt. 3 tablespoons butter. 2 tablespoons flour. Salt. Pepper. ½ cup freshly grated parmesan. ⅓ cup freshly grated gruyère. 1 tablespoon bread crumbs.

Preparing the cauliflower: Cut the cauliflower into quarters. Add the vinegar to a large bowl of water, and drop each quarter of the cauliflower into this mixture. Bring two quarts of water to a boil in a pot. Drain the cauliflower, and add the quarters to the boiling water. Cook for five minutes. Drain. (This is to parboil and tenderize the vegetable.) Fill another pot with two quarts of water. Add the one and a half teaspoons salt, and bring to a boil. Place the cauliflower in the boiling water, and cook at a slow boil for fifteen minutes.

The cheese sauce: Melt two tablespoons of the butter in a saucepan over low heat. Stir in the flour. Stir constantly until smooth. Add two and three-quarters cups of water and salt and pepper to taste. Bring to a boil, stirring constantly. Reduce the heat, and continue cooking for ten minutes over low heat, stirring the whole time. Add half the parmesan and all the gruyère to the sauce. Still stirring, continue cooking for another five minutes. Drain the cauliflower, and divide each piece into two parts. Place four sections of cauliflower in a buttered ovenproof dish. Pour half the cheese sauce over the cauliflower. Arrange the remaining four sections of cauliflower in the dish, and add the rest of the cheese sauce. Sprinkle in the remaining parmesan and the bread crumbs. Dot the surface with the remaining butter. Bake in a hot oven (425°) for twenty minutes.

To Serve: Serve as soon as the cauliflower comes from the oven.

AUBERGINES FARCIES

(Stuffed Eggplants)

There are several kinds of eggplant. The best kind to use in this recipe is long rather than round. The skin should be smooth and shiny, and the eggplant should feel firm when squeezed.

Ingredients (for 4 servings): 4 medium eggplants. 4 tablespoons olive oil. ¼ pound fresh button mushrooms, finely chopped. 4 shallots, peeled and finely chopped. 3 sprigs parsley, finely chopped. 1½ tablespoons flour. ¾ cup bouillon. Salt. 1 pinch cayenne pepper. Bread crumbs.

The eggplants: Wash the eggplants. Remove the green stem, and cut the eggplants in half lengthwise. Using a small spoon, remove the pulp inside each eggplant, leaving only one-quarter to one-half inch of pulp next to the skin. Make several X-shaped cuts in the pulp near the skin to facilitate cooking. (Save the rest of the pulp for the stuffing.) Place half the oil in a frying pan. Carefully sauté the eggplant skins three minutes on each side. Remove from the heat. Drain by placing the skins on a piece of paper towel.

The stuffing: Finely chop the pulp removed from the eggplants, and mix with the mushrooms, shallots, and parsley. Over low heat sprinkle the flour into the pan in which the eggplant skins cooked. Stir constantly with a wooden spoon for five minutes. Add the bouillon. Add the chopped vegetables. Cook for eight minutes, stirring constantly. Add some salt and the cayenne pepper. Simmer for four minutes more.

The final cooking: Put the remaining oil in an ovenproof dish. Arrange the eggplant skins in this dish. Fill each skin with some of the stuffing, and sprinkle with bread crumbs. Bake in a hot oven (450°) for ten minutes.

To Serve: Serve very hot.

LAITUES AU JUS

(Braised Lettuce)

Lettuce was probably used medicinally before it was used as a food. The oldest references to this vegetable are in ancient manuscripts which prescribe the juice obtained from squeezing lettuce leaves as a mild sedative. For centuries, lettuce was prescribed for nervous disorders and was believed to cure insomnia as well. Of course, gourmets soon found that lettuce was simply an excellent food and insisted on eating it (cooked or in salads) because of its taste, and now its medical uses are practically forgotten.

Ingredients (for 4 servings): 8 small heads leafy lettuce. Vinegar. Salt. Pepper. 6½ tablespoons butter. 1 bay leaf. 1 sprig thyme. Bouillon. 1 medium onion, peeled and stuck with 2 cloves. 8 slices bread, with crust removed.

Preparing the lettuce: Remove the tough outer leaves of the lettuce. Carefully wash the lettuce, without detaching the remaining leaves, by swirling the heads in a large bowl of vinegar and water. Rinse in clean water. Cook the lettuce for ten minutes in boiling water. Drain. Press in a dry cloth to remove any remaining water.

Cooking the lettuce: Divide each head of lettuce into two parts. Sprinkle with salt and pepper. Restore the heads to their original shape by tying the two parts together with a string. Place the lettuce in a large pot with half the butter, the bay leaf, and thyme. Add bouillon to cover. Add the onion. Cover. Simmer gently for two hours.

To Serve: Cut the bread into pieces about one inch square, and fry in the remaining butter. Remove the lettuce from the liquid in which they cooked. Take off the strings. Cut the lettuce sections into halves, and arrange them on a platter, interspersing the lettuce with the pieces of fried bread. Pour the liquid in which the lettuce cooked over the lettuce and bread. Serve immediately.

Salads

To most people "salad" means raw vegetables mixed with oil, vinegar, and spices. Yet from a purely etymological standpoint, it simply means "salt."

Just about anything can go into a salad: leaves, roots, cereal, eggs, shellfish, fish, pork, chicken, game, fruits, and cheese.

Salads were eaten by the kings of Persia long before the birth of Christ, and Roman soldiers, in order to gain strength and courage, ate *moretum*—a salad made of cheese and herbs. In ancient Rome, flagging appetites were revived with a third course of salad made of lettuce, chicory, and rocket plant (a sort of colewort) seasoned with other herbs and spices.

Old French cookbooks mention many salad greens still in use, such as chicory (escarole, endive, etc.) and lettuce (leafy, romaine, iceberg, and others). Other salad greens, mostly wild, were once popular but have been

largely forgotten in the twentieth century: milkweed, burdock sprouts, wild salsify, purslane, cardamine, garden cress, sea holly, sea fennel, lamb's-lettuce, valerian, saltwort, rampion, nettles, rocket plants, rue, and others.

Some old recipes call for seasoning the vinegar used in making the salad dressing with a variety of flavors. Some popular vinegars were seasoned with roses, gillyflowers, dianthuses, wild strawberries, and cloves. But whatever else they might contain, for centuries all salads were always made with olive oil. Mixed salads were often (and still are) served as an accompaniment to roast meats. In France, green salads are still served after the main course—never at the beginning of the meal. Today French cooks are much less adventuresome in their salad making than their predecessors, and subtle flavor combinations are the rule. Nevertheless, even the simplest salad could be improved, or at least varied, by the addition of the rose vinegar described by an anonymous author in the sixteenth century. Or a modern cook could follow Bonnefons' advice, given below, for making a mixture that would be a refreshing novelty today.

The Making of Rose Vinegar from the Buds of Red Roses During the Summer—*a recipe extracted from* La Pratique de faire toutes confitures, *1550*:

Take red rosebuds during the summer and cut off the bases. Place the rosebuds in a glass jar, full to the brim. Put the jar in the sunlight for an entire day. When you see the rosebuds closing and shrinking within the jar, add more rosebuds to fill the jar, then cover the jar so that not a breath or wisp of wind may enter or leave. Let the jar remain covered throughout the summer, until the month of September. Every day, put it into the sun; and, every night, take it into your house as soon as the sun goes down. In this way, the rosebuds will continue to be reduced in size within the jar, until they are transformed into the best rose vinegar that it is possible to make. Then, during the winter, keep the jar in a dry place.

Minor Herbs of All Kinds for Salads—*a recipe of Nicolas de Bonnefons, 1654*:

Tarragon, saxifrage, garden cress, watercress, lamb's-lettuce, pimpernel—all these and a thousand others, flowers as well as herbs, are useful in making salads to be served with oil or sugar. And, as a rule, the greater the diversity of ingredients in these salads, the more enjoyable they are. Pimpernel is also useful when placed in one's wine glass, for it gives its taste and fragrance to the wine. And the bud of the elder, when used in a salad, serves to relax the stomach.

Desserts and Sweets

The first real collection of recipes for desserts that appeared in France was the *Bastiment de recettes*, the translation of an Italian work published in 1541. The *Bastiment* dealt primarily with the preserving of fruits "so that a bunch of grapes may be as fresh and as tasty at Christmas as it was when it was picked in September." There were numerous recipes for preserving wild cherries, green walnuts, and melons, and the book explained how to "candy orange peels, which may be done throughout the year although the best time is the month of May, when the peels are large and thick."

The first work on sweets and desserts by a native Frenchman was written by Nostradamus about ten years after the *Bastiment de recettes*. However, it was not until the seventeenth century, when François de La Varenne and Pierre de Lune wrote their cookbooks, that dessert recipes similar to those of today began to appear. At the time there was a sudden interest in sweets, and French cooks began preparing marzipan, turnovers, puff pastries, macaroons, and custards, as well as jellies, preserves, and jams, all in enormous quantities.

It was Menon, however, toward the middle of the eighteenth century, who laid the foundations for the elaborate pastry cooking of today. He described such things as marzipan baskets, clusters of pastry swords, and various other constructions which would eventually lead to the incredible spun-sugar and pastry palaces that have made some critics call French pastry a branch of architecture.

Of course, French pastry is not all as pompous and showy as some of these constructions make it appear. Pies, custards, and puddings are typically French, and most French desserts are extremely simple. In France pastry cooks, like bakers, have always been specialists whose creations were rarely rivaled or imitated at home. And although professional pastry chefs have added to the prestige of French cooking, they have unfortunately given many cooks the impression that all French desserts are elaborate and difficult to make. The following section is composed of recipes by great chefs of the past, all of which are representative of French dessert cooking. Despite the diversity of the techniques employed, the recipes are relatively easy to prepare.

A native of Central Asia, the quince has long been known and cultivated in southern Europe. In the United States it is chiefly grown in New York and California, but it is also available in other parts of the country. The quince is never eaten raw but is always cooked. Since Roman times, it has been made into marmalades and jams or cooked with other fruits that counteract its extremely acid taste. Quinces were frequently preserved in honey, and honey can be substituted for sugar in the following recipe. Martial, the Roman poet, was fond of quinces preserved in honey and wrote that this was the way that the great god Jupiter had his nymphs prepare quinces for him. Preserved quinces can thus be called a food fit for the gods, and Nostradamus' recipe is certainly one of the finest ways of preparing this unusual fruit preserve.

INGREDIENTS
(for 6 to 8 servings)

8 ripe quinces
2 quarts water
6¾ cups sugar
Ground cinnamon
Ground cloves

The first step

- Peel the quinces. Wipe the skins to remove any fuzz, and save them. Cut each quince into eight pieces. Remove the seeds, and core the fruit.
- Pour the water into a pot. Add the quinces and their skins.
- Place the pot over high heat, and bring to a boil. Cook until you can easily insert a pin into the pieces of quince. Remove the quinces with a slotted spoon. Strain the liquid, and replace it in the pot.

The second step

- Add the sugar to the water in which the quinces cooked. Bring to a boil, and skim off the foam.
- When foam no longer forms on the surface of the water, place the quinces back in the pot. Simmer for forty-five minutes. (Do not stir or you will break the fruit.)
- Pour the quinces and the liquid into a large, shallow pan, and let stand for two days.

The third step

- After two days, cook the quinces and their liquid again for thirty minutes.
- Using a slotted spoon, gently remove the quinces from the liquid. Be careful not to break the fruit.
- Arrange the quinces in a large, shallow serving dish, and sprinkle with a pinch of cinnamon and cloves.
- Cook the liquid for another fifteen minutes. Pour it over the quinces, and allow to gel.

To Serve

- Slice the quinces, and serve.

Preserving the quinces

- This dish may be kept in the same way that one would keep preserves—that is, by hermetically sealing the quinces in sterilized jars covered with waxed paper or paraffin.

TOURTE ADMIRABLE
(Marzipan Pie)

Lemons can be used instead of limes in this recipe. In La Varenne's day both fruits had to be imported, and limes, especially, were very expensive. In either case this dessert lives up to its French name, which translates as an "admirable pie."

INGREDIENTS

(for 8 servings)

2 limes
2 cups ground almonds
6 egg whites (2 in one bowl; 4 in another bowl)
1¾ cups sugar
4⅓ cups heavy cream
8 egg yolks (each in a separate small dish)
1 tablespoon orange-flower water
3½ ounces candied cherries, finely chopped
Powdered sugar

The marzipan

- Finely grate the peel of one lime. Mix with the almonds and the two egg whites.
- Gradually add one cup of the sugar, mixing thoroughly.
- Spread this mixture in a buttered pie pan. Bake in a very slow oven (250°) for fifteen minutes. Remove from the oven.

The cream and meringue

- Cut off the white inner skin of the lime that was used earlier. Cut the lime into quarters, and remove the seeds. Cook the quarters in a pan over low heat. Add the remaining sugar and the cream.
- Over very low heat, stir in the egg yolks, one by one, until the cream begins to thicken.
- Add the orange-flower water to the four egg whites. Beat the mixture until quite stiff.

Baking

- Spread the cream mixture over the marzipan.
- Cover the cream mixture with the chopped cherries and another finely grated lime peel. Top with the meringue. Sprinkle with powdered sugar.
- Bake in a slow oven (300°) for fifteen minutes, or until the meringue is done.

To Serve

- Serve cold.

DAME SUSANNE

(Egg Bread Susanne)

This bread is similar to what is called a brioche. Both are unsweetened doughs that are made with large amounts of butter and milk instead of water. This bread would probably be eaten at the end of the meal (or for breakfast) with a little jam and a cup of coffee.

Ingredients (for 8 servings): 1 cup flour (for leaven). 1 ounce (1½ packages) baker's yeast. 6 tablespoons warm milk. 3⅔ cups flour (for dough). 8 egg yolks. 2 egg whites. 2 teaspoons salt. 1⅓ cups soft butter. 1 egg.

The leaven: Pour one cup of flour onto a table. Make a well in the center. Place the yeast and a few tablespoons of the milk in the well. (The milk will facilitate the leavening process, but make certain that the milk is warm, *not* hot.) Using the tips of the fingers, quickly mix the yeast and milk together; then gradually work in the flour. Add a little more milk, if needed, to soften the mixture. Let rise for one hour in a warm place.

The dough: Place three and two-thirds cups flour on the table. Make a well in the center, and place the egg yolks, egg whites, and salt in the well. In a small pot, heat the remaining milk along with the butter (the butter should be broken into pieces to speed melting). With the tips of the fingers, mix the eggs and salt together in the well; then gradually start working in the flour. Gradually add the melted butter and milk mixture to the dough until it is smooth and soft. When the leaven, prepared earlier, is ready, work it into this dough. Knead the dough vigorously. Shape the dough into a long, high loaf. Let rise in a warm place until the loaf doubles in size (about one hour and thirty minutes).

Baking: Just before baking, beat the egg, and spread it over the top of the loaf with a pastry brush. Using a sharp knife, make several rather deep slashes along the sides and top of the loaf. Place immediately in a moderate oven (350°). Bake for one hour until golden brown on top and firm to the touch.

PETITS METIERS

(Little Wafers)

These wafers are also known in France as *oublies*—a derivation from the Latin *oblata,* which means "an offering." And in fact, the original *oublie*—or *oublée,* as it was then known—was the large wafer, or host, consumed by the priest at mass. For centuries, wafers were sold by street vendors, especially in the city of Lyons, which became known as the wafer capital of Europe. "Here they are, ladies," the vendors cried, "pure pleasure for the asking!" This is the origin of the other French name for these wafers: *plaisirs,* or "pleasures."

Ingredients (for 4 servings): 1 cup sugar. 6 tablespoons cold water. 1¾ cups flour. 2 eggs. 1 tablespoon butter.

The dough: Dissolve the sugar in the water. Place the flour in a bowl. Make a well in the center. Add the eggs, and stir, gradually adding the sugar and water mixture as you incorporate the eggs into the flour. Mix until a smooth batter is formed. Melt the butter, and combine it rapidly with the dough. The dough should be smooth, and you should be able to roll it out with your hands.

Cooking the wafers: Using your hands, form about thirty small balls of dough. Heat a waffle iron. Butter it, and place a ball of dough into it. Close, and press down tightly. (You will have to butter the waffle iron after every four or five waffles.) If an old-fashioned waffle iron that is placed directly on a burner of the stove is used, it should be turned over after fifty seconds. Continue cooking for fifty seconds; then check to see if the waffle is done.

To Serve: Remove the waffle from the iron. Roll the waffles, or leave them flat. Serve hot or cold.

BENOILES

(Egg Fritters)

Fritters such as these are the ancestors of our doughnuts. They were once more common in France than they are today. The following recipe is for the type of fritter popular in France during the seventeenth and eighteenth centuries.

Ingredients (for 6 servings): 1 cup water. 3½ tablespoons butter, broken into small pieces. 1 pinch salt. 2 tablespoons candied lemon peel, cut into strips. 1 cup flour. 4 eggs. Oil for deep frying. Sugar. Orange-flower water.

The dough: Heat the water in a large pot, and add the butter. When the butter has melted, add the salt and lemon peel. Bring to a boil. As soon as the water comes to a boil, remove from the heat, and add the flour, stirring vigorously with a wooden spoon. Beat the mixture in this way until it becomes smooth. Place the pot over low heat, and stir constantly in order to evaporate any excess water. Remove from the heat once more. Add one of the eggs to the dough, and beat vigorously. Once the egg is totally incorporated, add another egg, beating vigorously. Add the two remaining eggs, one at a time, in this manner. If the batter is dry enough, it will have no difficulty absorbing the eggs.

Cooking the fritters: Heat some cooking oil in a deep fryer until it is very hot. Spoon a small amount of the batter into the hot oil. If the oil is at the proper temperature, the fritter will sink to the bottom and then immediately rise to the surface. Fry for four minutes on one side; then turn and fry the other side for four minutes. Remove with a slotted spoon, and drain well. Cook all the batter this way. If a large pot is used, several spoonfuls of batter can be cooked at once, but do not crowd the pot.

To Serve: Powder the fritters with a little sugar, and sprinkle with orange-flower water. Serve very hot.

RIZ MERINGUE

(Rice Meringue)

Rice is grown only in a very small area of France called the Camargue. The amount of rice produced there has always been small, and almost all the rice sold in France has to be imported. In the eighteenth century imported rice was a luxury and was rarely used in cooking. Even now there are few French dishes that use rice. But French cooks have consistently come up with excellent combinations whenever they do make a rice dish. The following dessert is an unusual variant on the rice pudding familiar to everyone today.

Ingredients (for 12 servings): 1¼ cups long-grain rice. 1 orange. 4⅓ cups milk. 1 pinch salt. ½ cup sugar (for rice). 2 tablespoons butter. 6 egg yolks. ¾ cup sugar. 3 tablespoons water. 4 macaroons. 4 egg whites. ¼ cup powdered sugar.

Cooking the rice: Wash the rice. Drain, and place in a large pot. Wash the orange. Use a potato peeler to remove a long, thin strip of the peel. Place the orange peel in a pot with the milk. Add the salt, one-half cup sugar, and the butter. Bring to a boil. Pour this mixture over the rice. Simmer for thirty-five minutes. Remove from the heat, and stir in the egg yolks. Pour into a mold (any shape you like). Bake in a moderate oven (375°) for thirty-five minutes.

The caramel: (Note: The caramel should be prepared at the very last minute; otherwise, it will harden.) Dissolve three-quarters cup sugar in the water in a saucepan over low heat. Stir occasionally to keep the sugar from burning. Cook until the mixture is light gold but not brown.

Baking: Turn out the rice from its mold onto an ovenproof dish. Crush the macaroons into a powder, and sprinkle over the rice pudding. Beat the egg whites until they are very stiff and firm. Using a spatula, spread the meringue over the surface of the rice pudding. Sprinkle with the powdered sugar. Bake in a hot oven (425°) for five minutes.

To Serve: Pour the caramel over the cake as soon as the latter is taken from the oven, being careful not to cover the cake entirely with the caramel. (The caramel should run down the sides.) Serve immediately.

TOURTE DE FRANGIPANE

(Frangipane Pie)

A sixteenth-century cook named Frangipani is said to have created the almond filling that gives this pie its name. La Varenne, on the other hand, can take full credit for the unusual puff pastry that surrounds the almond cream. His idea of rolling out thin sheets of dough and layering them in a pie pan has been abandoned today by French cooks, whose method of making puff pastry is more complicated—although not superior, in this case, to the technique developed by La Varenne three centuries ago.

INGREDIENTS

(for 8 servings)

6 tablespoons flour (for almond cream)
2 cups milk
½ cup blanched pistachios
½ cup blanched almonds
Orange-flower water (optional)
⅓ cup sugar
1 pinch salt
5 egg yolks (each in a separate small dish)
1¾ cups flour (for dough)
5 egg whites
½ pound soft butter

The almond cream

- Mix six tablespoons flour with several teaspoons of the milk. Place the remaining milk in a pot. Add the flour mixture. Cook for ten minutes over low heat, stirring constantly. Remove from the heat, and cool.
- Pound the pistachios and almonds in a mortar until a fine paste is formed. (A few drops of orange-flower water can be sprinkled on the nuts to prevent them from losing their oil.) Mix the pounded nuts with the sugar and salt.
- Stir the egg yolks, one by one, into the cool flour and milk mixture. Stir in the pounded nuts and sugar.

The dough

- Place one and three-quarters cups flour in a bowl. Mix with the egg whites until the dough is smooth and can be formed into a ball. Leave the dough in the bowl, and cover it with a cloth. Let stand for two hours before using.

The pie

- Butter a pie pan with one tablespoon of the butter.
- Divide the dough into two equal parts. Take the first part, and divide it into six pieces. Take one of these small pieces, and with the hands or a rolling pin, flatten it until it is paper-thin (almost transparent) and the size of the pie pan. Place it in the pie pan.
- Take the remaining butter, and divide it into eleven equal parts. Spread one part of the butter over the dough in the pie pan.
- Take one of the remaining five small sections of dough, and flatten it into a paper-thin layer identical to the first. Place it in the pie pan, and spread it with part of the butter. Repeat this operation until you have six layers of dough, separated from each other by the layers of butter.
- Spread the almond cream over the sixth layer of dough.
- Take the second half of the dough, and make six more paper-thin layers. Place these over the almond cream, separating each layer by a layer of butter, as you did earlier. Butter the top of the last layer.

Baking

- Bake in a moderately hot oven (400°) for thirty-five minutes, or until golden brown.

To Serve

- Serve either warm or cold.

"Le Ritz"

BEIGNETS DE FEUILLES DE VIGNE
(Vine-Leaf Fritters)

Vine leaves are seldom associated with French cooking and rarely thought of as a dessert. They are, in fact, popular in certain wine-producing regions of France, but they are usually stuffed with rice (Greek fashion) and served as appetizers. Menon clearly decided to replace the rice with an almond cream and then to deep-fry the leaves rather than stew them in the traditional way. It is always preferable to use fresh vine leaves for this recipe, but those canned in a salt solution can be used if they are soaked sufficiently before being cooked.

INGREDIENTS

(for 4 servings)

16 vine leaves
3 tablespoons brandy (for marinade)
1⅓ cups flour
Salt
¼ cup sugar
1 teaspoon olive oil
1 teaspoon brandy (for batter)
1 egg, separated
6 tablespoons dry white wine
1 cup milk
2 eggs
5 blanched almonds
1 bitter almond
2 macaroons
1½ tablespoons butter
1 teaspoon orange-flower water
Oil for deep frying
Powdered sugar

Preparing the vine leaves

- The vine leaves should be young and tender. Wash thoroughly.
- Marinate the leaves for twelve hours in the brandy.

The batter

- In a bowl, combine one cup of the flour, a small pinch of salt, and a small pinch of sugar. Make a well in the center of the flour.
- Into the well, pour the oil, one teaspoon brandy, one egg yolk, and the wine. As you add these ingredients, stir constantly with a wooden spoon so that they will mix with the flour without forming lumps. The batter should be somewhat thick so that it will generously coat the vine leaves.
- Beat the egg white until stiff, and combine it with the batter.
- Let the batter stand for two or three hours in a warm place before using.

The almond cream

- Bring the milk to a boil. Remove from the heat, and let stand until just warm.
- In a pot, combine the remaining flour, the remaining sugar, a small pinch of salt, and the eggs. Mix thoroughly with a wooden spoon. Gradually add the warm milk.
- When all the milk has been mixed with the other ingredients, place over low heat, stirring constantly. When the mixture reaches the boiling point, immediately remove from the heat.
- Pound the almonds (sweet and bitter) and the macaroons in a mortar until all are finely crushed.
- Add this mixture to the pot, along with the butter and the orange-flower water. Stir well.

The fritters

- Drain the vine leaves, and wipe them dry with a clean cloth. Using a small spoon, place some of the almond cream in the center of each leaf.
- Roll and fold the leaves into small packages.
- Dip each of the leaves into the batter. This must be done with great care to keep the leaves from opening. The best method is to place a vine-leaf package in a ladle and then to spoon in just enough batter to cover the leaf.
- Place the leaves one by one in a deep fryer containing very hot oil. As a leaf rises to the surface of the oil, turn it over. When the fritter is golden brown, remove it with a slotted spoon.

To Serve

- Drain the fritters.
- Sprinkle generously with powdered sugar, and serve hot.

OMELETTE CHARMANTE
(Jam and Nut Omelette)

Isabeau 1796

Omelettes are often filled with jelly and served as a dessert in France. The author of this recipe gives us a much more elaborate version of this sweet dessert—the simple jelly omelette is turned into a spectacular finish to any meal.

Ingredients (for 8 servings): 1⅔ cups blanched almonds. 2 eggs, separated. ⅓ cup, plus 2 tablespoons, sugar. ¼ cup flour. ½ cup blanched pistachios. 2 cups milk. 2 lumps sugar. 12 eggs. Salt. 2 tablespoons heavy cream. 3 tablespoons butter. ⅔ cup apricot jam. ⅔ cup cherry jam. Powdered sugar.

The almond dough: In a mortar, pound the almonds with the egg whites until a paste is formed. Place one-third cup sugar in a pot over low heat. Gradually add the pounded almonds, stirring constantly with a wooden spoon. Remove from the heat as soon as the sugar and almonds have combined into a single mass which no longer sticks to the pot. Place this mixture on a floured table, and roll out to a thickness of about one-eighth inch. Mix the flour with two tablespoons sugar, and sprinkle half of it over the almond dough. Use a glass or cookie cutter to cut the almond dough into rounds, each one about one and a half inches in diameter. Butter and flour a cookie sheet. Place the rounds on it, leaving a little space between them. Bake in a moderate oven (375°) for fifteen minutes. Remove from the oven, and allow to cool. Turn the rounds over. Sprinkle them with the remaining flour and sugar mixture. Put back in the oven for five minutes; then remove and set aside for later use. Keep them warm.

The pistachio cream: Pound the pistachios in a mortar. Bring the milk to a boil. Stirring constantly with a wooden spoon, add the pounded pistachios to the milk, along with two lumps of sugar. When the mixture begins to thicken slightly, remove from the heat, and stir in the egg yolks. Heat, but do not boil. Keep hot.

The omelettes: Beat six of the eggs with a pinch of salt and a tablespoon of the cream. Heat one and a half tablespoons of the butter in a frying pan. Add the eggs, and make an omelette, but do not fold it. Simply turn it out flat onto a plate once the eggs have cooked. Make another omelette with the remaining eggs, in precisely the same way as the first omelette. Keep both omelettes hot. They should be dry and firm.

The final steps: Immediately cover each omelette with half the pistachio cream, then with a layer of apricot jam, then finally with a layer of cherry jam. Cut into rounds with a cookie cutter. Place a round on each round of almond dough.

To Serve: Sprinkle with powdered sugar, and serve hot.

PAIN DES HOURIS
(Oriental Nut Cake)

Isabeau 1796

Houris is the French word for an Oriental dancer—specifically, a woman dancer with dark eyes. Since the almonds, candied lemon peel, and pistachios certainly give an Oriental flavor to this cake, some romantics like to believe that it was either imported into France (perhaps by a troupe of visiting "houris") or created in imitation of an Eastern specialty associated with these dark-eyed beauties. It is more reasonable, however, to assume that it was an imaginative creation labeled with an exotic name simply as a fanciful notion.

Ingredients (for 8 servings): 1⅔ cups blanched almonds. ½ cup blanched pistachios. 2½ ounces candied lemon peel. 1 cup sugar. 7 eggs, separated. 2 tablespoons butter. Powdered sugar.

The dough: Using a mortar and pestle, pound together the almonds, pistachios, lemon peel, and sugar. (Begin by pounding the almonds; next add the pistachios, then the lemon peel, and finally the sugar.) Add the egg yolks to the contents of the mortar, mixing well. Transfer the contents of the mortar to a large bowl. Beat the egg whites until very stiff; then fold them into the other ingredients.

Baking: Generously butter a loaf pan or ring mold. Pour the batter into the mold. Bake in a moderate oven (350°) for one hour, or until golden brown.

To Serve: Turn the cake out as soon as it comes from the oven. Sprinkle generously with powdered sugar. Serve after the cake has completely cooled.

PETITS PUITS D'AMOUR
(Currant, or Apricot, Pastries)

Viard 1820

The French name for these pastries literally means "little love wells." The puff-pastry shells are thought to resemble wells, and one supposes that the sweetness of their filling has led to their association with love, since the French have a tendency to associate pastry with romance. (A favorite endearment in France translates as "my little cream puff.") These pastries are traditionally filled with currant jelly, but any other jelly or jam (preferably homemade) will do as well.

Ingredients (for 8 servings): **For the puff pastry**: 1¾ cups flour. 1 tablespoon, plus 1 cup, butter. ½ teaspoon salt. 1 egg white. **For the pastries**: 1 egg yolk. 1 tablespoon cold water. Powdered sugar. Currant jelly or apricot jam.

The puff pastry: Make the puff pastry following the instructions given in the recipe for Tourte d'herbes, page 74.

Forming the pastries: Roll out two-thirds of the puff-pastry dough to a thickness of three-eighths inch. Dip a round, grooved cookie cutter about two and a half inches in diameter into hot water. Then, with a single, neat stroke, cut the dough into circles. Place the circles side by side on a greased cookie sheet. Do not allow them to touch. Roll out the remaining dough. Cut this dough into circles as before, but this time use a slightly smaller cookie cutter—about two inches in diameter. Then, with a three-quarter-inch cutter, remove the centers from these smaller circles, making rings. Dip a pastry brush into the water, and use it to dampen the edges of the large circles. Place the rings on top of them. Finally, take the centers you have removed from the rings, and without dampening them, put the centers back into place. Mix the egg yolk with the cold water. Carefully brush this mixture over the tops of the pastry—but *only* over the tops, for the slightest trace of egg on the sides of the dough will keep it from rising.

Baking: Bake in a moderately hot oven (400°) for fifteen minutes, or until golden brown. Remove the cookie sheet from the oven. Sprinkle the pastries with powdered sugar. Replace the pastries in the oven for one minute more to allow the sugar to melt and glaze the pastries. Then remove from the oven, and cool.

To Serve: Remove the centers or caps from the pastries. Using a small spoon, fill the cavities with thick currant jelly or apricot jam. Replace the caps, and serve.

BISCUIT AU CHOCOLAT
(Chocolate Cake)

Chocolate came to France from Mexico, by way of Spain. It did not take long for it to cross the Pyrenees, and one of Europe's first chocolate factories was built in Bayonne. Chocolate was so expensive at first that it was used sparingly and only in very rich households. But by the beginning of the nineteenth century the price had fallen, and desserts containing chocolate began to appear more frequently in French cookbooks of the period.

Ingredients (for 10 servings): 2 ounces unsweetened chocolate. 2¼ cups sugar. 12 eggs, separated. 2½ cups flour. 1½ tablespoons butter (for the mold). Powdered sugar.

The batter: Grate the chocolate. Place the sugar in a deep bowl. Add the egg yolks, and stir vigorously for ten minutes until the sugar has dissolved completely and the mixture is smooth and light-colored. Stir in the grated chocolate. Sprinkle in the flour, and continue to stir until the mixture is smooth. Beat the egg whites until very stiff. Fold them carefully into the batter.

Baking: Butter a large, rectangular cake pan or high-sided mold. Pour in the batter until the pan is two-thirds full. Bake in a slow oven (325°) for one hour and thirty minutes. At the end of this time, insert a knife or skewer into the cake, and immediately withdraw it. If the knife is dry, the cake is done.

To Serve: Allow the cake to cool; then turn it out. Dust the top lightly with powdered sugar. Slice, and serve.

FLAN DE NOUILLES MERINGUEES
(Noodle Meringue Cake)

The idea of noodles in a dessert seems strange to some people. There is no reason why it should. Pasta is made from flour, and so are pastries. Rice is sweetened and used in puddings, so why not do the same with noodles? In the nineteenth century noodles were frequently served this way, but the practice disappeared in France around the turn of the century. Beauvilliers' recipe should convince any skeptic that the use of noodles in a dessert is practical, logical, and tasty.

Ingredients (for 6 servings): 3½ cups flour (for the dough). Salt. 7 eggs, separated. ½ pound soft butter. ¼ cup warm water (approximately). 2 pounds flour (approximately—for first baking). 2 quarts milk. 6 ounces noodles. 6 macaroons. ½ cup sugar. 1 tablespoon orange-flower water. 1 tablespoon powdered sugar.

The dough: Pour three and a half cups flour into a bowl, and make a well in the center. Place one teaspoon salt, three egg yolks, and three-quarters cup of the butter into the well. Stir, gradually adding about one-quarter cup warm water until a smooth, soft dough is formed. (Work the dough with your hands if you prefer.) Shape the dough into a ball. Cover, and let stand for fifteen minutes.

Baking: Butter a hinged, high-sided mold (charlotte or soufflé mold). Reserve about one-tenth of the dough. Flatten the remainder with a rolling pin until it is about three eighths inch thick and large enough to cover the sides and bottom of the mold completely. Place the dough in the mold. Press it lightly against the sides and bottom. Fill the interior of the dough with approximately two pounds flour to about an inch from the top. Roll the reserved one-tenth of the dough into a circle so that it may serve as a cover to the mold. Moisten the edges of the dough in the mold, and seal the cover onto the mold. Bake in a hot oven (425°) for fifteen minutes.

Cooking the noodles: Bring the milk to a boil. Add the noodles. Cook for twenty minutes. Drain immediately. Crush the macaroons. Combine the macaroons with the noodles, along with the remaining egg yolks, the sugar, orange-flower water, the remaining butter, and a pinch of salt. Beat four egg whites until stiff. Carefully fold them into the noodle mixture.

The custard: Remove the cover from the mold, and pour out the flour. (Make certain that no flour remains inside the mold.) Pour the noodle mixture into the mold. Bake in a slow oven (300°) for forty-five minutes. At the end of that time, beat the remaining egg whites until stiff, and place them on top of the filling. Sprinkle with powdered sugar. Bake in a hot oven (450°) for five minutes, or until the meringue is browned.

To Serve: Remove from the mold, and serve hot.

PECHES AU GRATIN

Cuisinier Durand 1830

(Peaches Baked in Custard)

The name ''peach'' is believed to come from the word ''Persia,'' since this is the country that was long believed to be the home of this delicious fruit. There are two basic kinds of peach, clingstone and freestone. The freestone variety is preferred by most cooks, since the flesh of the fruit comes easily away from the seed. Yellow-fleshed or white-fleshed peaches can be used in this recipe, but the yellow-fleshed peaches are preferable since their color contrasts best with that of the custard in which they are served.

Ingredients (for 4 servings): 3 tablespoons flour. 5 egg yolks. 1⅓ cups milk. ½ cup sugar (for custard). ¼ teaspoon grated lemon peel. 2 macaroons. Candied lemon peel. 2 teaspoons orange-flower water. 4 ripe freestone peaches. 3 tablespoons sugar (for peaches). 1 egg white. 2 tablespoons powdered sugar.

The custard: Place the flour in a pot. Add the egg yolks, and stir until the mixture is smooth. Add the milk little by little, stirring constantly. When all the milk is added, stir in one-half cup sugar and the grated lemon peel. Place over low heat. Bring just to a boil, stirring constantly. At the first bubble, remove the pot from the stove, but keep the custard warm. With a rolling pin, crush the macaroons and a few pieces of candied lemon peel. Stir into the custard; then add one teaspoon of the orange-flower water.

The peaches: Peel the peaches. (Drop them into a pot of boiling water for twenty seconds, drain them, and place them in a bowl of cold water—the skin then peels off easily). Cut the peaches in half, and remove the pits. Place the peach halves in a pot with the remaining orange-flower water and three tablespoons sugar. Sauté the peaches over low to medium heat for about five minutes, or until the sugar has melted and begun to caramelize.

Baking: Spread a third of the custard over the bottom of an ovenproof serving dish. Arrange the peaches on top of the custard. Beat the egg white until stiff. Fold it into the remaining custard. Cover the peaches with this mixture, smoothing the surface with a knife. Sift the powdered sugar over the custard. Bake in a very hot oven (475°) for five minutes, or until golden brown.

To Serve: Remove from the oven, and serve immediately.

POUDING DE CABINET

Carême 1833

(Raisin Pudding)

The English ''pudding'' and the French *pouding* have the same meaning. Contrary to general belief, however, the English word comes from the French, not vice versa. According to some etymologists, ''pudding'' is the anglicized version of the French word *boudin* (blood sausage or black pudding in Britain). The word ''pudding'' was extended in English to cover both the original sausage and a number of cakelike desserts. It was as a description of these English desserts that the word migrated back to France and *pouding* became part of the French language. Pudding, in its broadest sense, can mean almost any dessert. Cakes, such as the one described here, would rarely be called puddings today, but in Carême's time this was a logical use of the word.

Ingredients (for 6 servings): 1 vanilla bean. 2 cups milk. 1 cup sugar. 2 eggs. 5 egg yolks. 1 tablespoon flour. ¼ cup dried currants. ¼ cup sultana raisins. ¼ cup Malaga raisins. 1 ounce candied lemon peel. 1 tablespoon vanilla-flavored sugar. ⅓ cup brandy. 1 large brioche or egg bread (see recipe for Dame Susanne, page 268).

The cream: Place the vanilla bean in a pot with the milk. Bring to a boil. Stirring constantly with a wooden spoon, add two-thirds cup of the sugar. When the sugar has dissolved completely, take out the vanilla bean. Remove the pot from the heat. Beat the eggs and egg yolks in a bowl. Gradually stir in the sweetened, aromatized milk. (Stir gently, and do not beat, or the milk will foam and give the surface of the cake a spongy, unpleasant texture.)

The raisins: Place the flour on a piece of cloth. Place the currants, sultanas, and Malagas on the flour. Fold the cloth shut, and with the fingers, roll the raisins in the flour. Cut the lemon peel into thin strips. In a bowl, combine the lemon-peel strips, raisins, vanilla-flavored sugar, the remaining sugar, and the brandy. Leave until the raisins have softened and begin to puff up.

The cake: Cut a large brioche or egg bread—one approximately equal in size to the cake mold that you intend to use—into one-quarter-inch slices. Butter a cake mold (a rectangular pound-cake mold, for example). Place slices of brioche in the bottom until it is covered. Over the brioche, spread a layer of the raisin mixture. Over the raisins, place another layer of sliced brioche, and over the brioche, another layer of raisins. Repeat until the ingredients are all used. Finally, pour three-quarters of the cream into the mold. (The brioche slices will absorb the liquid and expand to fill the mold.)

Baking: Wait about ten minutes before putting the cake into the oven. This will allow the cream to be absorbed thoroughly. (Slightly more cream can be added at this time, but some should be saved for later.) Place the cake mold in an ovenproof dish containing hot water. The water should rise no higher than a quarter of the way up the sides of the cake mold. Place the dish with the cake mold in a hot oven (425°), and bake for forty minutes.

To Serve: Remove the cake from the oven. Allow to cool; then turn it out. Heat the remainder of the cream over low heat, stirring constantly. (Do not allow it to boil.) When the cream is ready to boil, remove from the heat. Allow to cool. Serve the cake on a platter and the cream in a bowl.

SOLILEMME
(French Sally Lunn Cake)

Carême 1833

The name of this cake has baffled French etymologists, who simply define it as "a kind of brioche" and admit that they have no idea where its name came from. The mystery of the name "Solilemme" was solved by an Englishman (E. S. Dallas) in a work called *Kettner's Book of the Table*. He explains that Carême (the supposed creator of this cake) had visited England and tasted an English tea cake called a Sally Lunn (named for its English creator). Carême returned to France with a recipe for this cake and, using a garbled French pronunciation of its English name, claimed it as his own invention.

Ingredients (for 4 servings): ¾ cup flour (for starter). ⅓ ounce (½ package) baker's yeast. Warm water. 2 cups flour (for dough). Salt. 2 tablespoons sugar. 4 egg yolks. 1⅓ cups soft butter. 6 tablespoons heavy cream. 1 egg, lightly beaten.

The starter: Pour three-quarters cup flour into a small mixing bowl. Make a well in the center. In a cup, mix the yeast with two or three tablespoons warm water. Combine with the flour. Add enough warm water to make a soft dough. Cover the bowl with a cloth, and let the dough rise until it has doubled in bulk.

The dough: Place two cups flour, one teaspoon salt, and the sugar in a large bowl. Make a well in the center. Place the egg yolks, half the butter broken into small pieces, and the cream in the well. Mix the egg yolks and cream together, then gradually incorporate the flour and butter, working with the hands. When all the ingredients are mixed together, beat the dough with the hands for about ten minutes, lifting the dough up and slapping it back into the bowl. The dough is ready when it comes away from the sides of the bowl and no longer sticks to the hands. Add the starter to the dough, and mix it in thoroughly. Butter a large charlotte mold (or any other high-sided cake mold). Pour in the dough—it should fill the mold no more than halfway. Cover the mold with a thick cloth, and leave in a warm place for about an hour, or until the dough has almost reached the edge of the mold.

Baking: Using a pastry brush, paint the surface of the dough with the beaten egg. Bake the cake in a hot oven (400°) for one hour. If the surface of the cake browns too quickly, cover it with aluminum foil. The cake is done when it is firm to the touch and begins to come away from the sides of the mold.

To Serve: Remove the cake from the oven, and turn it out onto a serving platter. Cut it in half horizontally. Sprinkle each half with a pinch of salt. Melt the remaining butter. Pour half of it over each half of the cake. Replace the top half of the cake over the bottom half, and serve hot.

SAVARIN
(Savarin Cake)

Gouffé 1867

A Savarin and a Baba au rhum are basically the same thing. They differ only in that the Baba contains rum and the Savarin does not. The sweet syrup poured over the Savarin can be flavored with rum (as for the Baba), but Gouffé's recipe does not mention this possibility. Either cake can be made in advance, but the syrup should be poured over it only minutes before serving. If the cake is made ahead of time, it should be warmed in the oven before the syrup is added.

Ingredients (for 8 servings): ⅓ ounce (½ package) baker's yeast. 1 cup warm milk. 3⅔ cups flour. 5 eggs. 1¼ cups soft butter. 1½ teaspoons salt. 1 tablespoon sugar. 2 ounces candied orange peel. 1 tablespoon slivered almonds. **For the syrup**: ⅔ cup sugar. 1 cup water. Anisette.

The starter: Mix the yeast with two tablespoons of the milk. Pour the flour into a bowl. Make a well in the center. Pour the yeast into the well. Mix only a quarter of the flour with the yeast. Cover the bowl with a cloth, and let stand in a warm place until the yeast and flour mixture has doubled in volume.

The batter: Combine the starter mixture with the remainder of the flour. Stir in six tablespoons of the milk and two of the eggs. Beat until the batter is smooth and homogeneous. Stir in one more egg. Continue beating until smooth. Add still another egg and the butter. Stir until smooth. Add the salt, sugar, the remaining milk, and the remaining egg. Dice the orange peel. Stir into the batter.

Baking: Butter a ring-shaped cake mold. Sprinkle the sides of the mold with the slivered almonds. Pour the batter into the mold. (The mold should be no more than three-quarters full.) Cover with a cloth. Place the mold in a warm place, and let stand until the batter has risen to the rim of the mold. Bake in a moderate oven (350°) for one hour. At the end of that time, stick a needle into the center of the cake. If the needle comes out absolutely dry, the cake is done. Turn out the cake, and let stand for twenty minutes to cool.

The syrup: In a small saucepan over low heat, dissolve two-thirds cup sugar in the water. Boil for one minute. Let cool. Add anisette to taste.

To Serve: Pour some of the syrup over the warm cake. Let the cake stand for a while. Continue spooning the syrup over the cake until it has all been absorbed. Serve warm or cold.

POTS DE CREME AU CITRON
(Lemon Custard)

Gouffé 1867

This is simply an egg custard with lemon flavoring. A small amount of vanilla, coffee, or even chocolate can be used instead of lemon. Whatever the flavoring, it is important that it not overpower the delicate taste of the custard in this recipe.

Ingredients (for 6 servings): Milk. 1 lemon. ¼ cup sugar. 5 egg yolks.

The milk: Pour enough milk into a saucepan to fill four individual custard cups. Bring to a boil.

The lemon: Wash the lemon. Grate the peel, using a small grater in order not to remove any of the white pulp inside the skin.

The custard: Away from the heat, and stirring constantly, add the sugar and egg yolks to the hot milk. Stir gently to prevent the mixture from foaming. Stir in the grated lemon peel.

Baking: Pour the custard into six earthenware or porcelain custard cups—gently, so that the custard will not foam. Place the cups in an ovenproof dish. Add water to the dish until it comes no more than halfway up on the cups. Cover the top of the cups with aluminum foil, and bake in a hot oven (400°) for fifteen minutes. Test the custards by inserting a knife to see if they are done. They are cooked when the knife comes out clean.

To Serve: Remove the custards from the oven. Take them out of the water, and let cool on a rack. Chill in the refrigerator. Serve cold.

CROQUEMBOUCHE DE GIMBLETTES DE GENOISE

Gouffé 1867

(Genoese Ring-Cookie Basket)

A Croquembouche can be any French pastry that is crisp and crunchy when eaten. This particular Croquembouche is made of small cookielike rings called *gimblettes*. This elaborate dessert is sometimes prepared with little cream puffs instead of cookie rings and is served especially during Lent in France.

Ingredients (for 20 servings): 1 cup butter. 10 eggs. 2¼ cups sugar (for dough). 3⅔ cups flour. ¾ cup apricot jam. 2 cups powdered sugar. 4 egg whites. 1 teaspoon lemon juice. A few drops red food coloring. 1 tablespoon vegetable oil. 1 cup sugar (for syrup). 3 tablespoons water. Various candied fruits.

The Genoese dough: Butter and flour a baking sheet. Melt the butter in a pot over low heat. Do not let the butter darken. In a large bowl, vigorously beat the eggs and two and a quarter cups sugar until the mixture is smooth and foamy. Continue beating, and add the flour and melted butter. Do so as quickly as possible, in order not to work the dough too long.

Baking the dough: Spread the dough on the baking sheet to a thickness of about one-half inch. Bake in a moderate oven (375°) for fifteen minutes. Let cool.

Making the ring cookies: With two small cookie cutters—one and a half inches in diameter and one-half inch in diameter—cut the dough into doughnutlike rings. Mix the apricot jam with a small amount of warm water until the jam has become just liquid enough to spread with a brush. Spread the jam over the ring cookies and over the small rounds cut from the centers of the cookies.

Icing the ring cookies: Place the powdered sugar in a bowl. Stirring constantly, gradually add the egg whites. Stir until the mixture is smooth. Add the lemon juice. Divide the icing into two equal parts. Add red coloring to half the icing to color it pink. Ice half the ring cookies with the pink frosting and half with the white frosting. Let dry.

Building the basket: Grease a hinged high-sided mold with the oil. In a copper saucepan, dissolve one cup sugar in three tablespoons water. Place the saucepan over medium heat, and bring to a boil. When the bubbles become quite small and are very dense, the water has evaporated and the sugar has begun to turn into syrup. Run cold water over your finger, and very rapidly put the tip of your finger in and out of the syrup. Immediately run cold water over your finger again. When the sugar on the tip of your finger comes off as a clear, crisp film, the syrup is done. Use the syrup as a glue to attach the ring cookies to the sides of the mold (the icing should face the sides of the mold). Alternate the pink and white ring cookies in any design that strikes your fancy. Let cool.

The final decoration: Remove the ring cookie basket from the mold. Decorate with the small rounds cut from the center of the ring cookies or with the various candied fruits, such as cherries. Use the syrup to make the rounds or the fruits stick to the rings. Decorate the top of the basket, if you wish, with various spun-sugar ornaments.

To Serve: Cut into small pieces with a knife—although it is such a pretty confectionery construction one almost hates to demolish it.

TOT FAIT

Gouffé 1867

(Instant Cake)

A glance at this recipe will explain its name—it is so simple to make that some cooks regard its preparation as taking "merely an instant."

Ingredients (for 4 servings): 1¾ cups flour. 1 cup sugar. 1 pinch salt. 1 lemon. 4 eggs. ½ pound soft butter. 2 teaspoons butter (for the cake pan).

The batter: Mix the flour, sugar, and salt in a bowl. Make a well in the center. Wash the lemon, and grate a quarter of the peel into the well. Add the eggs and butter, gradually stirring these ingredients into the flour until a smooth batter is formed.

Baking: Butter a cake pan, and pour in the batter. Bake in a moderate oven (375°) for forty-five minutes. (Test by inserting a knife to be sure it is done.) Turn out the cake when it comes from the oven.

To Serve: Cool and serve, either plain or with homemade jam.

OEUFS A LA NEIGE

(Egg Fluff)

This is still one of the most frequently prepared desserts in France. Children especially like it because of the poached egg whites (their parents tell them these are actually little clouds that have landed on their plates).

Ingredients (for six servings): 4⅓ cups milk. 6 eggs, separated. 1 cup, plus 2 tablespoons, sugar. 1 lemon.

Preparing the ingredients: Bring the milk to a boil in a large pot. Beat the egg whites until they are stiff; then fold in one-half cup of the sugar.

Poaching the egg whites: Wash the lemon, and grate a quarter of the peel into the milk. Add two tablespoons sugar. With a spoon, take egg-sized portions of the stiff egg whites, and place them in the milk. (Do not crowd the pot—the egg whites should not touch.) Poach for four minutes. Turn the egg whites over, and poach for two minutes longer. Remove, and drain. Cook all the egg whites in this manner.

The cream: Take two cups of the milk, and let cool. In a saucepan, combine the egg yolks with the remaining sugar. Stir in the cooled milk. Place the saucepan over low heat, and stir constantly with a wooden spoon until the mixture thickens—it should not boil.

To Serve: Pour the cream into a deep platter. Arrange the drained egg whites in the platter on top of the cream. Chill before serving.

CHARLOTTE DE POMMES DE MENAGE

(Apple Charlotte)

As noted earlier, Gouffé divided his cookbook into two parts, "home cooking" and *grande cuisine*. This is his simplified version of a popular French dessert. In the *grande cuisine* version of this dish a special dome-shaped charlotte mold is used. The walls of the mold are lined with croutons, and the whole thing is baked in the oven. The charlotte is then turned out of the mold and spread with apricot jam before being served. The following recipe has all the taste of the *grande cuisine* version, but since there is no mold involved, it is quicker and easier to prepare.

Ingredients (for 6 servings): 3 pounds cooking apples. ½ pound butter. ⅔ cup sugar. 1 large loaf unsliced bread. 1½ cups apricot jam.

Preparing the apples: Peel and core the apples; then cut them in half. Cut the apples into slices about one-quarter inch thick. Place the slices in a pan with six and a half tablespoons of the butter and the sugar. Cook for fifteen minutes, turning the apples occasionally—but gently, so as not to break them.

Making the charlotte: Remove the crust from the bread. Cut the bread into twenty-four slices, each about three-quarters inch thick. Cut each slice in half. Fry the bread in a pan with the remaining butter until brown. Spread apricot jam, to a thickness of three-quarters inch, on each piece of fried bread. Arrange the pieces of bread around the edge of an ovenproof baking dish, leaving a space in the center of the dish large enough to hold the apples. Place the cooked apples in the middle of the dish. Cover with a layer of apricot jam. Bake in a very hot oven (500°) for five minutes.

To Serve: Serve hot.

BONNET DE TURQUIE A LA TRIBOULET

Alexandre Dumas 1873

(Turk's Hat Cake)

Dumas gives four different "Turk's Hat Cake" recipes in his famous cookbook. They are all prepared in a high-sided mold (either straight or indented) which is thought to resemble a "Turk's hat" (fez). These cakes are traditionally decorated with bands of colored icing or jam, the most popular colors being those of the Turkish flag—red and white. The cake can be made with either pistachios (as in this recipe) or almonds or both. It should be noted that neither yeast nor baking powder is used in preparing this cake—stiffly beaten egg whites make the cake rise. If jam is used instead of icing to decorate the cake, it should be spread over the cake only minutes before serving.

Ingredients (for 8 servings): 1 lime. 3⅓ cups pistachios. 1 cup sugar. 15 eggs, separated. 1¾ cups flour. 2 egg whites (for icing). 1⅓ cups powdered sugar. Red food coloring or another color of your choice.

Preparing the batter: Wash the lime, and grate the peel. Pound the pistachios with the sugar and grated lime peel in a mortar. Transfer the pounded ingredients to a large bowl. Add the egg yolks. Mix vigorously to obtain a smooth, foamy batter. Beat the fifteen egg whites until they are stiff. Fold them into the batter. Very carefully and gradually, fold the flour into the batter, a few tablespoons at a time. Do not stir it in.

Baking: Butter a high-sided cake pan, and pour in the batter. Bake in a slow oven (325°) for two hours. (The cake should rise considerably.) Turn out, and cool on a rack.

Icing the cake: Beat the two egg whites until stiff. Gradually stir in the powdered sugar to make the icing. Ice the cake, leaving a strip running around the edge of the top of the cake. Add a few drops of food coloring to the rest of the icing. Ice the bare strip around the rim of the cake.

To Serve: Slice the cake at the table, and serve.

Drinks

Heavily spiced and sweetened wines have been popular in France since the Roman conquest. These drinks were once served with meals, but were gradually relegated to a position before (*apéritif*) or after (*digestif*) the meal itself. At first, these drinks were generally considered medicinal; gradually, however, their therapeutic value was forgotten as people became accustomed to their pleasant taste. The French still consume enormous quantities of before- and after-dinner drinks, but rarely are they made at home in the traditional ways described in this section. Of course, some of the drinks described here were just passing fashions in France. Punch, for example, is rarely prepared in France today, although it was all the rage in the nineteenth century.

Outside France, French liqueurs have a well-merited reputation for excellence, but any Frenchman will tell you of his grandmother's recipe for cherry brandy or orange liqueur which surpasses any of the commercial brands. Since recipes for these liqueurs have practically disappeared from French cookbooks, this sampling of recipes from the past will permit cooks to prepare their own liqueurs for the first time in the traditional manner respected (though disappearing) in France today.

LIMONADE
(Lemonade)

Lemonade was once a drink that only the rich and fashionable leaders of Parisian society could afford. In the seventeenth century the drink had a snob appeal because the lemons (imported from Spain) were very expensive. La Varenne gave recipes for ''lemonade'' made with oranges or with jasmine, roses, or orange blossoms, but none of these concoctions ever rivaled the lemon, sugar, and water mixture that is still with us.

Ingredients (for 4 ⅓ cups): 4 lemons. ⅔ cup sugar. 4⅓ cups water.

The lemons: Wash and dry the lemons. Cut three of the lemons in half, and squeeze out their juice. Reserve. Squeeze the rinds to extract the oils contained in them. Add to the juice.

The lemonade: Dissolve the sugar in a pitcher with the water. Add the lemon juice to the water and sugar. Peel the fourth lemon, and cut it into thin slices. Remove the seeds, and place the slices in the pitcher with the lemonade.

To Serve: Keep the lemonade in a cool place. Stir before serving.

VIN DES DIEUX
(Wine of the Gods)

Pierre de Lune calls this preparation Vin des dieux—wine of the gods. If so, the gods in question were probably Spanish, since this wine punch is a close relative of sangría. Other specialties from Spain were introduced to France about this time by Marie Thérèse (Queen of France, wife of Louis XIV). She, of course, was Spanish and is credited with introducing such oddities (for the day) as hot chocolate to the French court. It is believed that she helped popularize many other beverages, including fruit-flavored wine punches like this one.

Ingredients (for 4⅓ cups): 4 lemons. 4 apples. 10 cloves. 3 cups sugar. 1 tablespoon orange-flower water. 4⅓ cups burgundy.

Preparing the ingredients: Peel the lemons. Cut them into slices, and remove the seeds. Peel the apples. Remove the seeds and cores. Cut into thin slices.

Making the punch: Place the lemons, apples, cloves, sugar, and orange-flower water in a punch bowl or large stoneware jar with a cover. Pour in the wine. Stir well. Cover, and let stand for three hours.

To Serve: Strain out the solids. Serve cool in large glasses.

HYPOCRAS BLANC

(White Hypocras)

Hypocras was the most popular drink in the Middle Ages; it was still being prepared during the seventeenth and eighteenth centuries in France but disappeared completely in the nineteenth century. Massialot's recipe is almost identical to one given by Taillevent three centuries earlier. Massialot adds a note, however, suggesting that a glass of milk or a tiny pinch of amber be added to the liquid before it is strained and served. It is doubtful that either of these additions improves the taste of this unusual drink.

Ingredients (for 4⅓ cups): 1 cup sugar. 1½ tablespoons ground cinnamon. 1 pinch ground mace. 2 white peppercorns. 1 lemon. 4⅓ cups dry white wine.

Making the punch: Place the sugar, cinnamon, mace, and peppercorns in a large pitcher. Peel and quarter the lemon. Remove the seeds. Add to the contents of the pitcher. Pour in the wine. Stir. Let stand overnight.

The finishing touches: Slowly strain the punch through a paper filter or folded cheesecloth placed inside a strainer. Filter three or four times, pouring the liquid over the solids each time. Store the punch in well-stoppered bottles in a cool place.

To Serve: Serve cool, in frosted glasses if you like.

POPULO

(Aniseed and Cinnamon Liqueur)

This is still a popular drink in both France and Italy, although few people make it themselves anymore. The essences of cinnamon and aniseed, which flavor the alcohol, are expensive and difficult to find nowadays, but are available in some specialty shops. This liqueur is best if left to age at least a year before it is drunk. Like all other liqueurs, it should be drunk at the end of a meal in very small quantities. Liqueurs such as this one are reputedly good for the digestion; thus they are commonly referred to in French as *digestifs*.

Ingredients (for 3¼ quarts): 2¼ cups sugar. Water. 2 cups grain alcohol (180 proof). 6 tablespoons essence of cinnamon. 6 tablespoons essence of aniseed.

The sugar: Stir the sugar in a pot until it dissolves in one cup water. Place the pot over low heat. As soon as it begins to boil, remove from the heat, and add one tablespoon cold water. (Audiger warns not to cook the sugar, or it will solidify in the liqueur and make it cloudy.)

Making the populo: Boil six and a half cups water. Allow to cool. Add the mixture of sugar and water, along with the alcohol, essence of cinnamon, and essence of aniseed. Stir. Pour the mixture into bottles. Seal them, and store in a cool place.

To Serve: Serve as an after-dinner liqueur.

RATAFIA ROUGE
(Red Ratafia)

Audiger 1692

Ratafia once meant any alcohol sweetened with sugar. Today the word "liqueur" means the same thing. This particular ratafia is made with a variety of red fruits, hence its name. It makes an excellent after-dinner drink that will rival the taste of any commercially prepared liqueur.

Ingredients (for 3 cups): Cherries. Currants. Strawberries. 1 cup grain alcohol (90 proof). 3 cloves, crushed. 3 white peppercorns, crushed. ⅔ cup sugar. 10 cherry stones (optional). 10 apricot pits (optional).

The fruits: The amount of fruit employed varies according to taste. Cherries should dominate this mixture. The amount of currants and strawberries combined should equal a quarter of the amount of cherries (*i.e.*, four times as many cherries as currants and strawberries). There should be enough of the three fruits to produce two cups juice when squeezed in the following manner: Crush the cherries, currants, and strawberries. Place in a clean cloth. Hold the cloth over a large bowl, and twist the cloth until it tightens around the fruits and squeezes out all the juice they contain.

The other ingredients: Pour the juice into a glass jar. Add the alcohol, cloves, and peppercorns. Add the sugar. Seal the jar, and let stand.

The optional ingredients: If you want to give an unusual flavor to your ratafia, crush the cherry stones and apricot pits with a hammer, and put them into the jar as well.

To Serve: Let the ratafia stand for four weeks. Filter out the solids, and store in a well-stoppered bottle.

VESPETRO

Menon 1746

According to the author of this recipe, it was "approved by the royal physicians" at Montpellier, who found it an excellent remedy for "stomach pains, chest pains, kidney pains, urinary difficulties, gall stones, depression, headaches, rheumatism, shortness of breath. . . ." It was, in short, a veritable cureall.

Ingredients (for 4⅓ cups): 1 tablespoon angelica seeds. 5 tablespoons coriander seeds. 1 pinch fennel seeds. 1 pinch aniseed. 4⅓ cups grain alcohol (90 proof). Juice of 2 lemons. 2¼ cups sugar.

Preparing the ingredients: Coarsely crush the angelica seeds, coriander seeds, fennel seeds, and aniseed in a mortar. The seeds should not be powdered, but they should be broken enough to yield their aromas and tastes.

The fermentation: Pour the alcohol into a stoneware bottle or jar. Add the remaining ingredients, and stopper the bottle or jar. Let sit for five days, stirring occasionally to dissolve the sugar. (Menon specifies "five days," but the liqueur can be left to sit for as long as a month.)

The final bottling: When the time is up, filter the liqueur. Store the filtered liqueur in tightly stoppered bottles.

To Serve: Serve as an after-dinner drink.

RATAFIA D'ORANGES
(Orange Ratafia)

Viard 1820

Since the peels of the oranges are used in this ratafia, be careful not to use fruits that have been treated with diphenyl or any other noxious chemical.

Ingredients (for 8⅔ cups). 6 thick-skinned oranges. 8⅔ cups grain alcohol (90 proof). 1 stick cinnamon. 2¼ cups sugar.

Preparing the oranges: Peel the oranges so that the skin comes off in one long spiral. (Be careful not to remove any of the bitter white pulp inside the peel.) Squeeze the oranges. Remove any seeds. Reserve the orange juice and peels.

The ratafia: Place the orange peels in a large jar with the alcohol and cinnamon. Dissolve the sugar in the orange juice. Add this mixture to the alcohol. Stir. Seal the jar tightly, and let stand for one month.

To Serve: Strain the liqueur (the orange peels give a bitter taste to the ratafia if left in it too long); then pour the liqueur into bottles. Stopper, and store in a cool place until wanted. Serve as an after-dinner drink.

FRUITS A L'EAU-DE-VIE
(Fruit in Alcohol)

Viard 1820

This is one of the most attractive after-dinner drinks and one of the easiest to prepare as well. Little pieces of the fruit are served in brandy glasses with just enough alcohol to cover them. The fruit is eaten with a small spoon before the flavorful liqueur that surrounds it is drunk.

Ingredients (for 12 small pears, or an equal quantity of peaches, apricots, or plums): Fruits. 1⅔ cups sugar. Grain alcohol (45 proof). 2 cloves. 1 small stick cinnamon.

Preparing the fruits: Select healthy chemical-free fruits picked slightly green. Wipe them thoroughly, and prick each fruit with a needle in several places. Place the fruits one by one in a pot of cold water. (Be careful not to bruise the fruit.) Place the pot over low heat. Simmer without boiling until the fruits become soft. Remove the fruits with a slotted spoon, and place them in cold water, being careful not to bruise them. Drain the fruits for seven minutes; then pour cold water over them once more. Drain again for seven minutes. Add cold water once more. Drain one last time.

The syrup: Place the sugar in a perfectly clean saucepan. Add one-third cup water. Heat slowly. Stir until the sugar is dissolved. Then increase the heat slightly until the water comes to a boil. If there is any foam, remove with a slotted spoon. Boil the liquid until the bubbles become small and dense; then remove from the heat. Let cool.

Bottling the fruits: When the fruits are thoroughly drained, place them in jars. Once more, be careful not to bruise the fruits. When the syrup has cooled, mix it with twice its volume of alcohol. Stir occasionally to dissolve the syrup in the alcohol. To each jar of fruit, add the cloves and cinnamon. Fill each jar with the alcohol mixture. If the fruits are not entirely covered, add extra alcohol. Seal the jars.

To Serve: Wait at least a month or two before serving.

KALDSCHALL A LA MACEDOINE
(Wine Fruit Punch)

Gouffé 1867

This is a remarkable cold punch that can be served at a large reception or before any meal. The fruits employed can be varied according to the taste of the person preparing the punch.

Ingredients (for 10 servings): 1 handful strawberries. 1 handful raspberries. 1 pineapple. 2 pears. 2 peaches. 6 apricots. 2 oranges. Juice of 2 oranges. 6 tablespoons raspberry syrup. 6 tablespoons kirsch. ¾ cup champagne. 4⅓ cups Rhine wine. Sugar (optional).

Preparing the fruits: Wash and clean the strawberries and raspberries. Place them in a large punch bowl. Put the bowl on a large tray full of ice. Peel, core, and quarter the pineapple. Cut it into cubes, and add them to the strawberries and raspberries. Peel and remove the seeds from the pears, peaches, and apricots. Cut the fruits into strips, and add to the strawberries, raspberries, and pineapple. Peel the oranges. Cut them into very thin slices. Remove the seeds, and place the slices with the other fruits.

Making the punch: Mix the orange juice with the raspberry syrup, kirsch, champagne, and Rhine wine. Pour over the fruits, stirring gently so as not to bruise them. Taste for sweetness. If the mixture is not sufficiently sweet, dissolve some sugar in a little water and add to the punch. (Sugar will not dissolve if you add it directly to alcohol.)

To Serve: Let stand in a cool place for one hour. Serve in frosted glasses.

PUNCH A LA FRANCAISE
(Hot Rum Punch à la Française)

Alexandre Dumas 1873

Alexandre Dumas must have had grog in mind when he invented this elaborate hot punch. A grog is simply rum, hot water, sugar, and lemon. This drink was invented by a British naval officer in the eighteenth century and became popular among seamen of all nationalities. It soon spread to restaurants and cafés throughout Europe, and it is still served (especially on cold winter nights) in France, where it is believed to be the perfect remedy for a cold or the flu. Dumas added tea, oranges, and arrack to his version of this drink—thus making the original drink into a beverage *à la française.*

Ingredients (for 5½ quarts): Tea. 2 pounds sugar. 4 cups rum. Juice of 8 lemons. Juice of 12 oranges. 1 cup arrack.

Preparing the ingredients: Prepare four quarts of tea—Dumas specifies Souchong tea.

The punch: Pour the sugar into a large punch bowl. Add the rum. Touch a match to the mixture, and stir constantly as it burns, so that the sugar may burn along with the rum. By the time the alcohol has burned out the quantity of sugar and rum in the bowl should have been reduced by a third. Add the hot tea, lemon juice, and orange juice. Finally, add the arrack (white Batavia arrack, Dumas says).

To Serve: Serve very hot. With the punch, serve macaroons or any other dry, delicate pastry.